To Hermione, Luke and Kit

Contents

CHAPTER ONE

The End

All golf tournaments come down to one last putt, but not all of them are high-octane occasions. At the climax of the 2009 French Open, for instance, Germany's Martin Kaymer found himself with two leisurely strokes in hand over Lee Westwood on the first play-off hole (Westwood having just knocked his approach, not to mention his hopes, into the lake). Kaymer, who would fly north to win the Scottish Open, on the extremely bonnie banks of Loch Lomond, the following week, poured the ball over the front lip for a relaxed, unnecessary, rubbing-it-in birdie. It was a formality. Not one hat was flung into the air. Not a single spectator's heart was racing; no one could hardly bear to watch.

While all such putts are final, however, some are rather more final than others, and the stroke facing Tom Watson two weeks later, after nearly 72 holes of tumultuous golf on the breezy links of Turnberry, had more drama and emotion riding on it than any other shot in the recent story of the game.

He was 59 years old, decades past his best, and was these days pivoting on a brand-new artificial hip, and leaning on memories for balance. At the start of the week he was a 1000–1 shot, with no serious chance. But here he was, on the 18th tee, requiring no more than the good golfer's fantasy score: par at the last. For four days he had taken the lead, faltered, and then revived again. He had just rolled in a putt for birdie to seize sole leadership once more. All he had to do now was finish the thing off.

The view down the 18th was familiar: he had played the hole many times, and won here twice before. He would have to clear a stretch of rough grass in front of the tee and land the ball on an invisible but roomy bulge of fairway in front of the dark-green television studio. From there the hole turned into the cavernous maw of three giant stands, surrounded by marquees. From the tee it resembled the jousting arena of a medieval tourney. Flags fluttered in the wind like knightly pennants, and yellow scoreboards sat on top of the crammed turrets like flowers on gorse.

Watson ignored all this and considered the yardage. 'Two hundred and fifty-eight to the right TV tower,' his caddie advised him, using the BBC's on-course presence as a navigational aid. 'Two hundred and eighty to the one on the left.' Watson drew out the hybrid club that had served him so well all week, settled into his neat, familiar stance and ripped his drive down the centre of the fairway. That was the hard part done with, and as he walked past the corporate boxes in the marquee away to his left, and entered the scurrying wings of the huge gallery that had assembled to cheer him on, a low, eager, grateful roar began to rise above the hummocks and dunes. It is a feature of all golf tournaments that the crowd swells at the end, because as each pair finishes, the gallery multiplies; but on this occasion no one had slipped away, and the stands were groaning. Watson was writing an epic story, and those who had followed him this far did not want to miss the end.

As the tournament leader, he was in the final pair (along with a little-known Tasmanian called Matthew Goggin) and almost everyone was willing him to prevail. He was much loved, and would have drawn warm sentimental applause had he been last, but he was not last, he was one shot clear of the field, and even the most sceptical fans, for so long doubtful that he could pull this thing off, found themselves believing that he could not fail. For the last four days he had been smiling and calm – 'I guess "serene" is the right word for it' – and seemingly able to control the boiling nerves that so often besiege golfers in winning positions. 'My nerves are too well fried by now to feel anything,' he said, but this was obviously a joke. His hands were steady; he looked the very opposite of edgy. He walked with a quick yet unflustered, apologetic gait – all business. If anything, he looked keen to get this over and done with.

The shot to the green, while not simple, was no great mystery either. The pin was on the left, behind a grassy mound and a bunker, near a bank that ran down to a gully. Hardly anyone had taken dead aim, not with the wind coming from the left: the chances of finding a landing spot on the front edge were slender. Watson and his caddie hummed and hawed.

The flag was 189 yards away, closer than it had been on the preceding three days, when he had faced shots of 206, 204 and 202 yards and bounded on to the green with his seven-iron. 'What are you thinking?' said Watson. 'I'm thinking eight,' came the reply. 'So am I,' said Watson. Of course this was not an unusual quandary: in his long career he had found himself between clubs thousands of times. 'When you're playing the wind, you always have two clubs in mind before a shot. At least I do.' Both men felt that a nine-iron would pitch short of the putting surface, and who could say what sort of bounce it might find: it might career off at a berserk angle to the right, or kick left into that ugly clump. In the end it wasn't a hard decision: Watson went with the eight-iron.

The spectators in the high grandstands had no way of knowing about these deliberations, but if they had they might have shuddered, because just 40 minutes earlier they had watched a 21-year-old English player, Chris Wood, come to this exact same point with a chance to become Championship leader, and fly a nine-iron over the back of the green en route to a bogey that would leave him one shot off the pace. 'I've never hit a nine-iron 210 yards in my life,' he said afterwards, torn between joy and chagrin. 'Probably a little bit of adrenalin, a bit of a flier . . . but you know, I couldn't do anything about it. I hit a good shot; it landed on the line exactly how I wanted. It just absolutely went miles.'

Watson was 38 years older than Woods, and there had been an awful lot of talk all week about the prime value of 'experience'; now, surely, was the time to make it tell. He settled into his unfussy stance, gave a brisk waggle, made perfect contact (as usual) and arched his ball with a strong, piercing flight straight towards the safe front tongue of the green. 'I like it,' he said as it flew high above Turnberry. 'I like this shot!'

The spectators tilted their necks to watch it soar, and an approving rumble rose in the stands as those in line with the ball saw it fly bang on track. It pitched exactly where he wanted, bounced a couple of times before settling and then, like a plane landing, began to taxi up the lovely smooth surface on this famous green. The crowd burst into applause when it touched down, and continued as it commenced its final roll forward, but now the hands were stopping with abrupt mid-air uncertainty because – oh, for crying out loud – the damn thing was not slowing down.

Many golfers had suffered this fate today: in seeking to keep the ball away from the trouble on the left they let it wander off to the right or at the back, and this one too just kept on running. The green had been firmed by hours of sun and wind, and the back edge was coming closer, and on the ball trickled, closer and closer to the drop-off. It tried to slow, and for one long, heart-stopping moment it did seem to be coming to a halt near the flag, but eventually, with a careless air (it was difficult at this point not to personify the ball), it sneered, sauntered over the edge, gathered pace and bobbled down the mound at the back.

Not everyone froze in horror. 'Christ,' muttered the caddie-master with a grin, hurrying away from the scene. 'A bloody play-off.'

This seemed premature. The dream was not dead yet. Surely.

Back in America his caddie would say: 'My dying words will be: "I should have made Watson hit a nine-iron"' – and he was only half-joking. Hindsight is the best historian, and even Watson, a day or two later, conceded that he might have erred. 'In retrospect I probably would have hit a nine-iron,' he said. But Jack Nicklaus called and told him bluntly: 'Eighteen, you hit two perfect shots. The ball should have stayed up.' This was cheering news. 'I didn't know,' said Watson. 'Nobody had told me that the ball was just barely trickling off the green. And Jack doesn't patronise you, and he doesn't patronise me. That soothed the wound a little bit.'

It comes as something of a shock to realise that top golfers, like leading performers in any sport, are not pundits, and have to make do without the close-up luxury of the televised view. And since they often do hit the ball, as the saying goes, out of sight, it should not surprise us that they are sometimes the last people to know what has happened to it. If Watson had known then what he learned from Nicklaus, he might not have reproached himself when he paraded up the final fairway (obliged by the crowd's euphoric cheers to act like a bashful Roman emperor enjoying a Triumph) and inspected his lie behind the green. The ball was sitting quite well, as it happened: it hadn't reached the dense rough, and though a delicate chip would be required to get it over the mound (land on the upslope and the ball would die; land on the downslope and it would skip past the hole), he could, if he wished, roll the ball up and over with the club that had performed wonders for him all week: his putter.

'I went with the theory that your worst putt is better than your worst chip,' he said. 'I could have stubbed a sand wedge and left it short.'

When he looked at the slope in front he saw too that the grass was growing towards him, leaving a shot that would run, as it were, against the grain. Aware of the danger of the ball dying on the bank in front of him, he tried to ignore the row upon row of well-shod feet that rose up behind his shoulders – he was so close to the expensive seats that those in front could count the freckles on his neck – and urged himself to be firm. He settled over the ball, stilling the crowd with the intensity of his concentration, and nudged it forward. Once again there was a greedy roar of approval that thinned into an agitated, nervous gasp. 'The ball started bouncing. It came out of that lie bouncing, and hot.' It darted past the hole and skittered on. Hands clutched heads in alarm.

In truth, it was a clumsy effort that inspired much should-he-have-chipped-it? debate in the days that followed. For a player of Watson's skill, it was not a testing shot: drop a dozen balls in that spot and he would get all of them nearer than this one. 'I just felt like I had a better chance to get it close,' he said, justifying his second queasy club selection. 'And I got a little too thoughtful. I was thinking it was going to be slow, and gave it way too much goose. I gunned it on by.'

Too thoughtful . . . now there was an interesting insight. Golf may seem an introspective pursuit, and much is always made of the so-called 'mental game', but it may be that thoughtfulness is the enemy of good play, an interfering, contrary force that needs to be tranquillised. The true goal of those expensive gurus and psychologists is to pacify the jittery mind, and replace it with the kind of pure, transcendent empty-headedness that produces good ball-striking. George Plimpton once wrote about the confusions that lay siege to his best intentions when he addressed a ball, and described his inner game as resembling the patchy chain of command in a Japanese aircraft carrier: resonant orders issued by brainy admirals high on the bridge were twisted and muddled by lazy, careless or drunk functionaries lower down the chain of command.

It was infuriating: in an ideal world Watson would have coaxed that approach putt up to the hole and enjoyed an easy tap-in before lifting his cap and smiling his modest, blue-eyed smile to the watching crowd, as well as to the billion or so eyeballs glued to television sets around the world (it was Sunday lunchtime in Watson's home state, Kansas), not to mention the poised pen of history. The world is not ideal, however, and to have to make this shot, on this day, for this title, in this place, was about as much as any professional golfer could reasonably wish for. Indeed, the whole essence of the mental inertia aspired to by the mind-gurus is that it declines to dwell on the past. What's done is done: spilt milk cannot be unspilt. The only shot that counts, in the sacred texts, is the one to come. This, roughly, is what golfers mean by 'taking the positives', and it is true of fans too. As Watson walked after his ball with a sag in his shoulders, the crowd forced itself to stay in the zone and think positive. It had to scrub away the painful fact that the shot to come was a putt of exactly the length Watson had become famous for missing, because on this splendid evening, with history beckoning, he might – you never knew – hole it. And if he did, it would be an even more beautiful ending.

Time always seems to stagger at the end of the Open, because the long, 150-year saga of previous championships, played over this same terrain, hovers over the scene like a grave presiding spirit. The ghosts of previous encounters drift through deep shadows on the sunlit turf and insinuate themselves into the present-day drama. The roars of ancient crowds rumble below the cries of modern fans. Watson was one of these ghosts himself, yet here he was, a flesh-and-blood golfer with one shot to play.

He had won the Open five times, most recently in 1983, more than a quarter of a century before. A sixth win would lift him alongside the great Harry Vardon, creator of the wrap-finger grip used by most golfers, as the most successful player in the history of golf's oldest championship. And while no one would wish to diminish the excellence of Vardon in any way, those titles were achieved in the Open's early years, against small fields of pioneering sportsmen, none as studious or skilful as himself. These were stirring times, when Old Tom Morris and his amazing son Young Tom Morris wrote the original chapters in the long history of this fabled event, but a Watson win would match anything in the game's legendary past. To let so many years go by before returning in triumph was not even slightly precedented: in 1984, seeking a famous hat-trick, Watson had come second to Seve Ballesteros, and in 1994 he made a better-than-brave run, missing a hatful of makeable putts before surrendering the trophy to Nick Price, but since then he had not laid a finger anywhere near the Claret Jug. A sixth win here – just one more putt – would equal anything ever done in golf; quite a weight to hang on one simple roll of a ball on smooth green grass.

Still, it could not have happened to a more deserving fellow. Watson (everyone agreed) was one of the good guys: a courteous, modest golfer of the old school. He accepted the often wearying attentions of the public and media with patience and grace, successfully pretending not to mind when he was waylaid between mouthfuls at dinner. More than any other competitor, he seemed to uphold the fair-play virtues that in most sports, these days, seemed honoured more in the breach than the observance.

He would later reject the suggestion that he was distracted by tremors of history-in-the-making ('Absolutely not . . . quite the contrary'), but if this is true, he was the only one who was immune. The thousands of fans in the grandstands had spent four days watching this semi-miracle unfold with slowly diminishing disbelief, and by now almost everyone felt it was somehow destined, written. Up in the hotel, managers were crossing fingers and toes, praying for the Watson victory that would make their refurbished resort the world's most momentous golf destination.

Even Watson's fellow players were holding their breath. The pair who had finished just ahead of him, Lee Westwood and Ross Fisher, broke off from post-round interviews with the media to witness the moment.

It was hard to believe, then – however necessary for his own composure that he deny it – that the echoes from his past did not reach Watson's hands at this time. This coastline was full of memories; it was a setting with which he himself was synonymous. Thirty-two years earlier, before his playing partner Matthew Goggin was born, he had snapped a one-iron into this fairway, then fired a seven-iron right at the pin.

On that occasion, after some celebrated heroics from Jack Nicklaus (who drove into the base of a gorse bush on the kneecap of the dog-leg, heaved his approach to the edge of the green and holed an absurd putt that snaked across it before diving into the cup), Watson wasted no time tapping in his own short birdie effort for the famous win. The pair of them had left the rest of the field so far behind (ten shots, to be exact) that it seemed a gladiatorial tussle, and went into the annals as the 'Duel in the Sun', a summer epic that had been replayed on loops and in souvenir pull-outs for years. Never more so than this week: all those watching had, in some corner of their mind, a memory-flash of Watson, in the kind of sickly tartan-effect trousers that give golf a bad name, leaving the fray arm in arm with his great, yellow-sweatered opponent in a gesture of sporting chivalry that completed the image to perfection.

The 18th hole at Turnberry was named after that grand day. It was 'Duel in the Sun', and Watson himself had given a speech at the renaming ceremony in 2003 (when he also won the Senior Open), announcing with a grin that those trousers were alive and well, and living on Jesper Parnevik.

The emotional resonance of the occasion stretched further. Not so long ago Watson had won another major tournament on this lovely Ailsa Course: the 2003 Senior Open. It was one of his favourite places in the world, and he was staying, as usual, in the Watson Suite, up in the hotel that overlooks the course (and which names rooms after its champions). His table for two in the dining room allowed him to breakfast and dine with his wife overlooking this very stretch of velvet turf, this emblematic horseshoe of grandstands that creates the theatre-in-the-round ending to all Open championships. And if he ever needed a nightcap, why, he had only to step into the 'Duel in the Sun' bar, where players lounged around a red-baize snooker table and propped their cues against the famous photograph of Watson and Nicklaus walking away from that fateful 18th green. The Turnberry clubhouse was equally full of Duel in the Sun memorabilia – indeed this whole landscape was impregnated with souvenirs: all week Watson had been able to recall that this spot was where Jack found his ball short of the gorse, and that fringe was where he had holed an improbable putt all those long, smiling years ago.

There were more recent, giddier memories. The first chapter of this week's sensational story had been written right here, three days ago, when Watson holed a sixty-foot putt across the green to become the halfway leader and 'roll back', as the papers were quick to have it, 'the years'. And in his three visits to the hole so far this week, he had needed only eleven shots (two pars to add to that euphoric opening-day birdie) on this last lap of the course. It presented, to say the least, a familiar challenge.

And now it came down to this. Immortality lay in that plain white cup just eight feet away. All week, Watson – a golfer as well known for his decades-old putting fragility as for his still-crystalline ball-striking – had been holing putts from implausible angles and distances. Time after time some force beyond himself, something uncanny, seemed to nudge his ball to the hole, lifting him towards the antique silver claret jug on which his name was already so many times engraved that it seemed his by right. One more smooth stroke was all he (and we) required. Just one more.

This for the Open. How many golfing children (or grown-up children) around the world have imagined such a whisper, such an invitation? It is a phrase that echoes across golf's fields of dreams (otherwise known as driving ranges) like a mantra. This for it . . . This for the Open. It can be sober or ironic, light-hearted or grave, but it always carries a bracing gust of conclusive fact. What happens now, it says, is irrevocable. This, right here, is the point where all the twists and turns, each of the lucky bounces and breaks that delivered us to this juncture, fade into the mist. This one straightforward stroke before us now . . . this is how the story will end.

And the mischievous golfing demon that eavesdrops on such moments is always there to underline a stark and undeniable fact:

Nothing is written. This could go either way.

It sounds obvious, or dumb. But most golf triumphs are eval-uated in retrospect, and drained of anything arbitrary or capricious. There is a reflex to present them as fated or willed (if nothing else, logical). So Padraig Harrington's great victory in the previous year's PGA (the season's last major) was casually ascribed to his work ethic, his attention to detail, his humility and the confidence that came from being a two-time Open champion. These are powerful factors, but in the end he won because his long putt on the final green trickled in, while Sergio Garcia's similar effort scraped the hole and missed. Not so long ago, Harrington was famous for repeatedly coming second, and it was widely mentioned that he lacked the little nugget of special-something that turned also-rans into champions. Few were happy to observe that coming second was both a heroic achievement and a cracking good sign: even Nicklaus came second more often than he won.

Anyway, no one could say anything disparaging about Watson's will to win, because it was not only his unusual age – two months short of his 60th birthday – that made his situation so remarkable. There was the astonishing fact of his new hip, installed as recently as October 2008. The world's media were so gripped by Tiger Woods's knee, the repair of which had kept him out of the game for nine months (including the year before's Open at Birkdale) that Watson's own encounter with the surgeon's knife had passed with little comment. It was evidently not fun, however. 'It took me two and a half months before I could hit a golf ball,' he said.

When he was able to swing a club, the old pleasure returned. 'I hit 200 drivers as hard as I could, and said, yeah, it feels good.' And now, six months later, here he was, rewriting the textbook on what was possible in elite golf. Watson had won his five titles in an eight-year burst between 1975 and 1983, and no one over 50 had ever won a championship of this stature. But this week he had led from the start, and despite many waverings he was still ahead.

He was not your average senior golfer: he was a much-garlanded all-time great who seemed to have a mystical affinity for the way the game was played in Scotland. He was serious-minded too. Like all great players of his seniority, he insisted that he was no mere 'ceremonial' golfer, and would not have entered if he did not feel competitive.

Everyone nodded and smiled at this, but few believed him: it sounded like a pleasant fantasy. Sure, it was plucky, virtuous and just what you would expect Watson to say: he was not the sort of man to occupy a spot in the Open that could have been filled by a younger combatant, just for the sake of an elderly ego trip. But golf, the reasoning went, had moved on. These days it was a game for youthful, gym-pounding dynamos with ball-bearings where waists used to be, a tight cadre of psychologists and swing analysts, and pink/yellow trim on their trendy white duds.

One or two people noticed, however, that the thing about the much-vaunted new technology in club design – the titanium-graphite revolution that was achieving vast distances and forcing even classic courses such as Turnberry to elongate themselves – was that it allowed older golfers to fly bunkers as freely as their better-muscled young comrades. Nor, in golf, was strength the be-all and end-all: one of Nicklaus's many trusty slogans insisted that to hit the ball further we must not make the mistake of trying to hit it harder – we must hit it better. Golf is a game of timing and accuracy, not mere brawn, and there was evidence to suggest that thanks to modern medicine and nutrition, 50 was not so elderly as it used to be. Only a year earlier, at Birkdale, the 53-year-old Greg Norman had snatched a headline-grabbing lead he did not surrender until the last hour.

Norman, however, was blatantly young for his years – he still had the streamlined silhouette of the young white shark he had once impersonated – and was patently rejuvenated (temporarily, it turned out) by the new love of his life, the tennis champion Chris Evert. She did look, some mean souls remarked, even more like Norman than did Norman himself, but their marriage seemed to have lifted the man's heart as well his game. Evert, he was happy to confess, had opened his eyes about the level of effort and commitment required from those who aspired to excellence.

Watson had few of these Aussie accessories. He was recently remarried too, but did not offer himself as a romantic lead. He wasn't a fast-lane, how-big's-your-yacht kind of guy like Norman; nor did he stride up the fairways, shoulders rocking like a man still trying to impress lissom models in a nightclub. He shuffled along with the suggestion of a limp, in a tired quickstep and with the grimace of a rambler determined not to give in to blisters. And where Norman really did roll back the years at Birkdale by leaking final-round shots to Harrington, Watson had spent the last few days clinging on like a stubborn Highland terrier.

He had not contended in one of golf's four major tournaments since the last millennium. He was officially ranked number 1374 in the world, and while this was not a realistic measure of his ability (ranking points are available to those who play regular Tour events, and these days Watson made his home on the Seniors

Tour), it certainly made him a very smelly outsider. Anyone fool-ish or sentimental enough to put a few hundred pounds on a Watson win was shaking with the possibility of becoming a mil-lionaire. For here he was, right in at the sharp end of things.

This for the Open.

Far out of sight, up on the hill, in the Duel in the Sun bar of the hotel, a gaggle of competitors – among them Nick Faldo, Robert Allenby, Boo Weekley, Chad Campbell and Darren Clarke – were having a drink and watching the denouement on television. When Watson walked up the 18th, his playing part-ner Matthew Goggin had stood to one side and sportingly applauded, as if he were a spectator, not a man two shots off the lead. And as the crowd rose to give Watson as thunderous and urgent an arm-waving ovation as has ever swayed an Open finale, these players had pushed open the doors, stepped on to the ter-race, looked down at the tiny figure in the pale-blue sweater (the same colour as his eyes) inching towards them on the toy-sized golf course beneath their feet, and clapped him home.

Down below, the crowd fell quiet as Watson prepared to putt. But something had changed. As he climbed the mound and chased after his errant first blow, there was an imperceptible hint of dismay and self-doubt in his hurried, let's-get-this-over-with demeanour. The serenity he had spoken of, the lightness of spirit that saw him seek out the hole with such unearthly calm, seemed to have dissolved. The crowd knew it: breaths stopped in mouths, hairs rose on necks, nails lay unbitten. The silence was heavy and nervous. For four days Watson had written a golf-ing fairy-tale – it seemed unthinkable that he might, at this last gasp, forget how the ending went. So effectively had he suspended reality this week that it made people's stomachs twist to see him stutter now.

It was often said, afterwards, that Watson 'suddenly looked his age', but this never had much merit as an argument, since it was held (often by the same people) that it was precisely Watson's advanced years – his superior canniness and experience – that had propelled him to the lead in the first place. In truth, it seemed only that in the tension of this moment *we* saw his true age. Only now did the fluttering images of a fresh-faced Young Tom, clenching his gleeful fists by this flag in 1977, clash with the sobering reality of Old Tom, who after a golfing lifetime spent in sunshine and wind was as creased and weather-beaten as an old fisherman. He had not changed, but we had. The rose-tints fell from our spectacles, and the enigmatic half-smile that all week had seemed wise, benign and ageless suddenly looked anxious, even world-weary.

It was hard not to feel that a cog had slipped, or a crack had appeared in the magic mirror. It had been a tightrope walk, and Watson seemed to have done the thing that high-wire artistes must not do: he had looked down. Please, the crowd urged. Just one more putt. But the trajectory of faith was twisted in a sour knot. Having been forced to set aside the conviction that Watson probably would not stay the course (having come, in effect, to believe in miracles), we had to face the fact that miracles are rare.

It is a function of crowds that at certain moments everyone has the same thought. True to form, that is how it was in the closing moments of the 138th Open at Turnberry. Please let there be things in life that are too good to be true, we prayed in silent unison. Please don't let him fail now.

It is interesting how strong these feelings can be. And while they may be inspired to a large extent by selfish hopes – we desire that memorable things happen while we are present, so we can boast for ever that we were there – a larger part has to do with the deep human thirst for stories. We are narrative creatures, and golf climaxes give us striking drama with terrific suspense. In structure they are a last-man-standing endurance test, but since they are tests of skill and nerve rather than mere drudge staying power, they engage more varied emotions. With each shot the field compresses and the story shifts; slowly, as the days pass, a diminishing number of endings becomes possible. Eventually the tournament sculpts itself into tangible shape, with both leading players and a supporting cast.

This is why tight finishes in golf tournaments can be excruciating. The story of the entire event does not exist until the ending has emerged; the ending shapes all that has gone before. We feel that it all hangs on the very last roll – because it does. In theory, Watson's first shot counted for as much as his last. When he cuffed that mid-iron off the 1st tee on Thursday morning . . . if he had skewed it into the sand he might have been unable to reach the green, might have been on a plane by now . . .

This is true. But it really is the concluding move that shapes both the tournament that has gone before, and the story we will tell into the future. What Watson did now would determine whether this was one of the all-time great days in the history of golf, or another damned close-run thing.

Watson has never been a slow player, so of course he did not allow such broodings to afflict his fans for long. He crouched over the ball, took a quick, familiar stab at it, and poked it short and right.

It was, as he said, 'a lousy putt'. It never looked like going in.

And that was that.

It was like falling off a cliff. And it was right, in a way, to call it a non-event, because the main thing that happened was that an enormous, rich thing did not happen. A few seconds earlier the world was swollen with possibilities; in the time it takes for a ball to veer off-line, the sun had darted behind a cloud and the world felt cold, shrunken and in shadow.

'During practice,' Watson told an interviewer, 'I made a slight adjustment to my putting stroke. I wanted to make sure I went more square to square. I kept that thought throughout the week, and that's what I was trying to think on that eight-footer. Square to square; do what you've been doing. But I took the club a little inside and never did get it in position. I blocked it with my left hand. Never released. Went right. Awful.'

Awful, indeed. And yet . . . He had not lost, but neither had he won.

This thing wasn't over. There would be a play-off.

The stands tittered with nervous static, and it was hard to know what to think. Something magical had died, but perhaps it could be retrieved. All week Watson had proved there could be second comings; what was to prevent him rising above this death and winning the four-hole decider?

That final putt, though . . . It would not be easy to remain sanguine after that. It was worse than feeble; it was enfeebling.

Weak putts cut golfers to the quick for a specific reason; the vocabulary of the game is unequivocal. Putts that blaze past are held to be 'bold', 'fierce' or even 'merry', slurs anyone can put up with: they make even bad players feel like buccaneers, pirates, rebels. But putts that fall short induce a grave, eyes-averted response, as if to a bereavement. Golf's most boring truism – never up, never in – is a folksy attempt to disguise the sense that short putts betray a defect of character. They are weak . . . timid . . . shy. They hit golfers where it hurts by attacking players' already suspect manliness (let's face it – golf is not rugby). This is true especially among the executive classes that love and sponsor the game. In their business lives they enjoy a certain deference from colleagues and underlings. They fancy themselves clear-eyed men of the world, who take no prisoners and expect no favours. Weak putts expose them as paltry bluffers; they carry a lethal whiff of cowardice and mental frailty.

None of this was going through Watson's mind. One of the strengths of his game – the reason he had won five Opens and almost, just now, a sixth – was the way he seemed able to accept the slings and arrows of seaside golf. One of the features of the Open is that it always takes place on a traditional links, over deep sandpits that stretch along a wind-battered coast. The uneven terrain and squally weather make luck, the careless run of the ball, a major element, and Watson understood this. He did not moan, and took care to emphasise the good fortune that came his way; he knew that luck was part of the game. 'The guys that are down in 50th,' he would say, 'I guarantee you, they got a lot of bad bounces, and didn't make some putts. I'm pretty realistic about that.'

This is a non-negotiable fact of all golf, but it applies especially to the game played on these historic shores. Indeed, the phrase that echoes through the marquees in any Open week (just ahead of 'Be interesting to see what happens when the wind blows') is 'That's links golf.' It fits almost every circumstance. A jagged bounce into a pot bunker? That's links golf. A haughty drive that curls into the heather? That's links golf. A splash of coffee on your slick Hugo Boss trousers? That's links golf.

In a way, that is how this play-off felt – like a crazy bounce. Watson would now play the 5th, 6th, 17th and 18th (a demanding little circuit, to be sure) against . . . hang on, could this be right? . . . Stewart Cink.

One didn't wish to be rude, but where the hell did Cink spring from?

In reality, he had never been far away. And half an hour earlier he had rolled in a firm birdie putt at 17 to stand on the 18th tee at one under par. It didn't look good enough to beat Lee Westwood or Watson, but on the 18th green he rolled in another, almost twice as long as Watson's – for birdie, not par – and clenched his fist in triumph. And I don't like to boast, but I watched it fall, nudged the man next to me, and said that we might have just seen the putt that won the Open. Naturally, I didn't mean it: it was black humour. And when Watson also birdied the 17th to stand on the final tee with a solid one-shot lead there seemed no way that Cink's brave effort would win him anything more than enviable prize money. The fact, however, stood: at the very last minute of the eleventh hour he had pulled off an abrupt two-shot swing against the leader. Coming at the end of a tournament as tight as this, it was a thumping turn-around.

Still . . . Stewart Cink? At the start of the day it looked as if Ross Fisher might run away with things, and for a long time Lee Westwood was the clear favourite. There was a flutter of excitement when two former champions, Ernie Els and Justin Leonard, made some putts to hoist themselves into the reckoning, and Chris Wood, the young Englishman playing only his second Open, somehow grabbed four birdies and an eagle to come within touching distance. Matthew Goggin, playing with Watson, was never out of the running, and for a few heady moments (when he rolled in a birdie putt on the 15th) it was possible that the 16-year-old amateur from Italy Matteo Manassero might come up with a fresh story altogether – a parable about the unbeatable value of inexperience, perhaps.

Jim Furyk, Retief Goosen, Luke Donald . . . the sudden landing of an eagle would have propelled any of them to the top of the leaderboard. But Cink appeared in none of these fluid last-day scenarios. 'I was never really out of it,' he said, with fine candour, 'but I was never really in it.' He was one of the few players to shoot better than par on the final day, however, and birdie-birdie finish is not to be sneezed at, so it wasn't his fault that he suddenly found himself cast as the villain of this piece. Watson had been writing a golden myth, and Cink, leaping out from behind a tree at this late stage, seemed every inch the pantomime baddie. Tall, strong and bald beneath his cap, he did not quite resemble a wicked witch, an ugly sister, even a big bad wolf. But something in the situation infused him with aspects of all of these baleful characters, and quite a few more.

In four days of Open golf it had never felt as though the two men could belong on the same page. Watson had blazed the trail and captured the headlines. Cink, a seasoned Ryder-Cupper and US Tour winner, had simply played his usual high-calibre game and not flagged. Some of the blame was ours: caught up in the soap opera of Watson's heroics we had been far too dismissive of Cink's chances. But it was still an act of bold disobedience on his part to ignore the script and actually compete for the trophy. For years he had been strictly supporting cast – this was his 12th Open, and he had missed the halfway cut more times than was decent – so it seemed astounding that he should wind up as joint leader.

There was some consolation, for Watson fans, in the fact that in most fairy tales the wicked witches and big bad wolves get their comeuppance in the end. But who said that this was a fairy tale? We still didn't know what sort of story we were watching here.

It was the Open, by its very nature unpredictable.

That's links golf.

CHAPTER TWO

The Beginning

Other things were being settled beside the small matter of the winner. The top ten players (and ties) guaranteed themselves a place in the 2010 Open at St Andrews. And while this was a matter of little relevance for some: the Open admits previous champions aged 60 or under, so former winners like Faldo and Norman could go right ahead and book hotel rooms for the following July. And players like Westwood, Donald, Goosen and Els . . . well, they were almost bound to be riding high enough in the money lists to be admitted. But some of the other high finishers could count this as a very valuable prize indeed. It would liberate them from the tense scrum of qualifying the following year, and allow them to plan their schedules in peace.

Since there were five players in joint eighth place, there were 13 eligible candidates in all. It goes without saying that they had won giddy handfuls of money, and for players such as Goggin (£157,000) or the young South African Thomas Aiken, or the US-Swedish Richard S. Johnson (both of whom won £90,400), this alone was a serious cause for celebration. But the exemption that accompanied it was priceless. Goggin had been a last-minute call-up, summoned to Turnberry at the eleventh hour, while

Aiken and Johnson had fought their way through the 2009 qualifying system before teeing it up in Scotland. None of them would have to suffer such indignities next time. They could already look forward to a midsummer crescendo in Fife, in the Open's 150th year, at the home of golf itself.

One competitor with more mixed feelings was Chris Wood, who had qualified this year through a fine performance in his debut Open at Birkdale in 2008. Tall, slim and scruffy-headed, he looked more like a student than a golfer, but at Birkdale he had played brilliantly for four days to come fifth, and win the silver medal that goes to the leading amateur in the field. With a proud father (four-handicap) toting his bag, and 60 pals and relatives from Gloucestershire cheering him on, he had floated in a daze through the week before playing the final round with Ian Poulter. In the end he finished tied with Jim Furyk, one behind Greg Norman and Henrik Stenson. It had been, he said, 'the best week of my life' – even though he had to wave aside a tempting cheque worth £168,500. If it wasn't seventh heaven, then it was certainly sixth, and even the absent-minded text message he had received from his sister ('Are you still at that Open thingy?') could not dent the happy mood.

This year was different: he was now a fully fledged (though novice) touring professional, whose rock-steady third place (only one stroke shy of the play-off) was a genuine world-class effort. This time he could bank the prize money (£255,000 – more than enough to pay for his new flat), bask in the glow from this dizzy continuation of his Open career, and ponder the pleasant possibility that, following a fifth and then a third place, he was almost destined to be in contention in 2010.

The drive south was a troubled one, however. He could barely speak, and not only because he was tired. 'I was just numb,' he said. 'If I was thinking of anything it was a bit of pride about a couple of clutch putts down the stretch to get back into contention.' The journey was more than 400 miles, and this time his girlfriend and

his sisters were in the back, but the car hummed down the motorway in dejected silence. 'They knew there was not a lot they could
say that would make any difference.'

He pulled up in Bristol at two in the morning, and began to
shake. 'It is hard to put into words just how devastated I felt. All
the negative emotions were there, the disappointment and annoy-
ance . . . It occurred to me then how close I had come to getting
my hands on the Claret Jug.' It didn't help to learn that he would
have been the youngest winner since Willie Auchterlonie in
1893. It was 'the dream of a lifetime' – and the loss was more
than enough to dampen his homecoming.

If losing were not painful, winning would scarcely matter. The
sharp consolation for Wood was the knowledge that his performance had won him entry not only to the PGA, the next
major, in August, but to the 2010 Open as well. There were
already plans to make it a memorable jubilee, and Wood did not
have to spend a single night (barring some unexpected injury or
illness) wondering whether he could be part of it. This was by
any standards a luxury: there were plenty of excellent players who
would have killed for such a golden ticket. Somewhere in the
depths of his sad ending was a bright new beginning. It is not
true in golf that there is always next year – the vagaries of form
and the whims of qualification are too tenuous and unreliable for
that. But for Wood, that third consecutive Open invitation was
as good as in the post.

This is how it always is: where one Open ends, another begins.
To the crowd, the television audience and even the media, it is
just one extra-long week in a mostly cloudless golfing calendar.
But in truth it is a deeply rooted part of the British sporting scene
that is never, even in the coldest pit of winter, entirely dormant.
The four days in July that comprise the Championship itself are
merely the glamorous tip of a huge qualifying mountain that
begins in February, and an even larger administrative effort that

begins more or less the moment the winner fills the Claret Jug with champagne, or Guinness, or Lucozade, or whatever golfers drink these days. By tradition, the secretary of the R&A 'concludes' the green-jacketed presentation ceremony by anticipating (and extending invitations to) the following year's event, and in this he is raising a glass to the idea that the Open, far from being a one-off pageant, is a continuous process, a wiry thread that runs, like the legend in a stick of rock, throughout the entire golfing year. The giant yellow leaderboard fixes its gaze on the future, and announces the following year's venue.

'We do try to take August off, to be fair,' said David Hill, the dark, dapper tournament director from Northern Ireland. 'But so far as we're concerned the Open really starts at the beginning of September. That's when we look to finalise accommodation for the following summer, and look at car parking, and even start to plan the tented village area.'

It helps that the Open rota makes a point of taking the event back to familiar sites, but it remains an awe-inspiring logistical effort. A year in advance, Hill knew that he and his team would have their work cut out. Turnberry is one of the more spectacular golfing venues, but also one of the more remote: despite being a mere half an hour from an international airport (Prestwick), it is not on the railway and is a good 90-minute drive from the nearest city (Glasgow). The reason it had not hosted an Open in 15 years was that, in 1994, it inspired a mind-numbing four-day traffic jam on the single trunk road (the A77) that runs south from Ayr ('It was bad,' said Peter Dawson, the R&A's chief executive, a Cambridge man and once a scratch player. 'There's no getting away from it.') There was also an acute shortage of hotel space in the immediate area, and nothing resembling a vibrant pub or restaurant culture.

This was part of its rough-and-ready charm: Ayrshire was not the Cote d'Azur, and felt closer to golf's hardy, windswept origins as a result. But from a practical point of view it was tricky. In

October 2008 David Hill emphasised, on the Open website, that the R&A was determined to 'take' its annual championship to 'all the top links courses', which might not have been ideally phrased (it made the Open sound like an elderly relative in frail health), but was a fair point. No one disputed Turnberry's merits as a golf course (though stern critics considered it a mite easy for the world's top players), yet no one could pretend that it was convenient.

'The village has 300 people in it,' said Hill, 'but we have to create a properly serviced facility for some 30,000 people a day, which means meeting all the statutory regulations regarding electricity, water, drainage, and so on. It isn't as easy as you might think.' Golf fans rarely pause to contemplate the labour that goes into staging their beloved majors (though they are not slow to complain if the coffee is too weak, or the queues too long), but Hill enjoys no such luxury. 'We had to spend, for instance, well over half a million pounds on utilities, and that's just to put in the basic things, that's before you hire any generators or anything.'

The first of these essential units was a new drainage system for the course and a 60,000-gallon water tank – a strange resource, some might think, in an area of epic rainfall. The next most pressing construction, as at any Open, was a high-calibre media centre. The modern world's press, television and radio personnel have high expectations (and needs), and the R&A is more than eager to help them get the message out. It takes a bit of planning, a task that fell (for the second time) to Malcolm Booth. He sighed at the thought of it. 'You're talking about a facility for around 750 working journalists, all of whom want phone lines and high-speed internet, in what is essentially a field in the middle of nowhere. They want to stream video as well. That's an awful lot of technology, and we have to get it right. There was a time when the media tent was literally that – a tent, with trestle tables on grass. But that obviously won't do any more.' These days the media get a marquee like an airport terminal, with long banks of desk space,

swivel-chaired views of giant screens, a live hole-by-hole scoreboard, a restaurant, drinks machines and a busy office churning
out piles of condensed facts, news announcements, schedules, statistics and up-to-the-minute player interviews.

'They are quite spoiled,' said Booth. 'We just hope they appre-
ciate it. To be fair, most of them do.'

In truth, the 138th Open began centuries before the first ball was
struck. The event is so soaked in history, and so proud of its con-
nections to a storied past, that all Opens bear the imprints of the
game's first stirrings. James II's famous anti-golf decree ('It is
ordaynt . . . that ye fut bawe and ye golf be Utterly cryt doune
and nocht usyt') is usually taken as proof that golf, or something
like it, was alive in the 15th century, and though this text is not
crystal clear ('golf' might at that time have been a game for village mobs, for all we know), the game was certainly taking shape
at Carnoustie, St Andrews and elsewhere by the time of the
English Civil War.

In 2010 the Royal and Ancient Golf Club has been a name to
conjure with for 256 years, and for most of that time it has been
one of those strange yet typical British institutions: a private club
that for historic reasons is also the ruling authority (tennis and
cricket have similar pedigrees). It actually predates the Open by
more than a hundred years. On 14 May 1754, 22 'Noblemen and
Gentlemen' from Fife formed themselves into a golfing society
on the St Andrews links. There is a widespread supposition that
Scottish golf grew up as a working man's pastime, but these pioneering golfers were clubbable types: a brace of earls, a pair of
baronets, several Honourables, two professors of philosophy, a
lieutenant-general and many other notables. They were not quite
pioneers; the Honourable Company of Edinburgh Golfers had
banded together in Leith some ten years earlier and had written
out the 13 articles (concerning how to play out of 'wattery filth',
and so on) that would form the basis of the rules.

In 1766 the two clubs joined forces to create an annual competition, with a silver stick by way of a trophy, open to members of both clubs; and as the years turned into decades the St Andrews club became the de facto 'home of golf'. In 1834 King William IV agreed to become its patron, thus bestowing on it the royal seal of approval.

At this early stage in its development, golf in Scotland was primarily a winter sport. It could not become a summer pastime until the industrial revolution delivered technology smart enough to cut grass in the growing season (the earliest horse-drawn cylinder mowers appeared in the 1840s). Until then, fairways had to be trimmed by sheep or rabbits. This was only one of many ways in which golf owed its growth to the industrial energy of mid-Victorian Britain. It often seems a pastoral idyll, full of exciting wildlife and birds crying on a sea breeze, but it is not a coincidence that the game is played with 'irons', and it was mass production (of both clubs and balls) that carried golf beyond the bounds of its original, upper-class champions. By the same token, it was the arrival of the railway that allowed urbane Scots to explore their new, wild-seeming seaside links. Trains reached Carnoustie on the Dundee and Arbroath Line in 1838, St Andrews in 1852, and soon afterwards the new railway opened up the magnificent golf coast in Scotland's south-west (Prestwick, Troon and Turnberry). Traces of this heritage are so integral that they are barely noticed. When Pete Dye (later a leading American golf architect) came to Scotland in 1963 to play the Amateur Championship, he was delighted (at Prestwick) to see bunkers lined with railway sleepers, and borrowed the idea for his own work at Whistling Straits and Kiawah Island.

In 1897 the Royal and Ancient was asked by a group of leading clubs (exasperated by constant squabbles and disputes) to produce a uniform summary of the game's laws, and ever since then it has been (except in America and Mexico: the United States Golf Association (USGA) was formed, with exactly the same purpose, three years earlier) the ruling body of the world game. In truth there was only one essential rule: the ball 'must be played as it lyes'.

Down the long years the Royal and Ancient has at times seemed stuffy and hidebound, but its historical right is incontestable. Nevertheless, in the 21st century it was hard to explain why a private club with 2400 members (none of them women) should continue to be the presiding body of a huge global sport, so the Royal and Ancient, on its 250th anniversary, launched a separate corporate wing to take charge of the commercial side, the rules and the running of the Open itself. This distinct arm was named the R&A: those evocative letters are no longer an abbreviation or a nickname, but a specific corporate brand. The R&A is a global concern, operating on behalf of some 30 million golfers in 123 countries. Apart from running the Open (the cash cow), it presides over major amateur championships, publishes the rules in many languages (distributing them free), and runs development projects in Africa, Eastern Europe and Asia.

All of this would be merely a historical aside if it weren't for the fact that the original golfing landscape – Scottish links – is the DNA of the modern game. The physical feature that binds the modern Open to these faded stories is the crumpled links landscape, what John Updike once called 'the medieval motherland' of golf. Glimpses of it can be seen everywhere, because it was Scottish émigrés from these corrugated sand pits who fanned out, first to England and then to North America. Where they could (on England's north-west coast, at Lytham and Hoylake), they created exact copies, but inland they echoed an alternative Scottish landscape – pine, heather and gorse – in commuter-belt miniature.

The many stories concerning golf's early years share something of the quality of myth. Early photographs show groups of men striking oddly formal stances, stiffly relaxed, or crouched in a pretend-stance over the ball. For the most part they look like

thick-booted, hard-drinking navvies, or off-duty soldiers; they
hold their clubs butt down, like walking sticks or rifles. The class
distinctions are painful: resplendent patrons stare at the lens, while
their far more skilled inferiors look weary, like scruffy gardeners.
It is from these complicated roots that the authority of the Royal
and Ancient derives, because every single Open, including the
138th at Turnberry, is rooted in this unique original landscape.

As it happened, Turnberry was one of the most famous and
spectacular courses in Britain, a gorgeous slice of Ayrshire coastline overlooking the humped outline of the Isle of Arran (and
occasionally, on rare clear days, the faraway silhouette of
Northern Ireland). Whatever happened on the fairways, this
famed sporting joust would be framed by the same magical
scenery in which golf had grown up. The drama – there is always
drama – would be acted out on the same hummocks on which
the game took root: it would put millionaire players with cashmere sweaters and private jets into ancient hillocks that dripped
with bleak, wind-swept traditions and gnarled folk wisdom. The
Open was a theatre of victory and defeat in which the finest of
fine lines – a cruel bounce or a momentary loss of composure –
could decide the outcome of a hole, a game, a tournament, or a
life; so it seemed more than apt that this one should take place on
rocks where Robert Bruce had once had a castle (the remains
having long since dissolved into the beetling cliffs below the 10th
tee).

Not the least of Turnberry's attractions is its queenly hotel,
which sits on the slope above the links – half fortress, half luxury
liner – high, white and superb, with a red-tile roof that added
a rakish splash of colour to a green-drab hillscape. It is historic
in its own right, a sporting child of South Ayrshire's 'Golfers'
Line', and the first grand golfing resort in Great Britain. It was
more than a hundred years old, and had seen plenty of social
finery, two world wars and three memorable Opens. No one
knew what would happen in tournament week, but one thing

was certain: rain or shine (rain, most likely) the setting would be second to none.

In its earliest days, the Open championship had little to do with the Royal and Ancient, because it was the brainchild of another new golf club, at Prestwick, on the opposite (west) coast in Ayrshire. In 1851 57 would-be members met in the Red Lion Hotel and agreed to form a club under the captaincy of – who else? – the 13th Earl of Eglinton. Tom Morris (at this stage child-less, and a long way from being 'Old') was asked to lay a 12-hole track over the lumpy dunes as its first 'Keeper of Green', and he did a grand job. The first hole, in particular, was a 578-yard mon-ster, a colossal and often dispiriting challenge for Victorian clubs and balls.

In 1860 Eglinton and his club paid £25 for a chunky Challenge belt – red Morocco leather, with a huge silver clasp – and invited Scotland's finest to tussle for it in the first 'General Open Competition'. Prestwick invited both Musselburgh and the Royal and Ancient, among others, to participate, but found no support, so pressed ahead alone. Eglinton was a belt man – he put up a gold equivalent for archery – but this golf one was (pardon the sacrilege) hideous: a prizefighter's trophy. Even so, it was deemed too valuable to give to the plebeian 'professionals' – cad-dies and clubmakers – who would compete for the right to hold it aloft; so it was stipulated that it should remain 'safely kept' at Prestwick Golf Club.

The year 1860 is just a date, so let's put it this way: Jesse James was barely a teenager, and had never robbed a bank. No one had heard of Abraham Lincoln (the newly elected President in Washington), and Charles Darwin himself had been famous for less than a year. Stanley had not begun to search for Dr Livingstone; and Florence Nightingale was only now setting up her nursing school. Snooker had not been invented, and soccer was in its infancy (there was no such thing as the Football

Association). *War and Peace* and *Middlemarch* were works in progress (if that), and excuse me, but what on earth was a telephone, a car, a bicycle, an Impressionist painting?

It was, we can safely say, a long time ago. But some little time before noon, on Wednesday 17 October 1860, a gaggle of men in thick, warm, buttoned-up suits made their way to the opening tee at Prestwick, some with sticks under their arms, others with pocket-sized cadets or caddies – boys with shoulder bags to ease the burden on the competitors. Each player was assigned a gentleman to act as a marker (the assumption being that unobserved professionals were bound to cheat), and in marked contrast to the modern habit, where rounds can take five hours, the field completed three circuits – 36 holes – in time for a drink before dusk.

In these early days it was original, almost eccentric, to have a medal tournament. Up to then the preferred golfing format was matchplay: more fun for spectators, and a jazzier vehicle for laying wagers. In the old days at St Andrews, Tom Morris and his mentor Allan Robertson had played for some famously high stakes. Morris and the Musselburgh-based Willie Park were regular opponents who often played for £100 or more, but the Open, at this stage, offered more glory than loot. In that first year the belt went to Park, who knocked his innovative gutta-percha ball round in 174 strokes, two shots clear of the local hero, Morris, and a tidy 58 strokes better than the hapless fellow who came last (that's links golf).

'They little knew what a candle they were helping to set alight,' wrote Bernard Darwin, the great *fin-de-siècle* golf correspondent for *The Times*. As the grandson of Charles Darwin himself, it was fitting that he was on hand to celebrate the origin of this strange new species: the pro golfer.

Ah, but the characters back in those days! By all accounts Park could play with one curved wooden stick, and to make it more amusing he would play one-handed or standing on one leg. On another occasion he used the face of a watch as his tee, and didn't so much as scratch it.

As for Tom Morris, he went on to win four out of the next seven Opens, with his young son clambering around the familiar Prestwick dunes, absorbing the approaches to each green. No one knew it, but in the coming years this father and son – Old Tom Morris and Young Tom – would become as famous as anyone in Scotland.

In 1863 money began to rear its ugly head: Tom Morris won £6. And then, a few years later, a meteor blazed in the Scottish sky. Young Tom Morris played his first Open at the age of 14, and it was immediately clear that he was destined to take the game to a new level. He had devised a new method of ball-striking, which none of his opponents could match. In 1868 he achieved his first victory at the tender age of 17 years and 161 days, partly thanks to a scintillating hole-in-one at the 145-yard par-three 8th, and three years later launched himself towards a hat-trick by securing an eagle – eagle! – on his father's impossibly lengthy first hole. That day saw him beat Willie Park's 1860 wining total (only a decade earlier) by 25 shots. He was playing a game no one in the world had seen before.

A hasty committee meeting at Prestwick decided it was 'not expedient' for the club to provide another belt – and given the way Young Tom was hitting the ball, they would soon have to surrender the original. In 1871 there was no Open while they fretted about the future. Eventually, both the Royal and Ancient and Musselburgh were enticed to join the party and, with each club chipping in £10, they commissioned, in September 1872, a new claret jug from an Edinburgh silversmith. It was called 'The Golf Champion Trophy'.

This time, to avoid some low-grade stripling ever taking possession of such a distinguished piece, it was decided that the Claret Jug should never be handed over for keeps: instead, the winner would get a medal.

It made no difference. At its first appearance, Young Tom Morris was too strong for everyone all over again (though only just: if David Strath had not found water on the last hole it might have been tight). But it seemed like destiny: Young Tom's name became the first to be engraved on the old heirloom. To this day, he is the youngest ever winner not just of the Open, but any major – a feat he achieved the year after his father became, at 46, the oldest such winner. Even in its infancy, the Open could produce fairy tales.

The first twelve Opens were all held at Prestwick. When the Claret Jug appeared on the scene it began to rotate between Prestwick, St Andrews and Musselburgh. But it was becoming clear that it wasn't, alas, very open: in those first dozen contests there were small fields – the largest was 17 golfers, nearly all local Scottish professionals (some of them related to one another). It was a closed shop: just two families (Morris and Park) won 15 of the first 25 Opens, and the early belts were shared between three men: Willie Park (three times), Old Tom Morris (four times) and his brilliant son (also four times – even in its earliest days, golf was a sport that could pit an oldster against a novice).

Facts and figures, however impressive, do scant justice to the story of the Morris family. Young Tom Morris came second in the first Open at St Andrews, in 1873, and second again the following year, at Musselburgh. He married a local girl, Margaret, and settled down to build a St Andrews golfing dynasty. Then, in September 1875, he was playing a challenge match with his father at North Berwick (against the Parks) when he received a fateful telegram. The good news was that his wife had given birth to a child. The bad news was that both of them were dangerously ill.

Tom and his father dashed to the ferry, but they were too late; by the time they arrived both Margaret and her new-born child had died.

Young Tom was crushed. 'He went about', according to one report, 'like one who had received a mortal blow. He lived as if in some trance, all his light-hearted buoyancy gone.' At the end of October he was playing a match with his father, and they were winning four-up with five to play, when he broke down entirely and lost each of the last five holes. On Christmas Eve he dined with a few friends, drank a bit too much, said goodnight to his mother and father, and retired to his room. When he did not emerge for breakfast on Christmas morning his father went into his room and found his dazzling, lovesick son lying quite still, quite dead.

He was 24 years old, the finest golfer that had ever lived, and a tragic hero. It seems he suffered a pulmonary event (a burst artery in his lung), but no one knows for certain. 'People say he died of a broken heart,' said his shattered father. 'But if that were true, I wouldn't be here either.'

Tom Morris Sr stayed at St Andrews and became the W. G. Grace of golf, designing 75 of Scotland's finest courses – Muirfield, Dornoch and Carnoustie, among others – as well as a few elsewhere, at Westward Ho! in North Devon or Royal County Down in Northern Ireland. He died in 1904, in the Royal and Ancient's 150th year. In the century since, the tournament has honoured its dead chiefly by revisiting the hallowed grounds where Morris and the other founding fathers made their first primitive balls, forged their antique clubs, hunched the collars of their tweed coats against the wind, and made golf the game it is today.

'We do like to maintain our traditions,' said Peter Dawson. 'We only ever hold the Open on a links course, and we have nine of what we consider the best links on our rota. We don't interfere with or manicure the land, and we like to let the weather dictate how the courses play.'

Fortunately, the requirements of tradition turn out to be convenient. Links courses are generous with 'open' (some would say desolate) space: there is room for marquees, car parks, hospitality zones, bars, television cranes, generator trucks, grandstands and all the features of modern golf – more, at any rate, than there might be at a tight inland course. Mature trees may be beautiful, but they don't half block the view.

In the end, however, it is the historical allure of these grand, peculiar, empty courses that makes the Open a singular event. Other majors have lush green pleasure grounds; the Open is a straw-coloured, wispy, windswept assault course where kestrels hang on the breeze and rabbits dart into dunes. The salt wind gives the trees (if there are any) a withered stoop, and the northern sea is usually a cold gunmetal grey. The aesthetic is primeval – those islands lie humped in the icy water like dormant dragons – but also martial, and not only because of the disused runways, or the fighter jets screaming over nearby gunnery ranges.

The term 'links' probably derives from the Anglo-Saxon *hlinc*, meaning a ridge or rise in the ground. In practice it refers to a very specific coastal formation: a band of sandy hummocks along a wild seashore, with wild grasses, and hardy clumps of gorse and heather, clinging to the dunes like barnacles on an upturned hull, with hardly a tree in sight. It is scenery that dates back to the aftermath of the ice age, when the melting snow withdrew to reveal a raw new coastline that was rapidly (that is, over several million years) covered with oceanic sand. Wind excavated the dunes into mysterious labyrinths of peaks and troughs, with shallow gullies nosing between high sandbanks, and Scotland's golf pioneers identified this as the ideal locale for their bemusing new pursuit. Busy streams or burns wriggled their way through the soft surface, while tough grasses invaded the otherwise infertile soil. It was land too weak to support crops, and not lush enough to suit cattle, so it became host to a sea-level form of hill-farming: small flocks of sheep grazed the sheltered spots, creating the smooth green alleys that would one day become fairways.

This is where golf took root, in a seaside moonscape that was roomy, exposed and of no value for anything else. The sandy soil made the game playable in wet weather (not rare in these parts), and also influenced the grass: deep rooted, with tiny blades, not at all the lush jungle matting that carpets today's more tropical golfing locales.

Golfing traditionalists (not a small tribe) have it as an article of faith that links courses are to golf what champagne is to sparkling wine: not just the original version but the proud summit of the game. Not everyone loves it; some players are flummoxed or worse. 'I don't know who designed St Andrews,' said Mark James, a one-time captain of Europe's Ryder Cup team, 'but I hear he's escaped.' Some, such as the 1954 US Open winner Ed Furgol, just hated it, period. 'There's nothing wrong with the St Andrews course,' he said, 'that 100 bulldozers couldn't put right.' Plenty of Americans do not trouble to overcome this angry first impression, and decline to cross the Atlantic even when they have earned a place. This was not hard to understand in the days before air travel – who wanted to spend ten days at sea in order to lose golf balls in a freak northern gale? – but these days it tends to inspire sharp rebukes from Open loyalists. When Kenny Perry relinquished his spot at Turnberry (for a perfectly decent personal reason: there was a tournament in his home state of Kentucky that he felt obliged to support), the golfing world was unanimous in its disapproval.

In a way, liking links is beside the point. Many golfers do not enjoy the experience, because if you like finding your ball, or playing holes in single figures, then you may well struggle to love the sea-flung gales that make links golf such a blast. But you do not have to like the game to revere it, because it is not, in the end, about anything so superficial as pleasure. To play one of the great links courses is to walk with epic ghosts. It does not require enthusiasm; it requires surrender.

Nor is it simply that this is where links golf was born. Virtually every modern golf course contains deliberate and unmistakable echoes of the original natural design (or absence of design). Parkland and mountain courses, meadowland courses, even desert courses – all take care, and go to grave expense, to incorporate the range of hazards spun from this same ancient recipe of water and sand. All over the world, fairways mimic the smooth, animal-nuzzled swales between wind-blown humps, and invite golfers to drive buggies up winding cart 'tracks' to greens perched on raised plateaux, surrounded by sandy gashes and ruffled pools. The fundamental topography of golf was laid down by nature long ago, right here; and the Scottish originals, like the great oil paintings, make all others – however superb – look like reproductions. Even their names (Carnoustie, St Andrews, Troon) sound like real places. As the Miami novelist Carl Hiaasen once pointed out, many of the new designer layouts are named after the very wildlife that was exterminated to make way for the golf course: Otter Creek, Quail Ridge, Falcon Heights, Leopard Falls.

The scrubbed, windswept terrain suggests itself as an austere training ground for tough fellows, and carries stark reminders of the game's hardy origins. Some of that fatalism lingers on. 'There's no such thing as bad weather – only the wrong clothes,' goes the auld Scottish saying; and this descends into an everyday fatalism out on the fairways. 'Aye, it's a wee bit breezy,' someone will say, moments before their cap goes spinning into the gorse. Fine wine has its terroir – the compound of geology, climate and history that is the cultural signature of each vintage – and so does Open golf. Year after year it connects the footslogging fan and the bloated armchair spectator with the long, rich history of the game.

Imagine an identical field of golfers assembled on a modern layout: however gripping the contest, it could not stir the blood so readily as it does on these time-honoured playing fields. The players themselves are its best promoters, quick (when pressed) to broadcast their affection for classic links. Gary Player, winner of Opens in three decades, calls them 'the finest courses on earth'

and few contradict him: they have meant too much to too many
for too long. 'There's nothing else like it,' said Ernie Els. That has
been true for an age. When Arnaud Massey from Biarritz – a
cloth-capped D'Artagnan of the links – won in 1907, he named
his (perhaps unfortunate) daughter Hoylake, in honour of his triumph.

The setting may have no bigger fan than Tom Watson. 'If the
Open didn't exist,' he said, 'I'd still take a trip over every year just
to play the great courses.' The first time he brought his game to
Scotland, however, he drove the ball straight down the middle
from the first tee, only to see it vanish into the mist. 'I couldn't
find it,' he said. 'My playing partners carried on while I took one
last guess, and there it was, buried in a tiny pot bunker. I had to
take a really awkward stance to get at it. And I didn't really like
that, having hit what I thought was a perfect drive. I was so con-
ditioned to play the ball high in the air. Links was the antithesis
of how I played. I only started to realize I had a love for it when
I made the decision to stop fighting and play the ball along the
ground, and not get upset when the bounces didn't turn out the
way I wanted.'

In the autumn of 2008, however, he did not even know if he
would be able to play the following summer. He was checking
into a hospital in Santa Monica to have 'anterior approach' hip
replacement. 'Hip rotation drives the golf swing,' said Watson,
and his joint was worn out after 40 years of top ball-striking. His
surgeon, veteran of a thousand such procedures, explained how
surgery 'minimizes hip muscle trauma and enhances the accuracy
of leg length' – balm to any golfer's ear. Watson stayed in the
clinic overnight, and left the next day, with a walking stick to lean
on. Teeing it up at Turnberry was just about the last thing on his
mind.

CHAPTER THREE

Past Meets Present

Hardly anything matters more to the R&A than the television contracts that broadcast the Open to the world and, true to the ideal of openness that governs (most of) its decisions, the R&A is unfashionably devoted to keeping the tournament available to terrestrial television. It may be the ringmaster of a great annual event, but it is also the guardian of the game and its past, and insists that the size of the audience matters as much as the size of the cheque. Peter Dawson rarely tires of pointing out that more people in Britain watch the Walker Cup (the amateur match between Britain and the USA) than the Ryder Cup, simply because it is on the BBC.

Television money remains the lifeblood of the R&A, however, so there are important negotiations ongoing almost all the time. In 2009 it transpired that America's Turner Sports organisation would not renew its contract and would thus withdraw after Turnberry ('We were unable to reach terms on future rights,' said the president of Turner Sports, David Levy). The R&A had persuaded ESPN to offer $25 million per year for the next eight Opens ($200 million overall – not bad) and there were also commitments regarding the brave new world of digital platforms, web rights and video on demand (the Championship may be ancient, but it has to move with the times). Dawson was pleased: 'It is all-important to the R&A that we preserve the traditions of the Open Championship,' he said. 'We know just how much ESPN respects the Open's heritage.'

George Bodenheimer, president of ESPN, sang from a more modern section of the hymnal. 'One of the most venerable of all sporting events has embraced the 21st-century worldwide media landscape,' he said. 'We're thrilled to showcase the Open Championship like never before.'

The negotiation was made easier by purely golfing considerations. Ever since Padraig Harrington, in July 2008, had blitzed that memorable five-wood past the left-hand bunker on Birkdale's 17th hole (and pretty much nailed down consecutive Open victories), the forthcoming Open looked mouth-watering. It was safe to predict that it would be unpredictable – melodramatic in the usual heart-in-mouth ways – because it always was. But this time it promised to be even more vivid than usual, for two simple reasons. First, it would see Harrington going for three Claret Jugs in a row – a rare hat-trick in the modern era. He had never played the course, despite growing up across the water in Dublin ('When I was young I couldn't afford the green fee'), but he had revealed himself to be a tough finisher on links courses, so, who knew, maybe he could pull it off.

The second proposition was, so far as the television companies were concerned, even more beguiling. After a distressing year without its superstar, 2009 would see the return of Tiger Woods after his painful and much-discussed knee injury. Harrington's 2008 victory was actually held by some to be somewhat devalued by Woods's absence (even though he had also won in 2007, when Tiger was present), so the reunion was a genuine face-off. After capturing that second Open Harrington had gone on to ruin Sergio Garcia's life by swiping the PGA as well, snaking in a wicked closing putt to scoop his third major in six attempts. He was industrious, modest, skilful and popular, a worthy opponent for the returning Tiger.

It was sometimes argued that Woods himself suffered from the absence of any significant opponents. Where Nicklaus had to cope with Arnold Palmer, Lee Trevino, Tom Watson, Johnny Miller and Gary Player, Woods had no one good enough to stretch him. This notion often seemed slack and self-fulfilling: Woods had cornered so many majors (14 so far) that he single-handedly diminished the number of major-winning opponents he could face. But now, with Harrington, there was the prospect of a serious joust. Even a year in advance it was possible to detect the outline of another duel in the sun: the best player in the world would be up against a proven links maestro.

Few were rubbing their hands more gleefully than golf's moneymen. Golf without Tiger, it turned out, was not like *Hamlet* without the ghost – it was like *Hamlet* without Hamlet. Viewing figures during his year off had plunged, and his commercial value had become even more striking than was thought. When first he signed for Nike, in a deal reckoned to be worth $90 million, the world gasped; but Nike's share price jumped for joy with such unfeigned enthusiasm that the company's market capitalisation grew, almost at a stroke, by more than double that.

In 2008 Woods's long rehabilitation had given television's ratings agencies a chance to quantify his impact on the viewing figures. The results were hard to swallow. On average, the man's presence in the final two rounds of a tournament pretty much doubled the couch-potato interest – in the United States, at least. In the months following the 2008 US Open (which he won, before retiring to fix his knee), Nielsen's ratings fell by 46 per cent against the year before. The worst-hit tournament was the PGA, which saw its numbers register a huge 78 per cent decline on 2007. The flow of visitors to the PGA website also fell, by around a quarter.

Even the Open could not claim immunity from Tiger's disappearance. In 2005 some 5.4 million Americans watched

Woods win at St Andrews; a similar number watched him do the same at Hoylake the following year. But his poor showing at Carnoustie cost the broadcaster a million pairs of eyeballs, and his absence in 2008 saw the number shrink to 3.9 million.

Pundits could debate the merits of a Tiger-free tournament as much as they liked; but there was no denying the fact that he was golf's central character. To some extent, of course, the media were reaping what they had sown, in that their own intense pre-occupation with Tiger had helped created this vacuum: his rivals had been under-televised, so only devout connoisseurs knew (or cared) who they were. For years we had seen every shot, blink, scowl, grin and swish of Tiger's haughty tail, and very magnificent it had been too. But it was little wonder that we were lost without him: the broadcasters had omitted to acquaint us with his understudies, had invested too many of their eggs in one superb basket.

Harrington or Woods? This was the story that would dominate the headlines in the months to come, but of course it was more than likely that, come the Championship proper, there would be others, for the Open was a reliable inspirer of grand tales. Could Sergio Garcia overcome a clutch of recent near misses and live up to his obvious talent? Might Colin Montgomerie have one last brave Scottish hurrah in store, on a course only a few miles south of the town (Troon) in which he grew up? In England, of course, the papers fretted over the chances of an English winner (while simultaneously pouring scorn on its most recent champion, Nick Faldo). But all the signs were that the golf world was enlarging, so perhaps some fresh star would be born that summer, an unknown youth or a visitor from golf's new worlds – Japan, India, Korea, China? Might an amateur make history, in this day and age, by beating the professionals (not inconceivable, as Chris Wood's fifth place at Birkdale had just proved).

The truth was that there would be 156 players in the field, and any one of them might form the basis of a surprising story. It was . . . open. That was the whole point. As it happens, another player, a one-time firefighter called Bruce Vaughan, had qualified a week after Birkdale by winning the Senior Open with a rousing comeback and a dramatic play-off at Royal Troon. At one point he trailed John Cook by three shots, but he watched Cook surrender a couple of strokes at the 11th, birdied the 16th, and then rolled in an emphatic 14-footer to win the first extra hole. Vaughan hit a superb drive, a pure five-iron and a dead-eyed putt. 'The three best shots I hit the whole week,' he said – bad luck for Cook. From a distance it was typical seniors golf: the winner had suffered six knee operations yet here he was, lifting the imitation claret jug. 'I don't give up,' Vaughan said.

Vaughan was from Kansas, so had a supreme regard for Tom Watson. 'He's like God there. I mean, you know, anybody thinks of Tom Watson, Kansas – he's still the man. That's what I tell my caddie, I say, There's the man! He only plays a few tournaments, and every time he plays, he's got a bad hip and looks like he can hardly walk, but he can still play.'

Vaughan would be back in a year's time for his third Open, and though no one expected him to win, there are many different ways to enjoy a golf tournament. Some would be there for sentimental reasons, teeing it up one more time before their exemptions ran out. Others – and they did not yet know who they were – would be thrilled simply to be taking part, to be inside the ropes for golf's grandest get-together. For yet others, the golf itself was a side issue – by no means the only show in town. As luck would have it, 2009 would also be the 250th birthday of Robert Burns (born 1759, just a few years after the Royal and Ancient), so the heritage industry was gearing up to celebrate. There was the thatched Alloway cottage where Burns was born, the famous 'brig' over the river Doon, the church immortalised in 'Tam o' Shanter' ('Kirk-Alloway was drawing nigh/Whare ghaists and houlets nightly cry'). Ayr had its Burns Heritage Park, and the Burns Monument Centre in Kilmarnock had been restored after a fire, and was now a smart new family-history archive as well as 'a spectacular venue for weddings'. It was sobering to think that the poet was only 37 when he died, the same age as Padraig Harrington, though sad to note that he was a resolute non-golfer (too busy writing 'Auld Lang Syne'). Who can say: 'The Ballad of Auld Tam o' Turnberry' might have been a masterpiece.

Tickets for the 2009 Open went on sale on 4 November. In a nod to the prevailing financial weather (harsh: Lehman Brothers had collapsed a month before, and the Royal Bank of Scotland, one of golf's most visible sponsors, had been all but nationalised), they were frozen at the 2008 rate − £55 per day. This was not quite cheap, but given that a day of golf runs from six-thirty in the morning until nine at night, it compared favourably (on a per-hour basis) with the cost of Premiership football or cricket.

So far, so good. Local hotel-keepers rubbed their hands in anticipation of a busy couple of weeks, while the *Ayrshire Post* predicted a welcome £65 million 'boost', and this was probably on the low side. The R&A's own studies showed that once you took the value of media exposure into account, the Open was worth more: around £200 million. But in links golf nothing (as we have seen) goes according to plan, and it was inevitable that something would come along to give the event a shake. Just days before those first tickets went on sale, the ground beneath the 138th Open shuddered when it was announced that the entire venue had been sold to a Dubai-based property-and-sport con-glomerate (Leisurecorp) for £55 million. Any day now, Turnberry would close down for the winter and undergo a £30 million refurbishment.

This was nerve-racking news. Everyone knows that significant building projects run into overtime − at the very least, the dead-line imposed by the golf tournament might give contractors a licence to name their price. The hotel was a dominant part of the package – it was where the players and officials would stay. An unready hotel would be close to disastrous.

That was only a superficial worry. Of much larger concern was the outlook for the whole Dubai-inspired concept. Everyone knew that the decades-long property bubble was bursting, and everyone also knew that Dubai, with its showy palm-tree developments in the warm blue waters of the Gulf, was one of the shiniest and most stretched parts of that bubble. Some years earlier it was said that a fifth of the world's cranes were in Dubai, and surreal new towers seemed to adorn the skyline every year. Nowhere on earth seemed more vulnerable to a property dip.

The only good part was that the hotel knew all this. The ownership may have changed, but the management was staying put, and was well aware that if the date was not met, Turnberry would be more or less finished as an Open venue, and they would be more or less finished as hoteliers.

'It was a guillotine deadline,' said the general manager, Stewart Selbie. 'We knew that if we missed it, we'd have our heads chopped off.'

Actually, Selbie was 'quite pleased' by the development. 'It was time. There had been investment in the past [a spa in 1991, a new golf course in 1993] but more was needed. A building this size needs a lot of work – in fact, the hotel had never had a refurbishment on this scale. It's an old building now, but the idea was not to start again, but to create a new building that was somehow more than faithful to the original idea, a better version of the original, if you like. The technology is all new.'

There were a few twitchy moments at the R&A, however. 'Let's just say I might have slept better if the hotel had been finished a few months earlier,' smiled Peter Dawson, when it was all safely done. But work on the course was well under way, and no one was chewing any nails over that side of things, because Turnberry was a much-loved nook. It had hosted only three Opens, in 1977 (Duel in the Sun), 1986 (Greg Norman) and

1994 (Nick Price), but each had produced a great champion. It was superbly picturesque – the rocky shore made a terrific backdrop – and the trim lighthouse (white, with lemon highlights) next to the 9th green was one of golf's great landmarks. Built in 1873, it was a noble monument, a beacon of calm bravery for thousands of shipwrecked golfers. In truth, the volume of rhetorical energy it inspired may have owed something to the absence of any other visible landmark (except the hotel) on the course. Turnberry's legion of admirers talk about the lighthouse's 'iconic' beauty as if it were the Matterhorn, and while it is indisputably fine, it is marvellous in part because it has so few rival attractions.

The course over which it presides, however, is undeniably a classic. Half a dozen holes run along the thrilling coastline, with spectacular sea views, and each hole seems subtly framed and individual: you do not feel, as you often do at St Andrews, that you might be on the wrong fairway.

In 2003 Tom Watson, fresh from winning the Senior Open, told Peter Dawson that he thought Turnberry was playing a little short. Since 1994 it had been set up for holiday golfers and was no longer, given improved modern weaponry, a genuine Championship test. At just 354 yards, the first hole, for instance, was within range for a good number of top players, and the R&A was not keen to begin with an open goal. 'Today's professionals are bigger, stronger, fitter and have more technology at their command,' said Dawson. 'It's important that we keep our great links courses relevant.' Together, Turnberry and the R&A commissioned a study from the golf architect Martin Ebert, and work began in 2005. The brief was unusual: the course needed to test the world's best, yet it also needed to be benign enough to tempt post-Open tourists into parting with a top-of-the-range green fee of more than £100.

For the most part the course was merely tweaked. The tees were nudged back to create extra distance, and some 21 new bunkers were strategically placed to make Tiger Woods, John

Daly and the other long hitters think twice on the tee. Two holes were given an even more dramatic upgrade. The 10th was already a signature hole, with the tee beneath the lighthouse and a fairway that ran along the wild shoreline. But now a long-cherished idea of the estates manager, George Brown, was realised in a new tee even closer to the cliff, obliging players to fly their drives across crashing waves. Two new bunkers were carved in the centre of this fairway to create options, or sow doubt (or both). Keep left of them (flirting with the Irish sea) and you would need only a short knock to the green; stay right (the safer route) and you would face a much harder 200-yard approach.

The alteration to the 16th hole was equally radical. A once-straight fairway was shoved inland to create a left-to-right dog-leg, which meant that the steep-banked stream in front of the green was now a lethal trap. Any ball moving sideways would gather pace on the slope and disappear into the water. It was not hugely long, so most approach shots would be played with a lofted club; but an errant wedge would face the most severe penalty. The R&A planned to put a grandstand behind this green; while Scottish fans may be the most 'knowledgeable' in the world, they enjoy a car crash as much as the next man. The stand would certainly be full.

So far as the course was concerned, closing for the winter was no great loss. A six-month rest was just what the doctor ordered. The hotel didn't mind either ('Winter is never the easiest time,' said Selbie) and it gave Ebert's earth-movers the links to themselves. Golf was no longer a cold-weather sport. But Leisurecorp's arrival was troubling on a deeper dimension, because it illuminated a profound fault-line in the modern game – or, at least, the industry that is modern golf.

In most respects the Open is golf's jewel in the crown, the highlight of its annual calendar. Just as Wimbledon stirs people who never touch a racquet, so the Open impinges even on those who detest golf. But in other ways it is an anomaly, a throwback. If the European tour resembles the Premier League, then the Open is the FA Cup, homespun relic of a bygone age. It is not a coincidence that the headquarters of the European Tour are at Wentworth, because this better represents the modern vision of golf as a game held in a gentle embrace (using the interlocking grip, as P. G. Wodehouse might say) by the imperatives of property development.

It was happening everywhere. Spanking golf villas were being planned, excavated and marketed across the known world. And all of them were in some way based on an original idea by Walter Tarrant, who dreamed up the collaboration between property and golf on the Surrey/Berkshire borders. In 1922, following his creation of St George's Hill, Weybridge, Tarrant teamed up with the finest golf course architect of the day, Harry Colt, to build a luxury gated 'community' around two prime courses at Wentworth. Colt's aesthetic was Scottish: he wove heathery bumps and hollows through the sandy Surrey pines, creating a heavenly slice of Walter Scott countryside in the commuter zone near Virginia Water. It was consistent with what Willie Park Jr (son of the first Open champion and himself winner of two 19th-century Opens) had done at Sunningdale, just down the A30, and it was a triumph.

Not everything went well (Tarrant went bankrupt in 1931), but the dream did not die. It was here, in 1926, that Sam Ryder had the brainwave that gave birth to the friendly game between Britain and America. This was a fine response to a moment of golf genius: Bobby Jones had just shot 66 in a British Open qualifier, a 33 followed by a 33 – a near-perfect round in which he missed neither a green nor a fairway. 'We should do this again,' said Sam, taking defeat like a man – and the Ryder Cup was born (it was held at Wentworth in 1953).

The business rationale of a place like Wentworth depended not just on having a nice golf course, or even a great one. It had to be a famous one. A prestige tournament was essential, and it arrived in 1964, with the first World Match Play tournament, the brainchild of Mark McCormack. Happily for all concerned, his money-spinning protégé Arnold Palmer won it, and without further ado Wentworth was launched as a world-class venue. Other big names followed – Nicklaus, Tom Weiskopf, Player, Ballesteros – and their photographs and scorecards began to decorate the imposing club-house. Members and visitors alike could march in the footsteps of the golfing gods. House prices tripled.

The West Course became known as the Burma Road when it was cleared by hard-working German prisoners of war. But Wentworth was already a desirable milieu for wealthy patrons, tucked in stockbroker-belt pines, within easy reach of central London and Heathrow. A whole new formula sprang into life: golf plus real estate plus television exposure equalled luxurious property prices. Mansions built for discreet grandees from the City began to attract marquee names from light entertainment (Bruce Forsyth, Cliff Richard), up-against-it dictators (General Pinochet), mil-lionaire footballers (Andrei Shevchenko), golfers (Ernie Els, Thomas Bjørn), other sports stars (Eddie Jordan, Prince Naseem Hamed) and Russian moguls (Boris Berezovsky). The grandest properties on the estate soon cost upwards of £10 million, but the recent (often Russian) fashion has been to knock down the orig-inal 1920s mock-Georgian mansions in favour of something altogether more ostentatious. The green fee rose accordingly. By the time of the 138th Open, a round at Wentworth cost £285 – the priciest game of golf, it was said, in the whole of Europe.

The importance of golfing prestige in this arrangement can hardly be overstated. For the last two years Padraig Harrington, the two-time Open champion, had skipped Wentworth's mid-summer tournament (the BMW PGA Championship) because, he said, he did not like the greens. There were giddy rumours (unconfirmed, of course) that he was offered more than €250,000 in appearance money to change his mind . . . but declined. A tournament unable to attract the top players cannot thrive, so Wentworth had no option but to dig up those traduced greens (which were like billiard tables, by the way) and prepare for a full complement of top golfers in 2010.

The Wentworth model is familiar the world over – in Florida, Arizona, Spain, Portugal, Ireland and everywhere else that golf is played. Housing developments around a signature golf course (preferably designed by a Nicklaus, a Palmer or a Norman) were popping up everywhere: from Argentina to China, Mauritius to China, St Lucia to Slovenia. In 1981, the American PGA moved into a spanking new HQ in West Beach, Florida, a luxury development which put four well-groomed layouts (hosting tournaments like the Honda Classic and the Ryder Cup) with a golf academy, a short-game school, a spa, a racquet club, pools, hotels, restaurants and so on, in the middle of 5000 homes, built on reclaimed pieces of the Everglades and with fine mosquito mesh around their backyard swimming pools.

Nowhere was the boom boiling so hard as in Asia. 'Johan Edfors loved Black Mountain Golf Club so much,' ran an advert for a new Thai resort, 'after he won the Black Mountain Masters 2009 he purchased one our luxury B-type villas.' There were Nicklaus layouts in Korea and Brunei, a Greg Norman monster outside Delhi, a Gary Player in Burma and scores of new ones in China. Norman was building an 'ultimate' oasis in Vietnam, of all places! At Mission Hills, north of Hong Kong, there was a Nicklaus Course, a Norman, an Annika (Sorenstam) and seven others, making 180 holes of golf in all; but two new tracks were on the way. 'Our members were getting bored with only ten,' said Tenniel Chu, the complex's executive director. China had 300 courses, mainly in the south, and some projections envisioned a further thousand in the years to come. 'In China, living in a golf community is the ultimate feather in your cap,' said one happy architect. 'It's like moving to Beverly Hills.'

For the last decade golf's new favourite territory had been Dubai. And Leisurecorp was one of its star performers. The purchase of Turnberry was a bit more than a topical sign of the times, because Leisurecorp was also behind 2009's rebranding of the European tour, which would now come to a climax with a big-money end-of-season tournament in Dubai. It would be played on the 'Earth' course, a Greg Norman design that looked, at this unfinished stage, like an emerald mat in the middle of a building site. In a few months' time it would be a made-for-TV golf zone with fluttering trees and acres of broken bark (neither exactly native to this region). It was part of a costly quartet of courses (the others would be called 'Wind', 'Water' and 'Fire') at Jumeirah Golf Estates (ultimate owner: Leisurecorp), which sold itself as 'golf's glorious new home'. The final purse would be an astonishing $10 million, with a bonus of $2 million to the winner of the season-long ranking – enough, it was hoped, to tempt a few Americans to play east of the Atlantic. Phil Mickelson and Camilo Villegas were mentioned. Even Sergio Garcia, people said, might be tempted home.

The courses were surrounded, naturally, by 'secure' communities or 'neighbourhoods' (there would be a thousand homes around the Earth course). One of these, 'Fireside', offered air-conditioned mansions in the 'Jersey' or 'County Down' style, so even the buildings seemed to carry careful if unseasonal echoes of links golf in the pouring rain. Prices ranged between one and two million pounds.

Dubai was putting up the money, and what it wanted in return was the name. The 'European' season – quotation marks rendered necessary by this new Gulf backing – was now 'The Race to Dubai'. Some golf fans resented this fervent courting of the petrodollar, with its tiring principle that all golf tournaments be auditions for the next big TV spectacular, but others were happy that 'Europe' could at last glance at American budgets without envy. Europe had made many such overtures to Asia, with its

'European' events in Hong Kong, Malaysia and China. Now it
was establishing itself as a true rest-of-the-world super-tour.

'Our ambition,' said Leisurecorp's Australian CEO, David
Spencer, 'is not necessarily to change the format of golf, but to
enhance it and to make it more relevant to the next generation.'

Not necessarily? This sounded ominous. Did Leisurecorp plan
to build a thousand villas on the hills above Turnberry, or on the
wind-bashed beach that made the course so stunning? As the
evenings began to draw in, an unexpected (but predictable) problem began to appear. Golf had hitched its star to a housing
bubble, and the bubble had burst. In Dubai alone, golf property
values stood at 50 per cent of their 2006 value. The BBC was
saying that $185 million of property projects were being shelved.
Newspapers began to scoff that golfers heading to Dubai would
not need a hole-in-one to win that sporty car, tethered on the
man-made lake like a goat to lure tigers. They could help themselves to any number of flash convertibles left behind by fleeing
expats: there were stories of cars (some 3000) being abandoned
at the airport in the rush to get away.

There was a historic symmetry to all this, because while
Turnberry might be a stately antique, a century earlier it had itself
been the brash arriviste. A luxury golf destination? Preposterous!
Who would stay in such a ludicrous eyesore? Perhaps, in 2009,
things were coming full circle; perhaps this was no more than a
giant leap backwards.

But then David Spencer mentioned that it might be nice, in
future, if Turnberry held other elite events – the European Open,
for instance. This time the R&A felt obliged to sigh in public. 'I
don't think,' said tournament director David Hill, 'that it would
be ideal from an Open point of view.' In a curt warning that
Turnberry would be gambling with its place on the regular Open
rota, he added that the world had changed, and Scotland could
no longer assume a divine right to hold the Open whenever it
wished.

'The authorities in England are all over us, and want to pay us to go there . . . Kent council, for example, would pay handsomely to have the Open every five years at Royal St George's.' He had a point: regular tournaments on the Ailsa Course would diminish its charm as an Open location. It was equally easy to see Leisurecorp's reasoning, however: a single Open Championship every 15 years was quite a weak incentive for a golf 'destination' as ambitious as the new Turnberry.

Was one British Open worth 15 European Opens? Surely not.

There existed a genuine tension here between two different concepts of golf. For the R&A the Open is the cash cow that funds its governance of the amateur game, but it still relies to a huge extent on volunteer help. Some 2000 unpaid workers support the Open as marshals, stewards, scoreboard operators, sign-carriers and in a slew of other under-appreciated roles, and this is part of its enduring appeal. It carries the flag for an old-fashioned concept of golf that is rooted in the landscape where the game was born, and in the people who love it. To a touching and unfashionable extent, the atmosphere is half Formula One, half village fête.

The most modern incarnation of 21st-century golf was the new Tiger Woods course beginning to rise in the sands of – where else? – Dubai. It was called Al Ruwaya, and its desert location meant it was the opposite of the early Scottish links, shaped as they were by millions of years of divine erosion. Al Ruwaya was a blank piece of paper, 55 million square feet of scorching desert (three times the size of London's Hyde Park). Some 25 million cubic feet of earth, 6500 tons of concrete, 460 tons of steel, 16,000 construction workers, 3.3 million square feet of freshwater lake, a huge carpet of imported grass (from Georgia, USA), 30,000 trees, 48,000 shrubs and $130 million later, Al Ruwaya (Arabic for 'serenity' – not much of which was evident during the construction period) would be one of the most lavish golf 'destinations' in the world. A lot of that trouble and expense would go into including all the identifying marks of golf's Caledonian roots: bunkers, mounds and snaking water hazards. There would be a super-amazing clubhouse designed to look like a Moorish palace, an 80-suite 'boutique' hotel, 197 luxury 'residences', and 22 palatial mansions (prices ranging between $20 million and $60 million). The hotel, with its 'trickling streams and waterfalls', would look over lush green lawns that, with summer temperatures regularly sweating up to 40 degrees celsius, would drink thirstily from a purpose-built water recycling plant (30,000 cubic metres per day).

The concept was Wentworth-on-Sea, or Golf-sur-Gulf: the elite game as a magnet for luxury property deals. Before a brick was put in place, 70 properties had been sold, but that was in the boom time. Now, things looked less promising. And Al Ruwaya was only one part of a larger concept – 'Dubailand' – that aimed to be a glamorous Western playground in the sun: hotels, shopping malls, restaurants and 'several' theme parks.

This was modern golf. One of the ironies of today's professional tours is that they rarely play on resonant, famous courses. This is partly because the older ones are often too short to put up much of a fight against the new booming hitters, and partly because they were not built to hold the necessary infrastructure (Prestwick, host of those first 12 Opens, was declared obsolete in 1925, when it was overwhelmed by the crowd that spilled out of the railway station). But there remain tensions between the grandeur of the old game and the commercial thirst of the contemporary industry. There was a fine storm brewing on Scotland's east coast, where Donald Trump was hoping, in the teeth of defiant local opposition, to build another glitzy golf estate on an ancient coastal wilderness.

It was hard to believe that Scotland, of all places, really needed a new golf course (especially one on a new access road called 'Donald Trump Boulevard'), since it had so many magnificent old

articulate. 'I'm like Frankenstein,' he said. 'What I have achieved medically is far beyond anything I can achieve in golf. The greatest shots I ever hit were in the hospital.'

It was a heart-warming story, and everyone wished him well. But it wouldn't be golf if there weren't a thistle in the Bermuda grass somewhere. In his first round in Dubai, in searing heat, he was penalised for slow play. He ended up missing the cut by three strokes.

A week later, in Melbourne, the second of the qualifiers came within a few miles of being cancelled. So far as the rest of the world knew, the city was on fire. But the flames that scorched the air, drove people from their houses and drew the television cameras fanned themselves mainly on the northern fringe, and the golf course at Kingston Heath lay to the south. It was decided to press ahead, to play the ball as it lay.

'Our thoughts are with all those touched by this tragedy,' said Peter Dawson. 'We have sought local opinion, and have decided to proceed as planned.'

The blaze consumed 750 houses and killed 181 people; there was even talk that it had been started deliberately. 'There are no words to describe this other than mass murder,' said the Prime Minister, Kevin Rudd.

Golf, anyone?

Kingston Heath had the requisite historical background. After the First World War a Melbourne solicitor wrote to Harry Vardon and his almost-as-famous contemporary, J. H. Taylor, seeking advice. These days they would be on the next flight with a lap-top and a contract, but back then they urged him only to build a course that would stand the test of time. He tried. In 1926 it was a 6312-yard par-82. It had tightened up since then: Greg Norman had once taken a nine on the tricky 16th.

There were only 44 men in the field. Some of them – Peter

Senior, Peter O'Malley, Peter Fowler and Craig (why couldn't he be called Pete, for Craig's sake?) Parry – were experienced campaigners. Parry had played 18 of the last 21 Opens; the previous summer, at Birkdale, he hit the first ball of the Championship. At Carnoustie in 1999 he led with seven holes to play, but tripled the 12th and ended up one shy of the Jean Van de Velde–Paul Lawrie play-off. O'Malley, for his part, had won seven European tournaments, including the 1992 Scottish Open at Gleneagles. Golf, while sentimental about its legends and 'characters', can be hard-headed too. These fine players had to take their chances alongside those taking their first steps in the game.

Parry was out in the first group, at 7.15 a.m. (golfers are early risers, and like to practise for an hour before hitting the tee too), along with Josh Geary, a green-shirted 24-year-old from Tauranga, New Zealand. Geary had shown good form of late, winning the 2008 Saskatchewan Open, and he came out of the traps fast, slamming home five birdies before dropping a few on the back nine to finish on two-under. 'I felt I had a chance,' he said.

He was back on the course soon after midday, and matched his morning score for a four-under-par total of 140. 'I had no idea what was going on. There were other guys on three-under and four-under.' He was an early finisher; he was up there, but could only chew his nails and wait.

Not much more than 20 minutes later, Tim Wood holed a putt to finish on exactly the same score. He had been attracting quite a bit of attention with a strange, elbow-flapping pre-shot routine that led to him being nicknamed 'the Seagull'. He pointed his toe into the grass like a chunky ice-dancer, rested the butt of his club on his (conveniently generous) stomach, and shook his arms like someone trying to open a stuck drawer.

It is a rational, if inelegant, move to get him to brace his weight on the balls of his feet. 'I pretend I'm going to catch a big, heavy medicine ball,' he said. He was not proud of it, and at the recent New South Wales PGA, in Sydney, tried to do without it. He began the day five shots off the lead, took driver off the first tee, aimed himself at the 300-yard par-four, and hit the flag. But then he hit two shanks in a row, and his caddie sighed. 'You've got to go back to the Seagull.' He did, and finished well, picking up AU$28,000 – good news for a man who had taken out a $20,000 loan to finance his golfing hopes. 'I hate it,' said Wood. 'But it works. You've just got to laugh about it. I've just got poor posture.'

He faced a tense wait, but when the fiery Melbourne dust settled, he and Josh Geary were the joint winners.

Both of them said the same thing. 'I feel like I'm going to wake up and say, damn! That was a great dream,' said Wood. 'It wasn't so much a goal,' agreed Geary, 'more a childhood dream.' It would be Geary's first ever trip to Europe.

These two were joined by Michael Wright, a Brisbane father-of-two who came in one shot behind. A professional for a decade, he had played on the Asia Tour for the last two years (and had qualified for the 2006 Open) so was no newcomer. But he still pronounced it 'a huge thrill' and said: 'I intend making the most of it.' On his website he was looking for a 'hat sponsor' to help defray the (not small) expenses of the trip.

Peter Senior missed out by one shot on what would have been his 18th Open. He was about to turn 50, and would soon be able to join the old-geezer tour that had been named in his honour, but that hardly made him feel better: he was just one lousy putt shy of having a last crack at the real thing. He needed a birdie-birdie finish, and managed only a birdie-par.

He can't have felt worse than Cameron Percy, who led at the halfway stage with 67, but struggled badly in the afternoon, ending with a 75 that also left him one shot the wrong side of happiness.

The R&A pledged a donation to the Victorian Bushfire Appeal, and that was that. The circus moved on.

In the old days qualifying was staged locally, somewhere near the Open venue, at the beginning of tournament week. It was, in effect, the start of the Championship, part of the whole weave of the Open. Back then, even top Americans like Arnold Palmer played their way in, like anyone else. If the big-name players thought they were better than the weather-beaten old professionals from Fife and Ayrshire, well . . . go ahead and prove it.

In recent years the R&A, in a laudable attempt to open up access to the Championship, had staged pre-qualifiers in Africa, Australia, Asia, America and Europe, so players who had furthest to travel could win Open spots well in advance. 'We felt it was the best thing for us to go to them,' said David Hill. 'The old local Final Qualifying was great, and we all loved it dearly, but for young overseas players to travel all the way to Scotland and then not qualify, it was long odds and a lot of money. Final Qualifying is still an option for anyone who wants to take that route. But the new way is much appreciated by the players, I think.'

These far-flung qualifiers were just part of an enormous entrance exam. The best players in the world could still 'exempt' themselves through stirring deeds elsewhere, but this too had evolved into a mind-numbing patchwork of allowances. It goes like this. Take a deep breath.

The top 50 players in the world ranking are automatically exempt. So are the top 30 on Europe's Order of Merit (now the Race to Dubai), the top 30 on the US money list and the top two on Japan's ranking. The highest echelon in Europe and America, in other words, sweeps in by right. Most of the marquee names are waved straight in.

Now the fun starts. As noted, past Open champions under 60 are welcome; the top ten from the previous year are urged to return; the last five champions from the other three majors (Masters, US Open and PGA) are invited, along with the Japan Open champion. Winners of the Orders of Merit in Asia, Australia, Japan and South Africa, members of recent Ryder Cup teams, the Senior Open champion and the Amateur champions from Britain, Europe and the US . . . step this way. There are a few last-minute ways in: the leading non-exempt player in the two tournaments before the Open (on both sides of the Atlantic) earns a spot, so long as he finishes in the top five; the top two on a mini-order of merit based on five recent tournaments are given the nod; and the top four players (if they are not exempt in other ways) from the Mizuno Open in Japan.

Most of the field is assembled through these fiddly means, but that still leaves a handful of spots. The qualifiers in South Africa and Australia produce six competitors; Asian qualifying produces four; America produces eight, and Europe ten. That leaves nine places for the mighty qualifying pyramid in Britain itself. The first stage, Regional Qualifying, takes place in June, at 16 venues. Each attracts a field of 90 or so golfers – the prize, for the top ten, is a spot at Final Qualifying in Scotland the week before the Open. There, three large fields (between 80 and 100) compete for just four places (twelve in all) at the Open itself.

It is a monumental undertaking. It would be easier (not to mention cheaper) to swipe 12 more players from the world ranking and be done with it. But then it wouldn't be open, would it?

And this was why Tom Watson, for one, called it 'the World Open': it embraced a wider range of international players than any other major.

The news from Scotland was mixed. The Ailsa was shaping up well, and estates manager George Brown, for one, was not concerned that it would be overpowered. 'I tell you one thing: the way things are at the moment, nobody is going to dominate Turnberry. Golf is a game of skill, not brute force.' Greg Norman (winner here in 1986) had been invited to pass his eye over the changes, and was optimistic too. 'It's great,' he said. 'From a player standpoint, Turnberry has it all, because you stay in the hotel, walk down the hill, and never put a key in the ignition of your car.'

That was right, in theory. But in the middle of March the contractor engaged to refurbish the hotel, Miller Construction, was fired. Roughly 100 workers did not know if they had a job or not: they arrived on site to find the security arrangements had been changed, and that there was a two-week 'transition period'. The lifts weren't done, and there was wiring all over the place. Local newspapers ran photographs showing it to be a 'mud-spattered' building site entirely wrapped in scaffolding, with excavators where the pot plants should be. It didn't look good.

Miller was itself feeling the pinch, or the crunch (it had just reported a £170 million loss) and had taken its eye off the ball. 'It wasn't a big contract for us,' said its chief executive, Keith Miller, not sounding too troubled. 'I think the client has a pretty tight deadline.'

This was almost comic. The 'client' was one of the central pillars in the majestic Victorian inheritance of sport. It took, as they say in Scotland, the shortbread.

On a lighter note, it was also being reported that investigators searching for the Loch Ness monster had come up empty-handed, but had found the bottom to be coated with golf balls, pounded into the deep, cold water by careless drivers. Actually, it was clear to most people that these 'balls' were spherical monster eggs. There was writing on them, but why should not Nessie's spawn be branded? Everything else was.

At the end of March it was Asia's turn to open the door to Turnberry (a crack, at least). But before the field could gather, a meteor streaked across the Arizona sky. Tiger Woods made his comeback in Tucson. No one was sure which Woods would appear: the convalescent invalid or the proud defending champion, but on the first hole he bombed a drive down the right, nailed an iron to five feet from the flag, and holed for birdie.

It was like a thunderclap. He was back.

On the next hole: eagle.

'I told Stevie,' said Woods, 'it felt like we hadn't been gone.'

The TV industry threw its hat in the air. The show would go on.

There was much less fuss at the Sentosa Club in Singapore, a groomed grass-and-water paradise with views through palm trees across to the city. Huge cranes swung over the docks across the sparkling water. It was hot and breezy: anywhere less like Turnberry was hard to imagine, but there was a Claret Jug sign over the entrance (and a copy of the original inside somewhere) and this was one way to grab a piece of it. Asia mattered. It was golf's Klondike, its boom town, and Sentosa was a good advert for what it offered: vivid foliage, the brightest grass you ever saw (paspalum on the tees, zoysia on the velvet fairways), with generous jigsaw-shaped bunkers and a cool, colonnaded clubhouse housing upscale restaurants (with 'award-winning' chefs) and a 'golfer's terrace'. The class divide in golf lingers on. The sponsors sip bubbly and nibble salmon; the players (some hugely wealthy) grab burgers and head for the range. 'Nowhere else,' said Sentosa's blurb, 'can golf and business mix so eloquently.'

There were only 37 in the field, and this time four would qualify, a softer ratio than the first two, and a sign of Asia's growing importance as a golf nursery. The favourites were Liang Wen-Chong, one of China's top players (as number one on the Asia Tour he made the cut at Birkdale in 2008), and the Finn Mikko Ilonen, an established international. Ilonen played well the first day and went to bed the overnight leader, but nothing went right in the second round: he shot 77 to finish some way out of the running.

Such is golf. Even the best players work within a ten-shot range: on their good days they shoot 65, on bad ones 75. They just pray they don't throw in a loose round when it matters (like now). Ilonen, a former British Amateur champion, was not riding high enough on the money lists to earn an Open spot that way, so this had been a good chance to play in his sixth Open. 'I putted really bad all day,' he said.

The winner was a young Indian called Gaganjeet Bhullar. A number of hopes were pinned on him, because India was looking for a bright new golfing attraction, and the personable Bhullar seemed to be it. It was hard not to think of him as a cricketer, since he looked and sounded just like one. He played better than steadily, and finished with a barrage of birdies (three on the last four holes) to hoist himself two strokes clear of the pack.

Afterwards he spoke to the *Indian Express* and said he had 'no words' to describe how he felt. 'I've been watching the British Open since I was a kid,' he said. 'To actually get to play there is truly a dream come true.'

They were all saying this, but while it was certainly a cliché, it was also a fact. Sport is rich fuel for fantasy, and nearly every player at Turnberry would, almost by definition, dream it in detail before checking in.

Bhullar was a fine prospect, and might be a great story too: he could be the Year of the Youngster and the Year of Asia rolled into one.

Liang Wen-Chong's excellent 66 earned him second spot, and then things began to get tense. It wouldn't be the Open if there wasn't a tall tale, but this was one of those days when the back end of the field blew up, leaving the leaders in the clubhouse high and dry. Australia's Terry Pilkadaris was one of the first in, and didn't like the look of things. 'I thought I'd blown my chance,' he said, after four bogeys on the front nine. 'I thought I took one too many.' But as the hours passed his rivals fell away, and he found himself in sole possession of third place. One player with a chance to beat him was his fellow Australian Tim Stewart, but he parred the last to finish on two-under, sighed, packed his bag and climbed into a taxi. He was halfway to the airport when a call on his mobile told him he was in a play-off. 'I said to the driver, "Turn around! Now!" Gave him a handsome tip to get back as fast as he could.'

Perhaps this was more relaxing than sitting by the 18th green in a cold sweat. On the first hole of the crowded (eight-man) play-off Stewart sent an 18-foot birdie putt tracking down a line just left of the hole and watched, with mounting joy, as it curled right and fell in. Only one other player made birdie, the impressive Singaporean amateur Danny Chia, but he celebrated by losing his ball in the water on the very next hole, leaving Stewart two putts from three feet to claim the last qualifying place.

'It's pretty heart-stopping stuff,' he said.

It seemed rummy to have two Australians playing their way through this qualifier, when they have one of their own, but schedules are schedules.

And there we had it. Turnberry had four more entrants.

The International Qualifying system is impressive, and the R&A is right to emphasise the importance of the Open being open to all. There is one respect, however, in which golf (and the R&A in particular) has never been open, and that concerns its attitude to women. There are many aspects of golf's reputation for grubby male pomposity, but this is the biggest. What kind of barmy aesthetic could bar women from an arena that permits (encourages!) tubby men to wear shorts? Yet even now golf was making only reluctant 'concessions' to modern life. Augusta National, where the Masters is staged each year, is enduringly men-only, and while the R&A has women on its committees, the Royal and Ancient Club, to which it remains connected and devoted, is all-male. Even the MCC dropped its men-only rule in 1999, but some of the clubs on the Open rota – Royal St George's and Muirfield – resist change. Muirfield would be the venue for the 2013 Open, and there was certain to be trouble there. The subject was also cropping up with respect to golf's Olympic hopes: the Games was a determined equal-opportunities employer.

This year (the subject frothed up most years) it was Scotland's First Minister, Alex Salmond, who raised it by complaining in public that the new principal of the University of St Andrews had not been invited to join the Royal and Ancient thanks to her sex. There is no written-in-stone law about this: but the last two principals of the university had been welcomed as members, and it was a symbolic shame that the new principal, Dr Louise Richardson (an American expert on international relations and terrorism, and not, by all accounts, a golfer), was not invited to join.

Like all political gestures, this one had its posturing aspect. Salmond did not insist that the two ladies' golf clubs based at St Andrews should also, on grounds of fairness and equality, admit men. The head of the Ladies' Golf Union, Shona Malcolm, was reluctant to echo his words. 'We don't have a difficulty with single-gender clubs for either men or women,' she said. 'It's up to the individual clubs to decide what they want to do.'

Either way, for the first time in its 250-year-plus history the R&A found itself at odds with Scotland's ruling authority. The blunt fact was: the R&A was not any old club, but the guardian of the game's rules and the custodian of its image. Barring women seemed clumsy, at best: it encouraged the outside world to persist in seeing golf as a sexist, seedy, smug-bastard pursuit. There was a widespread perception that golf, like many British sports (tennis, cricket, football), was run by a bunch of elderly chaps in blazers; why was golf happy to let this endure? When Prince Andrew was captain of the R&A, he presided over a club from which his mother was banned, and in 1978 a reporter assigned to cover the Open was thrown out of the Royal and Ancient clubhouse. The last thing golf needed was evidence that this would never end.

It is important, of course, to detach the game from the social scene that has claimed it. It is, as has been noted, possible to love golf while disliking golf clubs, just as it is possible to love skiing without loving electro-pastel Gore-tex, or football without enjoying the four-letter barrage that streams from 'loyal fans'. But the charge remained: for how long could golf in general, and the R&A in particular, pretend that 'tradition' made progress impossible?

It may seem a simple issue, but there were some subtleties here. The Open is a 'bastion' of the old ways, right down to the good-old-Tom maunderings of the commentary unit. But while the old ways are by no stretch of the imagination perfect, neither are they quite imperfect. One of the charms of the Open, when you attend it, is that it carries unpretentious reminders of the car boot sale – children run laps in the champagne tent. Many of the voices that protest against the fusty ways of the Open are themselves spokesmen for a bigger, more conventional establishment rooted in the mass market; and somewhere in that oily bathwater is a healthy baby. Peter Dobereiner once wrote that golf had been 'soaked in male chauvinist piffery for five hundred years'; it was impractical to think it would change overnight.

Some of the old rationales were pragmatic. In an era when men were obliged by etiquette to surrender their chairs to women, there was selfish logic to a men-only zone. But none of this was relevant any more. These days the only freedom left to protect was the freedom to tell crude jokes.

Not that British golf was unique. When Martha Burk campaigned, in 2003, against the fact that Augusta National was men-only, she drew scant support from the game itself. Arnold Palmer and Jack Nicklaus were busy pleading with Hootie Johnson, chairman of Augusta, to raise the age limit for ex-champions – happy, it seemed, to speak up on behalf of a few crocked legends who might struggle to break 80 (Palmer himself shot 89 the year before); but on the matter of women, they remained ostentatiously silent. Tiger Woods, usually not one to court controversy, said simply: 'Should women be members? Yes.'

There had been a few cautious steps forward, few of them happy. In 2004 the R&A agreed that if a woman qualified, she could play, a fine alteration spoiled slightly by the fact that it was sparked by the emergence of the highly talented young Hawaiian golfer Michelle Wie, whose marketing advisers were urging her to play men's events. She took a fine picture, but was not yet the best player in the women's game – should she really jump the queue just because she was young and willowy?

So when Laura Davies proposed to play a tournament in Australia, to address the intriguing question of whether her booming game was strong enough to compete with men, Greg Norman denounced it as a 'marketing gimmick'. There was much mirth in the idea that a man who had branded himself a great white shark, with 'Attack Life' emblazoned on his golf balls, might be in any way opposed to marketing gimmicks. But his point was shared by almost every golfer. Davies was deemed to be claiming a space to which some deserving young male golfer had a right.

In theory, women were now permitted to play the Open, so long as they qualified – which seemed fair enough. But the Open also remained a place where ageing champions with no chance even of making the cut could indulge themselves (at someone else's expense) by turning up year after year. This small step at least encouraged us to imagine a future in which golf's dividing lines were drawn not by sex but by ability. Perhaps the forward hitting area – the ladies tee – should be reserved not for women but for weak players, male or female. The best women could play off the back tees and the determining factor would be skill, not sex.

It may be that the arguments about women are not honest. The real issue may not be sex so much as money: what golf objects to may not be women per se so much as crowded courses and clogged fairways. Opening up the game to the other half of the world might well lead to some overcrowding. But the obvious solution – to discriminate not by sex but by ability, obliging everyone, in effect, to qualify before playing a course – would hamper all novices and stink of exclusivity in a different way. And it would give golf's treasurers heart murmurs, because the game as it stands does rely hugely on the financial power of male duffers.

Nothing like this was on the horizon just yet, and Alex Salmond, by picking a fight on weak ground, made sure that his protest was fleeting. But the R&A was in a cul-de-sac, with the future nipping at its polished heels. Tiger Woods could not single-handedly erase the gin-and-jag image that had dogged golf for so long. He didn't even seem to want to.

However humourless in this area, elsewhere the R&A was happy to poke fun at itself. When Al Shepherd struck his six-iron on the surface of moon, in 1971, in the NASA Invitational (his first effort was an airless-shot, but he clipped his second 200 yards, with a slight fade), the R&A soared to the occasion by sending a telegram ('Warmest congratulations') to Houston, chiding the astronaut for his glaring, televised failure to rake the galactic dust. 'Please refer to Rules of Golf section on etiquette, paragraph 6, quote,' it read. 'Before leaving a bunker a player should carefully fill up all the holes made by him therein, unquote.'

CHAPTER FIVE

Texas and Berkshire

The International Qualifying tournament in America attracts a high-class field, and this year it convened in Plano, an affluent suburb north of Dallas, Texas, in May. There were 78 players, eight of whom would win the golden ticket to Turnberry; some came straight from the Byron Nelson Championship, a few miles down the road, which had finished the previous evening.

Four players qualified out of the Byron Nelson by lifting themselves into the top 50 in the world rankings (this was the cut-off date). Dustin Johnson, Brian Gay, Charley Hoffman and Charles Howell III could take time off, and so, after a nerve-racking couple of days, could David Toms. He was the world number 47 going into the tournament, but missed the cut. Naturally he feared that he might be overtaken, but when the arithmetic settled he was in 50th spot, the right side of the line. He did not have to tee it up in Plano. Everyone else had to take on the golfing gods once more, along with a bunch of hard-hitting lesser lights.

The most notable player in the line-up was Davis Love III, but he was still sent out early, at 7.10 a.m. He did not hesitate, however. The Open was his 'favourite major' because of 'the way they set up the course, the tradition'. He had the memory of 21

consecutive Championships, and five top-ten finishes, to help
him sleep, and he was in good form from the off, firing a nippy
67 on day one and following up with an even better 65 (seven
birdies and two eagles) on day two. The standard was so high that
this was only just good enough. Indeed, when he missed a 15-
footer for eagle on the final hole he thought he might have
missed out, and had to settle in for a two-hour wait alongside his
caddie, Joe LaCava. 'Joe said he didn't think we'd get in,' said
Love. 'Reverse psychology. I've been sweating. But a lot of guys
ran out of gas on the back nine.'

One of those was Jesper Parnevik, who was trying to tap into
his own ambivalent memories of Turnberry (he should have won
there in 1996). He pulled out a terrific first-round 64, but could
not hang on and ended up falling two shots short of the mark.

The eventual winner was Matt Kuchar, a distinguished player
(US Amateur champion in 1997), who made mincemeat of the
course with 63 on the first day, and a 66 second time around. 'I
wanted to keep the gas pedal down,' he said. 'I knew if I just
steered it around the back nine I would not qualify.' His Open
record was not strong, but he wasn't about to let that spoil his
fun. 'I'm excited. I've never made a cut over there, but I sure do
love going over and giving it the good old American try.'

Jeff Overton had an up-and-down sort of day. 'I missed two
five-footers and had three balls in the water,' he said. But he was
hitting the ball well enough to survive these setbacks, and booked
himself a trip to Ayrshire.

Richard S. Johnson was a curious figure, the Swedish-born all-
round sportsman now living, possibly for weather-related reasons,
in Florida. As a boy he had been a hot tennis prospect, played
high-level handball and was a championship-standard skate-
boarder until he broke his rib (not to mention a hand and a foot)
for the seventh time: 'You have to be crazy to do the stunts.' He
started golf late, didn't think much of it at first, but then got the
bug. He played on the European Tour in 2002 (winning the

ANZ Championship in Sydney), but now played in America. He had only enjoyed one top-ten finish all year, and for the first hour and a half there was nothing to suggest that this would be his day: he parred the first six holes. But then he played the next 21 holes in minus-12, and barged into contention. He bogeyed the last but by then, who cared?

Tim Wilkinson, a left-handed New Zealander, stormed home with six birdies on the back nine; the American James Driscoll (thanks to two eagles on the par-five 8th) slipped in; and Sweden's Fredrik Jacobson recaptured his old sharp-shooting form, pinged the ball at pins, and finished with a 64.

Listing the players who prevailed makes it sound like a procession, but the day was full of groaning twists and nippy turns; players looked at the sky one minute, at their feet the next. It was not easy to exaggerate the difficulty of getting through a qualifier as strong as this. You only had to glance at the names that fell behind. There were seven tied on nine under par, one shot out of things. All might have contended at Turnberry had they secured a place. Alex Cejka (like Parnevik) had a fabulous first round and then fell back. Ben Crane, whose world ranking, 53, made him the top player in the field, shot 65 in the afternoon and still didn't make it (though he did later on, thanks to withdrawals). The Australians Rod Pampling and Aaron Baddeley, skilled performers on their day, came up one putt short. Scott McCarron, Woody Austin, Nick O'Hern and the hot new upstart, Danny Lee . . . all of these astonishing players made just one birdie too few.

The last and most delighted qualifier was Martin Laird, a Scot making his way on the US tour, who shot 65 in the second round to tie with five other players in joint third. 'I've never even played a professional event in Scotland,' he said, trying not to whoop. 'This is going to be great.'

On the very same day, at Walton Heath in Surrey, European golfers were going through the same exercise in reverse: trying to qualify for the US Open. Walton Heath was a famous course, a heathery masterpiece where W. G. Grace himself used to play. It is possible that golf was not his game: it was said he achieved more centuries here than on the cricket pitch.

It ended with high drama, in a seven-man play-off (for five spots). Four of the players birdied the first hole, leaving the other three to fight over the last place. They went to the 206-yard par-three 17th, and the Swedish player Peter Hanson popped a six-iron straight into the hole ('It was just a perfect shot') to break the hearts of Richard Bland and Stephen Gallacher.

No one heaved a bigger sigh than the Italian Francesco Molinari. A week earlier, at the Irish Open, he had been leading the tournament, and playing out of his skin, when this same Peter Hanson made a marking error that led to Molinari being dis-qualified. Now, thank goodness, the Italian had qualified for the US Open by birdying the first of those play-off holes. Golfers are not jockeys; they rarely get kicked by flying hooves. But they do get pummelled. 'This game is so stupid sometimes,' said Hanson.

When Angel Cabrera won the Masters it looked like being the Year of the Established Pro (for a while there, until Kenny Perry missed his final putt, it looked like being the Year of the Middle-Aged Spread), but then Shane Lowry came along and did the same as Danny Lee had done in Australia. In vile weather, he outlasted the field and won the Irish Open – as an amateur. The Year of the Newcomer was back on the menu again.

The last qualifying event, at Sunningdale, took place against a backdrop of grave financial alarm: the global 'meltdown' was incinerating some of golf's best friends. Apart from US Bank, which ended its support for the Milwaukee event where Tiger Woods had made his debut, there had not been many outright sponsor withdrawals, but the big picture was gloomy. Golf's most significant backers – automobile companies and banks – were exactly the sectors most violently buffeted by the storm. Buick,

Volvo, BMW, Wachovia, Morgan Stanley, Barclays . . . institutions like these were having to scrutinise their spending, fast. The Royal Bank of Scotland, which had backed the Open for as long as anyone could remember, had been semi-nationalised, and its chief executive was a laughing stock (so much so that the Royal and Ancient was obliged – to the delight even of its enemies – to blackball his application for membership).

There were other casualties. Nike had announced 1400 job cuts; Footjoy was closing a plant in Massachussetts. Celtic Manor, home of the 2010 Ryder Cup, was looking for 70 redundancies, and Gleneagles, home of the 2014 Cup, was asking for voluntary retirees. Several top golfers, such as Henrik Stenson and Vijay Singh, were reported to have lost 'millions' when the Texan-Antiguan mogul 'Sir' Allen Stanford belly-flopped into a humiliating bankruptcy. And it seemed like only the beginning.

For the Open, early signs indicated that the hospitality market had dried up, and the decline of the pound meant that the Open's once generous prize money was suddenly, in dollar terms, only average – in the space of six months it had sunk from $8 million to $6 million. When Harrington won at Carnoustie in 2007 the prize money converted into €1.106m; victory at Hoylake produced, from the same number of pounds, €938,565; this year's winner would get 'only' €866,577. 'We were once the most lucrative major,' said Peter Dawson. 'Now we're at the bottom.'

It was a grey day, pressed by fat clouds, full of drizzle and midges. It was too warm to be Scottish weather, but this was not Florida, Spain or the Emirates. It was British golf, and as the combatants trussed themselves into light rainwear, it had some of the hallmarks of a camping trip. The field would play both of Sunningdale's courses, the New and the Old, and the players gathered on the putting green behind the first tee like a group outing, exchanging considerate glances and words of encouragement.

'Have a good one.'

'Luck, mate.'

'Play well'

'Get stuck in.'

'You too.'

'Seeya.'

The first tee at Sunningdale is one of golf's hallowed spots: James Braid, Vardon, Player, Bobby Locke, Bernhard Langer, Norman, Ian Woosnam and Faldo had all won big tournaments from this shining sliver of commuter-belt grass. When Bobby Jones achieved his so-called 'perfect round' here in 1926, he said: 'I wish I could take this golf course home with me.' Modern players could only gulp at the fact that his top score on any hole was four, and that on ten occasions Jones was hitting approach shots with a two-iron or a wood.

These are the kind of things that make ageing members sigh. Were those the days, or what? A modern player who needed a two-iron to reach the green on a par-four would be regarded as an absolute dud – and would probably berate the course set-up as ridiculous . . . unfair . . . a disgrace.

It was a shame about the Coca-Cola wheelie bin by the first tee, and at the real thing the courtesy apples and bananas would be in a neat basket, not a plastic crate; but in other respects there were exciting hints that this was a special day. Caddies pulled Claret Jug bibs over their heads, careful not to dislodge their cigarettes; the players had expensive tropical tans.

The highest-ranked player in the field (95th in the world) was Sweden's Johan Edfors, and he was out early, in a bright turquoise shirt he declined to tuck into his trousers – a racy bit of dressing-down, by golf standards. He birdied the 1st (an easy par-five for these professionals), missed a putt for par at the tricky 2nd (where the green slips away from you more than you think) and took dead aim at the green on the short par-four 3rd. This was a nice risk-reward hole: the green was drivable but small, and surrounded by trouble. Edfors drove his ball to the front edge and

watched it roll out to the flag. He had a 15-footer for eagle:
Turnberry here he came.

He was feeling optimistic, because he had just made it
through the US Open qualifying round at Walton Heath. He
had played three consecutive Opens since 2006, and wanted to
make it four.

It wasn't even eight o'clock, but one golfing truth was emerging with clarity: every shot counts. If Edfors made his eagle, he
would be two-under after three and would feel launched, irre-
pressible. Miss, and even though he was under par, he would feel
bereft, as if he had let shots go. Golf is subjunctive: it measures
rounds against what might have been, could have been, should
have been. One of its favourite phrases is 'on another day'. On
another day, goes the saying, it could have been four or five
under, easily. Edfors's partner, Lee Slattery, began less well. He
struggled for par at the second and dropped a shot at the third
when he drove into sand, splashed out and left an approach putt
woefully short. But when he ripped his tee shot at the par-three
4th about two feet from the pin for a gimme birdie, there was –
since Edfors missed his eagle putt – only a single stroke between
the two. Edfors seemed to know it was not his day. Before long
he was trying to whack it extra-hard off the tee, and flaring it up
the right-hand side.

The road that cuts across the second fairway was proving a fair
indicator of the players' ball-striking. David Frost, the genial
South African, didn't quite make it, but Peter Lawrie, a small,
neat Irishman, cracked it 30 yards past. Danny Willett, a newcomer who was still bleary from an excellent fourth place in
Wales the evening before, drilled it a dozen yards past that, and
Christian Cévaër actually bounced on the road and went another
60 yards, into the light rough on the far side of the elbow. Gary
Orr, Robert Dinwiddie, Simon Khan . . . these might have been
the European Tour's lesser lights, but they were fearsome hitters
of a golf ball: all of them flew the access road.

As water dripped from the pines, there was a bit of ill-feeling simmering on the course, partly because of what had happened the night before. The Wales Open at Celtic Manor (just on the Welsh side of the Severn Bridge) had been delayed by downpours, obliging the top finishers to pay for their success with a late-night drive up the M4. They had been promised a kind tee-time, and the officials did their best (Oliver Fisher, who came joint sixth, restarted here at 8.46 a.m. – the golf equivalent of a lie-in). But they still had to be up and about sharpish to prepare for the two-round slogathon.

One notable absentee was the Wales Open winner, the young Danish player Jeppe Huldahl, who appeared as if from nowhere to win the event. Some saw proof here that this might be the Year of the Unknown, but he wasn't unknown to those who knew him. He had made a similar splash back in 2004, when he tore through the six-round Q-school near Barcelona in a blur of rapier-like irons and clouds of cigarette smoke. Now, without warning, he stunned himself again ('I couldn't feel my hands on the last three holes'). It was so exciting, he didn't know if he could face getting himself to Sunningdale for the Open qualifier.

'I haven't decided,' he said. 'I'm a bit tired. Thirty-six holes tomorrow sounds like a lot. I might go home and celebrate this.' There was the small matter of his winnings to tot up: 300,000 euros, and it struck someone that this might even get him to Turnberry automatically.

'I have no idea,' he said. 'Anyone in here know?'

In the end he decided not to come, influenced in part by the fact that he was handed a 6.48 a.m. tee-off time.

Paul Broadhurst took the opposite view. He was not in good form, and missed the cut at Celtic Manor, but he was joint holder of the Open low-round record (63) – so there was pride to consider. 'I was in two minds as to what to do.' He hit a few warm-up balls and decided to have a go.

'It's frustrating,' he said. 'I am playing great on the practice range, but not on the course. It's like someone else takes over. But I will soldier on.'

It pays not to give up. He got off to a steady start at Sunningdale ('I got to one under early on and played reasonably well'), made no mistakes, picked up birdies here and there, and had a first-round 65.

All over the course, crucial shots were going in or staying out. At the par-five 14th Edfors hit a career drive, nailed a thrilling iron at the distant flag to leave himself a four-foot eagle putt . . . and missed. At the 16th his birdie putt hit the hole and spun out. Angry, he ballooned his next drive into the trees and bent to unzip his (pink) bag for another ball. Like an attentive butler, his caddie held one out. Edfors took a huge swipe, and watched it soar into the same tranquil stand of ancient oak, pine and birch.

Shane Lowry, winner of the Irish Open, whacked it off the first tee of the New Course, stuck his hands in his pockets to keep them dry and ambled off the tee, scattering magpies. On the practice green to his right, not even glancing at the players setting off, Thomas Bjørn was chipping over bunkers with metronomic ease. Up and over, up and over, up and over. Three in a row landed softly, took a hop forward, then stopped by the flag. How on earth was this man not winning tournaments any more?

Bradley Dredge was there too, feathering chips over the hump with immaculate ease. Again, how a chap like this could possibly have to qualify for anything that involved hitting golf balls . . . it was a mystery.

At the 1st, Bjørn nailed a drive up the middle, middled an iron shot to three feet, nudged it with his long putter, and leaked it a few inches past.

Was that the putt that would cost him a place at Turnberry?

At the 2nd another magnificent iron shot left him inside 15

feet, but the putt ground to a halt an inch or two short of the hole.

If Bjørn managed to reach his 13th Open, he would embellish a record that included four top-tens and two second places. He had once seen off Tiger Woods during a final-round nail-biter in Dubai, a feat thought virtually impossible, and had been a big part of Europe's winning Ryder Cup teams in 1997 and 2002. If there was a society for those who have had one hand on the Claret Jug, Bjørn would be its secretary, if not its president-elect (no one can wrestle pride of place from Jean Van de Velde). At Royal St George's in 2003, he took a two-stroke lead into the bunker beside the 16th green . . . and left it there. By the time his third shot found the putting surface, he had tossed away his chance.

Golf is fond of the notion that a youthful putting stroke, unclouded by failure, may be steadier than a weather-beaten one. Bjørn seemed to be the living proof. But there are plenty of instances to show that novices can be ambushed by the same affliction. Back in January a promising young (18-year-old) Surrey golfer called Max Williams won the Qatar Amateur, and was invited back soon afterwards to compete in a full-blown pro event, the Qatar Masters. First time around he shot 68 and 75 to win; two weeks later, on the same course, he shot 79 and 81 to be dead last.

Inevitably, he was invited to consider the reasons for such a decline. There was one strategic consideration: the pins were in more difficult spots. But mostly it was mental: 'The feeling that I didn't deserve to be there.' On the range he was swinging next to Henrik Stenson ('It's hard not to feel awestruck'). Unease of this sort is a game-wrecker. 'On one green I hit my first putt to three feet, and both my partners stood back as if expecting me to finish. Normally I would have marked, but I felt like I was in the way. I putted out. And missed.'

Something else was new: spectators. 'You don't want to hit a bad shot; you're thinking about how they're going to react to you, and feeling you need to prove yourself. It's weird.'

Like any new pro, he was trying to learn ('take the positives') from this experience. In this context he needed to look no further than Tiger Woods, who had written the set text (it was already in lists of self-help quotations): 'There's no such thing as a setback. If anything goes wrong, it is an opportunity to learn and improve. The greatest thing about tomorrow is, I will be better than I am today. And that's how I look at my life. I will be better as a golfer, I will be better as a person, I will be better as a father, I will be a better husband, I will be better as a friend.'

The future would provide an interesting gloss on this maxim, but that didn't mean it wasn't wise. It chimed with what Williams had just learned in the Gulf. 'Tour players have world-class attitudes,' he said. 'They can come away from anything and say they've got better.'

They need to. Golf punishes its disciples by confronting them, more often than not, with failure, or at least defeat. Even Woods lost more often than he won. Jack Nicklaus once said that golf was 'the only sport where, if you win 20 per cent of the time, you are the best', and this was a simple statement of the facts. Golfers spend most of their time losing (if beating all but one of your rivals counts as losing), and one of the reasons why golf psychologists charged such lavish fees was that players required armour-plating against the reversals in their professional lives. Most of them were, in their youth, by some margin the best player they had ever known, or could imagine: only on the top stage did they fall short.

Those golf mind gurus had an interesting task: to install stupid optimism in their charges. Golf does not require its adherents to be subtle, sceptical or sensitive to nuance; it insists instead on bulletproof self-belief. 'It has been observed,' wrote Sir Walter Simpson, 'that absolute idiots play the steadiest.' It is a cliché to assert that the game is played 'between the ears', but once a high level of skill has been attained, a resilient attitude is decisive. It won't cure a bad swing, but can bolster a good one.

Was anyone tougher-minded than Gary Player? Ask him – he may well say no. Those who used to watch him over four-footers in his glory days knew that if there had been any stones in the vicinity, each one would have been thoroughly turned. He scrutinised lies, it was said, 'like a laboratory technician with a blood sample'. In the famous Duel in the Sun Open he was paired with Nicklaus and also with Peter McEvoy (then Britain's leading amateur), whose recollection remained crisp.

'I cannot believe,' he recalled, 'that Jack ever played better than in the opening two rounds. He was as near to perfect as you can possibly be. His striking was just so clean. And no matter whether he came a little short or a little long or really close, he missed the putt. If anyone had putted for him in the first two rounds he'd have won by ten.' McEvoy's thoughts of turning professional began to melt. 'I was slightly depressed by him. I thought I wasn't good enough. He scared me off, in a way.'

Player, on the other hand, was floundering – but didn't notice. 'I recall Jack asking him how long he had been hooking it. Of course, Player being Player, he could only think in superlatives. "I've never hit the ball better in my life," he said. Which wasn't true. He was snap-hooking everything. He was in denial, which was probably his greatest strength. If he had suddenly realised how ordinary he really was, he would never have achieved half of what he did.'

Wishful thinking as a practical asset? If that were true, everyone would win, all the time.

At the halfway mark you could have bet your house on Graeme Storm making it to Turnberry after scorching round the New Course in a course-record eight-under-par 62. He wasn't one of those golfers who lived in Sunningdale (like Nick Dougherty) and knew the greens like the back of his hand. He had walked the course the previous evening, but had never played a full round. An eagle at the 18th helped, but otherwise it was just one of those days.

It isn't always easy to remain calm after hitting such heights, but Storm threw himself at the afternoon with a vengeance, hitting a five-iron to six feet and holing out for eagle on the 1st to help him relax. He gave one shot back, but steadied the ship with a birdie on the 9th, and from then on his participation in the Open was not in doubt. His two-under-par 68 was, by the standards of his morning, a mild effort, but it was good enough to make him joint winner. 'That eagle at the first gave me a secure feeling,' he admitted. 'It would be nice not to have to qualify this way, but I have to. In my eyes the Open is the biggest event in the world.'

For Johan Edfors the morning was turning into a struggle. He was proving it was possible to play badly and brilliantly at the same time. The 17th hole, however, showed what was needed to be a force in golf. When he carved his drive right and hit a provisional, he didn't give up, even though he needed about eight-under on this hole to catch the leading group. He searched in the woods and found the ball, but could see no visible route back to his own fairway. Undaunted, he marched out the other way, where a group was still playing, and spied an opportunity. Fifty yards away, surrounded by long grass, was a ladies tee; if he could squirt his ball on to that, he might get a decent lie and a line to the target: there were dozens of tall trees in his path, but nothing else to worry about, except the bunkers.

Edfors returned to the ball, gritted his teeth and shoved it on to the pale green stage on the far side of the clumps. Then he blazed an iron over the trees to seven feet, and holed out for a magnificent, redundant par. A knot of spectators nodded their heads. Even when all was lost, golf offered the possibility of such redemption. Edfors had endured a poor day, but had played one of the shots of his life. At the 18th he sent the ball up the fairway, stopped to relieve himself in a waist-high gorse bush, hit it into a bunker and splashed out to two feet for a closing par that typ-ified his round. He had hit some awful whiffs, but had scrapped over every shot and finished with a level-par 70. Maybe the after-noon would be better.

When he looked at the halfway leaderboard, however, he could see he was in trouble. Graeme Storm had broken the course record. Andrew Coltart and Raphaël Jacquelin had shot 65; Rafa Echenique and Michaël Lorenzo-Vera were in with 66; and Grégory Havret was five-under for the front nine. A dozen other players had also gone low; there were too many ahead of him, if he was honest. The rain had eased, and it was a mild, still day, with receptive greens. Turnberry was slipping out of reach.

On the 18th tee, the French player Grégory Havret could hardly believe it. Par would give him a round of 63. He snapped open a bottle of fizzy water, blew on his fingers, and poured a drive up the middle. Up ahead he could see the clubhouse, the tents, the smoke of grilling sausages and bacon, and hear the rumble of conversation beneath the oak tree by the green. He plonked his second shot safely on the putting surface, but his first putt was a little heavy and then he missed the return.

He grinned. It wasn't the sort of day a chap could afford to drop shots like that, but 64 was the third best score so far – *pas mal*, to be sure.

Six players picked up their ball after one round and went home, burning with disappointment. One was Lee Slattery. And it didn't take long to see why this was frowned upon, because it left his playing partner, Johan Edfors, in an awkward spot. At the par-three 2nd, playing on his own, he missed the green on the left, fluffed a chip, rattled it on and missed the putt for a hope-ruin-ing double bogey – and then, to add insult to injury, he was asked to join the group ahead and play as a three.

The atmosphere was damp and strung out. At midday two of the first-round leaders, Alastair Forsyth and Jan-Are Larsen, set off down the first hole of the New Course, and not a soul followed them up the fairway, even though they were up there with the leaders. It was just two blokes playing golf. Away to the left a strimmer buzzed in the trees of a grand house – buffing up the edges of the badminton court, perhaps. Sun gleamed on wet leaves, rabbits scampered on lawns; squirrels darted on high branches.

The caddies pulled off their sweaters. This was hot work.

Up the hill, Graeme Storm was tugging a stream of fans along the first hole of the Old Course. From a distance you could see him crouching over his eagle putt, and then – a second after he marched decisively towards the hole, came a sharp explosion of applause. There is a delicate calibration to such noises. The polite smattering that greets a par putt is markedly different from the firm clamour that greets a birdie, and an eagle noise is something altogether more emphatic and astonished.

That's what it sounded like, and sure enough, only a couple of moments later, walkie-talkies crackled under the old oak tree, and Storm was credited with a three. He was eleven-under after 19 holes, and marching on.

In the middle of the second round it is impossible to keep track of the big picture. Shots are flying in all over the place, and though the scores are rung in after 5, 9, 13 and 17 holes, and patterns do emerge, there are phases when players simply fall off the radar.

It looked as if the leaders were keeping their games together, though. Scotland's David Drysdale flicked an iron from the raised 10th tee and left himself nine feet for birdie (he missed); Jacquelin, slim as a pencil, struck it in close to the 9th flag, and then again at the 14th, and settled for two tap-in pars.

Spectators crunched on stony paths, oblivious of the players trying to concentrate a few yards away.

'Turned out better than I thought.'

'Yes, quite warm when the sun breaks through.'

In quiet moments you could hear the motorway rushing south to Camberley, and there were lulls in which to wonder why people liked watching these young millionaires playing golf. It was partly (chiefly) for the exalted standard of their play: it was a thrill to see talented sportsmen negotiate the zing of competition. But there was something else; they looked so neat and well drilled, so composed and resolved. Even the young ones seemed assured. And their clothes, however silly, were pin-fresh. The typical demeanour of the golfer – calm, intent, optimistic – seemed to mock the fans' own edgier, in-two-minds sense of things.

Edfors was continuing to have a strange day. Now part of a three-ball, he whacked it into the trees up the right of the 6th, came out sideways, flailed it back in, punched to the green and sank a 50-footer for bogey.

'It wasn't very nice,' he said. 'I hit quite a few good shots, but never had any rhythm.'

It was a brave display, but it wasn't doing him any good. Graeme Storm was signing for a 68 to keep him comfortably in the lead; Rafa Echenique was blazing his way to a 64. Jacquelin was stealing through the woods like a bleached-blond pickpocket, nicking birdies here and there, treading lightly in cat-burglar black, and capturing his second 66 to be safe in the winners' circle with an eight-under-par 132. Bjørn was finding the range with his putter with four birdies on the front nine; South Africa's Branden Grace was lighting up the greens; Paul Broadhurst was nursing a score back to base. Only a great score, it was clear, would do.

The first player to post a target had been Simon Griffiths, a Wentworth professional whose most glittering (and relevant) golfing achievement was back-to-back victories (in partnership with the young Ross Fisher), in the venerable 'Sunningdale Foursomes' on this very course. This year he had won a bit of money in Malaysia and Indonesia, but had missed cuts in Hong Kong, Australia and Madeira; he was exactly the kind of player the Open, with its qualifying structure, was all about. He started at quarter to seven in the third group of the day, and finished with a two-round total of 134, six shots under par. It was a tremendous effort; whether it was good enough, only time would tell. He settled in for a long wait.

The scoreboard was under the great old oak tree by the 18th green. This was where, as the afternoon went on, players, caddies and their friends gathered, to keep an eye on how the big picture was developing.

An hour or so after Griffiths a young Dutch player called Taco Remkes went one better, and signed for a score of 133. He was another for whom this event was intended. He was just 24 years old, and in his first year on tour. He had won three times on the Challenge Tour in 2008, but was struggling to make the most of his chances this year. He came 12th in the Johannesburg Open, but then flew to Abu Dhabi as fifth reserve, on the off chance that five people would drop out. They didn't, so he flew back to Spain to work with his coach. His shoulder had been aching too. Success at Sunningdale would give him a more than welcome boost.

Gary Orr birdied the last two holes, always a good idea, to secure a 63 and ensure that Scotland had someone to cheer for at Turnberry, and set a new target: 131. He hadn't played in the Open for eight years, and hadn't been to Turnberry since missing the cut there in 1994.

Ten minutes later, Peter Lawrie and Danny Willett joined Taco Remkes on 133, and crossed their fingers. At this stage it seemed that minus-six would be good enough, and these were all on minus-seven. But looking at the scoreboard it was clear that there were some low rounds coming this way.

Willett, in a bright-pink shirt and showy, alligator-skin belt, was the very image of the Poulteresque modern golfer – some people tried to call the look 'punk', but that was a strong term for a bit of hair gel and some Hugo Boss spiv-wear. He was having quite a time. It was his first year on the Tour (he had come fourth at Q-school the previous November) and he had come joint fourth in the Wales Open this time yesterday. A spot at the Open would make this a year to remember, and it looked likely now.

Mark Foster jumped into the reckoning when, on the final hole of the New Course, he laid his second shot dead for an eagle that clipped two more shots off an already imposing score. Another one on 133 – there was quite a cluster forming there.

As if it weren't tough enough, he had made it more interesting by getting off to a textbook bad start. 'I three-putted the first two holes and thought, Here we go, but I got it working after that.' This is not a recommended tactic, but driving the green on a par-four (which he did at the 9th) and then holing the eagle putt – everyone agrees that this is a good idea.

It might have been a hasty decision to make that 18th hole a par-five, because so long as they didn't lose their tee shots in the trees, the players could comfortably reach the green in two shots. True, there was trouble around the raised green, but for golfers of this calibre it was a serious eagle chance, and a near-certain birdie. It was making for some dramatic last gasps, but it also meant the qualifiers might just turn out to be the chaps who happened to hole an eagle putt on this final hole.

This was the opportunity that soon faced Scotland's Richie Ramsay. It had been an unusual day or two, and he was absolutely exhausted. In Wales he had led at the halfway stage, and was only one shot off first place in the third round, in heavy rain, when something happened that ruined his weekend. He was in the middle of the 16th fairway, and pressed his foot behind where he was about to place his ball – the tournament was playing preferred lies – to see (he said later) how much water there was. When the round was called off in the fading light, he was summoned before the rules officials for a two-hour grilling (no one's idea of a jolly evening). They informed Ramsay that his fate would be decided in the morning. 'I didn't sleep,' he said. 'I was concerned about what people might think.' When the time came he was cleared of any wrongdoing, but he clearly had the jitters. On the very next hole, in full view of the watching referee, he took relief and dropped his ball without marking it first. The penalty was one shot: a par-five became a bogey-six and though he scrambled well, he fell back to joint 10th.

All this was only a day ago, but Ramsay couldn't afford to think about it now, because he was coming up the 18th hole of the New Course on minus-six, near enough for someone to have communicated his position. He needed eagle at the last to reach minus-eight and qualify for certain, and this was the best eagle chance on the course. Even the scorers were confused: when eagles started flying in early in the day, they thought players must be holing six-irons. Ramsay was safely on the fringe in two. He discussed it at length with his caddie, and so did the crowd.

'Two putts from here,' said a man in a suit; probably a member, fresh from the office. 'It's a done deal.'

'I suppose,' said a Scottish voice, kind yet fatalistic. 'Though there's a fair few have pushed it a way by from here.'

If Ramsay holed this one, he would jump inside the play-off line, leaving four of them to haggle over the last place. If he two-putted, he would be part of a five-man team digging for just two tickets.

He coaxed it three feet short and became the third player on minus-seven.

There was still half the field to come. Michael Lorenzo-Vera looked good at lunch, after a heady first round of 66, but his afternoon 68 looked like one too many, especially when, within minutes of each other, Rafa Echenique and Graeme Storm both posted 130, ten under par.

Echenique had missed the cut in his two most recent tournaments. Not surprisingly, he was 'really, really happy'.

The next player to punch the air was David Drysdale, who matched his morning 65 with an afternoon 66 to join fellow Scot Gary Orr on 131. He had a feeling it might be his day when he holed in one at the 217-yard 10th in his first round. After that, anything seemed possible.

Drysdale carried a couple of intense Open memories in his bag. A long time ago, in 1992, he played as a make-up-the-numbers 'marker' in the Open, first for Roger Chapman and then, next day, for John Daly.

'I was 17, and it was a big buzz,' he recalled. 'It would be just great if I got to play with Daly again – he was fantastic.'

His other memory was sterner, more useful. In 1999, at Final Qualifying for the Open at Carnoustie, he outplayed another Scot, Paul Lawrie, by a whopping six shots. But while Lawrie roared back in the afternoon, Drysdale faltered. Ten days later Lawrie repeated the trick and won the Claret Jug. It was a reminder that all things were possible, but also that winning positions could slip away in a flash. Drysdale had tried to qualify nine times already, in vain. This time he kept his swing tight and prepared himself to defy the rumble about the weakness of Scottish golf: the home of the game no longer had a single top-ranked player.

'I can't wait,' he said, looking forward to his week at Turnberry. 'I've got the next two weeks off and I'd love to go over and have maybe a couple of games there.'

Raphaël Jacquelin needed no last-gasp heroics. He had played well all day, and he swung his nimble way to 132. He had won the equivalent qualifer for the US Open two weeks earlier.

'I guess I'm pretty good at these things,' he said.

Half an hour later he was joined by Paul Broadhurst, who had enjoyed a strange afternoon. At the lunch break his playing partner, Jyoti Randhawa, decided to give up, so Broadhurst was on his own. Unlike Edfors, he managed to turn this to his advantage. 'I found myself having to slow down,' he said. 'It gave me time to start thinking more.'

On the 14th hole his eagle putt horseshoed out. Oh God, he thought.

He was six-under at the time. On the next hole he hit it into what looked like a ditch. 'Got up there, there's no ditch. I pitched it in for two.'

When it is your day, it is your day. Broadhurst birdied the 16th to get himself to minus-eight and, like the old campaigner he was, parred the last two holes.

Oliver Fisher came to the 18th of the Old Course with an exciting chance. His drive flew left into the light rough, but he hit a lovely wedge close to the flag. The putt missed, but he could still celebrate: he had joined the other minus-sevens – Remkes, Lawrie, Willett, Foster and Ramsay, on 133. There were enough of them to make a play-off certain, but it was not yet clear how many spots they would be playing for.

There was one fewer when Branden Grace came up the 18th of the Old Course. People tried to find out what his score was, and what he needed. At one point he had been on minus-nine, a grand effort, but no one knew what had happened on the last few holes. He seemed to have a good idea himself, however. He eased the ball up to two feet, popped it in, and smacked happy palms with his caddie. He had hung on, and joined Orr and Drysdale on 131. It was, he said, 'just a wish come true'.

By now the crowd around the final green was swollen by people who sensed there would soon be blood in the water. This was the sharp end of the day, when matters would be settled for good. Down the hill, the practice tee lay empty. It was too late for all that now.

There were seven men on 132 or better, so only three more qualifiers were needed. There were already six men tied on 133, so it was curtains for Simon Griffiths and the others on 134. But even those minus-sevens were not safe. The information coming in was patchy, but there were four men out there – Havret, Rhys Davies, Bjørn and Marcus Fraser – who could, in theory, still beat them. If all of them came home in 132, then they would play off for the last three spots, ejecting the seven players on 133. This was getting fiendish.

I made the mistake of sharing this thought with the man next to me. He had been making agitated growling noises for a good while.

'What!' he said, horrified. 'Are you serious?'

I admitted I might be wrong, and beat a hasty retreat. But the damage was done. I soon realised my faux pas: my agitated neighbour was Oliver Fisher's father, and I had just about given him a heart attack.

Grégory Havret was 120 yards from the pin: up and down would get him into the play-off. He would have accepted that at the start of the day, but given his brilliant first round it was a bit disappointing. Did he know that the line had moved from minus-six to minus-seven in the last 40 minutes? He licked a nice approach into 15 feet, but didn't look stressed when he two-putted for par. He smiled at a friend, winked at his caddie and ducked under the rope. It looked as if he thought he had made it. But he hadn't: he was a shot shy.

If Havret wanted to reproach himself, he could have looked back to the fourth, an uphill par-three, when he carved a mid-iron on to a steep bank away to the right, bunted it up short and then three-putted for a card-ruining double bogey. Or maybe the way, on the very next tee, he had a detailed consultation with his caddie before selecting a rescue club for a safe lay-up, and then bashed it straight in the bunker. In truth, it was the simplest of matters to replay the round in his mind and improve it by a shot or two. Either way, the card he had to sign contained one shot too many.

Rhys Davies made no such mistake. Tall and slim, he had out-played his fellow Welshman Bradley Dredge all day, and now stood on the brink. He hit a fine approach to eight feet and ran it in to join Broadhurst and Jacquelin on 132. It meant that there were only two places left.

In the group after Davies, the Australian Marcus Fraser came, missed and went. After a superb day, he too fell short by a single shot. And while golf is polite, certain people under the famous oak tree were jumping (silently) for joy. The minus-sevens could not now be denied a play-off. There were no longer two play-ers who could barge ahead of them.

Lawrie and Orr were already down at the range, loosening up. 'Anyone know which are the play-off holes?' said Danny Willett, hurrying past.

The machine ground on.

A quarter of a mile away, down at the bottom of the hill, Thomas Bjørn stood tall and impassive on the Old Course's 18th tee. On this closing hole there was no possibility of an eagle, not unless he holed from the fairway. But a birdie would put him in the play-off, and that was a realistic hope. It was a short hole, just 423 yards. A firm tonk up the left, and he could go at the flag with a lofted club. He had been in these situations before. In some ways – foolish as it sounds – it was more straightforward (though not easier) than needing to make par, since there were no awkward decisions to be made. Nothing was more infuriat-ing, when par was the target, than the dropping of a shot through either aggression or caution. Bjørn's programme was clear: he needed to pierce the fairway with his drive and attack the pin with the approach. No half measures.

He thumped it away with that familiar, sawn-off follow-through and watched the ball roll out into a perfect spot. He knew he needed to get it up and down from there to hit the mark, but didn't waste time over his approach, throwing it high above the green and holding the finish (often a good sign) as the ball came down over the flag. It landed with a plunk and stopped dead, four feet from the cup. There was warm applause: people knew how things stood. He had a straightforward putt to make the play-off. These are often called 'character-formers', though in truth they seem not so much to form character as to reveal it.

He pressed into his chest a long-shafted putter, that ugly broom-handle which is, of course, the putter of choice for the gentleman whose nerves have been scraped to ribbons. Did Bjørn's thoughts drift back to his first putt of the day, a putt of about this length? Almost certainly not. But the result was the same. He stood over the ball for a long time – an instant too long – then rolled it at the edge in search of a non-existent break. It slid by.

It is a cliché to put this missed shot in a ball-game down to 'pressure'. Golfing pressure is artificial, and no one would dream of comparing it to the life-or-death stress faced by soldiers, fire-men or anyone else on life's troubled frontline. But it does create dramatic contexts fraught enough to make the players' hands shake, and Bjørn had shown that even wise old campaigners could not evade such tremors. Earlier in the afternoon he had holed half a dozen – in his golfing life he had holed thousands. But on this warm afternoon, with a place at the Open hanging on the outcome, he had not been able to keep his stroke calm. He strode to the marker's cabins, reached for a cigarette, and con-soled himself in a cloud of smoke.

The day's second most disconsolate figure was the Frenchman Thomas Levet. He was not impressed when handed a start-time of 6.39 a.m. Golfers like to reach the course a good hour before their tee-off time, so they can go through their bag of shots on the practice green and absorb the pace of the greens. He played dreadfully ('like a monkey') and knew he would have to shatter the course record in the afternoon even to have the ghost of a chance. Things got worse when he discovered that, thanks to his early start, lunch was not ready. *Mon dieu* – was nothing sacred?

He played the second round, but his game was off. He finished seven shots short, then signed an incorrect card and was disqualified.

All in all, a good day. Wasn't he lucky to be playing the game he loved?

Bjørn and Levet weren't the only big-name players to miss out. As the car boots slammed, and Swedish and French golfers sat on the rear end of their rental hatchbacks and changed out of their shoes, a number of fine players were heading home empty-handed. As in the American qualifier, the intensity of the contest was most clearly visible by looking at the calibre of those who fell by the wayside. Christian Cévaër, winner of the European Open two weeks earlier, missed by five, and the Swedish Ryder-Cupper Niclas Fasth, runner-up at Celtic Manor only a couple of days before, missed by seven. Philip Archer, Nick Dougherty, Bradley Dredge, Johan Edfors, Shane Lowry, Jean-François Luquin, Scott Strange, Steve Webster – this was an impressive troupe. On another day, as the saying went, they might all have qualified.

There were four other so-called losers – Alexander Norén, Simon Dyson, Michael Jonzon and Ross McGowan – who would go on to win big-money European tournaments (in Switzerland, Scotland and Spain) before the year was out. This hadn't been their day, and that was all.

There were six players competing for two slots. After a flurry of activity in the R&A inner sanctum (the scoreboard in the press tent), it was announced, by word of mouth, that they would go out in two groups. There were three Englishmen (Oliver Fisher, Mark Foster and Danny Willett), a Scot (Richie Ramsay), an Irishman (Peter Lawrie) and a Dutchman (Taco Remkes). It sounded like the beginning of a joke, but no one was smiling: they were all too tense.

It was getting late, and the sky was wet. While a six-man group would have been eccentric, it would also have been a grand spectacle. At the Open play-off in 2002, four players (including Thomas Levet) were sent out in two groups, and while this was ideal for the armchair viewer, it was impossible for those at the course to know how things stood.

Ours not to question why. Off they went.

Remkes, Foster and Fisher went first, punching drives at the generous fairway on the first hole and finding the green in two. Foster and Fisher two-putted, but Remkes was tentative with his first (a sticky downhiller) and then missed the follow-up. He hurled his ball at the rhododendrons and stormed off towards the car park without a backward glance, his caddie trailing behind, and his girl-friend 30 yards behind that. Golfers do not always behave well when things fail to turn out as they hope. Half an hour earlier he had been jubilant; now he was a picture of dejection.

It was beginning to rain.

The second group parred the hole and joined forces with the first. Now we were talking.

The next hole was the short par-three where Edfors had tripped up when he played it alone. From the tee it looked straightforward, but anything that missed on the left would shimmy down a sharp slope into thick bushes. Birdie was possible; so was double bogey. Fisher went first and slammed it nine feet from the pin; Foster followed him, and was only a couple of feet further away. Ramsay flew a beauty all the way to the back of the green, but Willett, a touch conservative, left it short, and on the lower tier. There were four balls on the green facing Lawrie, and the suspense led him to tug it left, down the hump, into the long grass at the base of a small tree. He thinned it out and the ball scuttled across to the far side of the green, a full 60 feet away from the flag.

It was still his honour. This is one of the humiliations golf can offer: a player in Lawrie's position has to walk around the putting surface while everyone else watches and waits, avoiding his eye by pretending to repair pitchmarks; somehow he has to gather himself and have another go. Amateurs usually apologise for holding things up, but professionals are made of sterner stuff. They need you to mess up, and you know it.

'No worries,' they say, glad it is not them in this jam. 'Take your time.'

Lawrie didn't crumple, but his approach rolled six feet past, leaving him in grave danger. Willett, perhaps registering the pace of Lawrie's, hit a meek putt of his own and left himself a curving five-footer for par.

The others relaxed. Ramsay rolled it up to a foot and marked his ball; Foster trickled over Ramsay's coin and marked as well; Fisher's birdie putt died just a couple of inches from the cup. There was a fair mount of loose change around the hole by now: it looked like a wishing well.

That was three certain pars, which meant that Lawrie was done for. For appearance's sake he tried to hole his putt for bogey, but missed.

Now it was Willett's turn. He had played beautifully in Wales and well again here, but it came down, as it so often does, to this. He needed to hole this putt to stay in the play-off, and the fourth place cheque from Celtic Manor (€95,000) wasn't going to help him one jot.

He missed. Did his mind flash back to the moment, at Final Qualifying for the Open at Birkdale a year before, when he reached the 18th with a two-shot cushion, made a badly timed double bogey, and allowed Jean Van de Velde's birdie to seize the last available spot? If so, he didn't show it. A flicker of disbelief ran across his face, then disappeared. He looked like a quick learner. He knew that players couldn't afford to beat themselves up over every reversal, because golf is so generous with them; it would be suicide. You win some, you lose some. You take your chances and move on. That's all there is. C'est la vie.

Only three men now, and still two places to fight for: this was a proper eliminator. Shifted over to the 17th on the Old Course, which ran down into a dip, with trees both sides, and then up again to a roomy green. Fisher played a safe iron up the left, Foster gambled with a wood and clubbed it down to the bottom of the hill, a mere wedge short of the green; Ramsay split the difference and left it halfway down the slope.

Fisher slapped his ball into the middle of the green, and Ramsay rifled it even closer. From his flat lie, Foster hit it close too. All had a chance.

Fisher's putt broke early and dribbled 18 inches below the hole; Foster's nine-footer also fell away on the low side. But Ramsay took the deepest of breaths, stayed ice-still and rolled it in. He had claimed one of the spots outright – he could walk up the hill and buy himself a strong drink.

The golfing day had been running for some 14 hours, and the light was heavy and grey. There were two men still standing, and one of them was going to have to give way. On the next, Foster swiped the advantage when his drive found the perfect centre of the fairway. Fisher thumped it up the left-hand side, and from where the crowd stood, up by the green, it seemed to have bounded into the bunker. These chaps could certainly still reach the green from the sand, but it was advantage Foster.

As they walked up the fairway, Foster had to fight to keep his emotions in check. But he could not afford to smile, because Fisher's ball had missed the bunker and was lying nicely in some light rough. Foster bore down and hit a lovely iron dead at the pin; it bounced, checked and slammed on the brakes about 15 feet short of the hole. He would probably have that for it.

But things were about to change. Fisher's ball was close to where he had been a couple of hours earlier. He knew the way

from here, and he was flooded with relief at his narrow escape.
He felt on top of this one.

His wedge flew high and slammed down about a foot from the
hole. The crowd gasped. He might as well have stuck a dart in
Foster's chest.

On the green, Foster walked around his putt, trying to ignore
the roaring in his ears. He could do this. He'd done it before and
he could do it again.

But the putt did not fall; Fisher tapped in; and that was that.

People stood around under the tree for a little while, letting
the day's events sink in. Ramsay pulled out his phone to relay the
good news; Fisher stood giving interviews to a camera, light glaring on his already shining face. 'I was in that spot earlier, so I
knew the shot,' he said. 'But any time you are in the semi-rough
like that, you are guessing a bit, so I was a bit lucky there. But it's
the British Open. It's great. I can't wait.'

Golf is so absorbing and time-consuming (the Sunningdale day
ran from six in the morning till nine at night) that the rest of the
world seems to dissolve into the cloudy distance. When I reached
the car, it felt strange and out of kilter that the news on the radio
was not about Graeme Storm's course record or Bjørn's missed
putt, Ramsay's success or Echenique's burst of form. Instead, this
being the day when the British National Party had won two seats
in the European Parliament, someone was trying to explain why
banning black members was not racist. It was a basic freedom, it
seemed, that a party could discriminate against black skin without being called names by the 'politically correct brigade'.

And people said golf was stupid.

The first and simplest qualifying stage was over. Some 295
golfers – all exhilarating players who had spent their youth winning junior events and hearing lavish predictions of greatness
from the noisy, have-another-half enthusiasts at their clubs – had
tried to qualify for the Open; 267 of them had failed. Some fell

short by margins thin enough to leave them crushed. And the fiercest part of the crap-shoot had not even begun. Nearly 10 per cent of the players in the qualifiers up to now had made it through. That percentage was about to plummet. In ten days' time, some 1500 hopefuls would attempt an even more arduous and quixotic challenge.

There were twelve spots left. The dream was still alive.

This for the Open.

CHAPTER SIX

Regional Qualifying

The next step on the pyramid, Regional Qualifying, is a dispersed pageant held, with surprisingly little fuss, on 16 courses in Britain and Ireland. With 100 entrants at each venue, it asks the nation's best golfers, amateur and professional alike, to compete for an exciting but remote prize: a place in the next, final round of qualifying. No day in the calendar reveals so clearly the extent to which each Open candidate, even the sad dreamer who comes last, is a winner. It reminds us that the Open is the conclusion of a tense obstacle course that weeds out almost all of its participants. The odds against are extreme. Back in 2002, only three out of nearly 1800 players made it through to the Open itself. Yet still they come.

The rules are simple. At each site, ten or so spots in the next round are available (the R&A inspects scores as they come in, weighs their relative strength, and assigns precise numbers in the afternoon). But by the time the greenkeepers and officials gather, at five in the morning, to sweep dew, plant flags, complete the paperwork and heat the coffee, it is certain that 90 per cent of the day's field is destined to trail home empty-handed, thinking, as they duck into cars and head for the motorway, that if only it hadn't been for the putt that slid by on the 4th, or that blasted divot on the 9th, or that absolutely bloody passer-by who had a coughing fit on the 16th and made me fluff my chip, this could have been their day.

By rights, Regional Qualifying should be one of the congenial high points of the British sporting summer, a dashing festival of stick-and-ball skill, an off-Broadway Derby day. The players certainly dress for the occasion – there is enough co-ordinated pastel and blond fringe to make it look like the annual golf day of the local hair salon. A tiny sprinkling of spectators (mostly chums or relatives) chit-chat along the fairways; the myth-making eye of the media is fixed elsewhere, on Wimbledon.

This is a shame: Regional Qualifying binds Scotland, Ireland, Wales and the shires of England together in a green web of golfing aspirations, and while most are doomed to be shredded in the wind, it is still a carnival of competitive golf. The setting shifts from Gog Magog (it sounds like the wild coast of Ireland, but is in fact south of Cambridge, on the Colchester Road) to Ferndown, a classic amphitheatre in Dorset (where Peter Alliss's father Percy was the professional, oh, gracious me, goodness knows how many moons ago now). It links Pleasington, on the Pennine slopes above Blackburn, to the wooded heath of Royal Ashdown Forest, in the heart of Sussex. It binds the salt-whipped links of Royal Dublin (Ireland's second oldest) to the groomed alleys of Old Fold Manor, near Potters Bar.

Actually, the 2009 venues had plenty in common. Most were 100 years old or more: all had roots in the Open's grand ancestry. Lindrick, near Worksop, was laid out by the Sunningdale architect Willie Park Jr, while Yorkshire's Alwoodley (which drags lovely Dales scenery into the suburbs despite being only a few bus stops from the centre of Leeds) opened in 1907 under the watchful eye of Dr Alister MacKenzie, a Boer War surgeon who, though an average player himself, was the celebrated creator of Cypress Point in California, Royal Melbourne in Australia and, most famously, with Bobby Jones, Augusta National.

The courses spanned the country, but shared a heritage. Musselburgh held six Opens in the early days, and had been the cradle for eleven Open winners (America might call it Britain's 'winningest' club). Royal Ashdown (1888) was home to Horace Hutchinson, the first English captain of the Royal and Ancient, and also to Abe Mitchell, England's best Ryder-Cupper – he is depicted, mid-swing, on its gold lid. Royal Ashdown is equally proud of Alf Padgham, the Robert the Bruce of West Sussex, who came third in 1934, second in 1935, and first in 1936.

Golfing folklore was blowing down these courses (five of which were designed by one man: Harry Colt, renowned for spreading echoes of Scotland in English pastures). The R&A does pay the clubs, but not much (the fee is little more than a thirsty golf society would generate on a hot summer's day), and it relies hugely on the bottomless goodwill of the members, scores of whom are needed to act as spotters, marshals and dogsbodies on the day in question. It is hard work for everyone involved: caterers, greenkeepers, managers and volunteers. But it is an honour to be involved – akin to being informed that a medieval royal progress was on its way: would dinner for 500 be too grave an imposition? Hosting a qualifier boosts prestige (clubs use the Claret Jug logo on notepaper and websites) and the morale of members and staff, and puts greenkeepers on their mettle and chefs on their toes. In the fullness of time, if all goes well, it might even permit a modest increase in the visitor's green fee.

The Open's openness is a cherished asset, but also a hard-headed stance. With an entry fee of £125, the field generates nearly £200,000 for the R&A. And since these qualifying events depend almost entirely on volunteer workers drawn (some with twisted arms) from the clubs involved, this has many of the benign, earnest overtones of a charity day. Even the R&A officials, in their trim green blazers, are mostly unpaid.

Reasoning (I was quick on the uptake) that it would not be possible to attend all 16 qualifiers on the same day, I headed for a course that on the surface had little in common with Turnberry. Effingham lies on an unspoilt flank of the North Downs near Guildford. On a clear day you can hear traffic crawling along the M25, and from the top of the course (the 14th tee) you can see, across miles of rooftops, the new Wembley Stadium, the Millennium Wheel and the strutting pillars of Canary Wharf. You could enjoy a striking view of West Horsley, if East Horsley weren't in the way. It is by no stretch of the imagination a seaside links, in other words; it is the suburban commuter belt. Turn off the A3 out of London, and you nose past well-mown lawns, neat hedges, crooked parish spires, clumps of neat rhododendrons, well-fed sprays of climbing rose and old red-brick pubs that are now Thai restaurants. Between the nice houses, past hand-painted signs for toddler groups, lies a dozy woodland haunt of plump rabbits, contented squirrels, bright thrushes and lazy crows.

Behind this homely façade, however, are historical gleams even the Open cannot match. The handsome Georgian headquarters (1770) stands between ancient cedars on the site of a grand manor house that was confiscated by Henry VIII, as part of his monastery-dissolving land grab, and given to his admiral-in-chief, Lord William Howard. His lordship's son, Charles Howard (of Effingham), went on to command the trim Elizabethan navy against the lumbering Spanish galleons in 1588, a rout commemorated in the golf club by a silver 'Armada dish' mounted on the wall in the bar (where one of the oak beams is dated 1591).

As luck would have it, Regional Qualifying was on 24 June, the exact 500th anniversary of Henry VIII's coronation. This was auspicious, but for whom? I scanned the list of tee-off times, but was sorry to find no one called Henry, or Howard, or VIII. Clearly, this thing was wide open.

*

Regional Qualifying doesn't sound like a high-grade golfing event. No one arrives by helicopter or private jet; the car park is full of hatchbacks, and the players often use family or friends as caddies.

'Dad,' says one. 'Did you remember to pick up the drinks?'

'They're in your bag.'

'Have I got time for a leak?'

'Best hurry. We're next group but one.'

On the evidence of previous years (this was Effingham's third time as a qualifying host), anything below par would probably be enough – but it was a beautiful morning, and the course was running fast. In the second group of the day, a more-than-promising youngster called Curtis Griffiths was already attracting a murmur of interest. He was only 15 years old, yet a few months earlier had set a new course record when, on greens damp with spring rain, he shot a blistering eight-under 63 in a junior tournament (completing the back nine in just 29) to become something of a local hero. The entry form allows the competitors to choose which course they would like to play, and it was no surprise that Griffiths chose this one.

'I knew there was professional qualifying at Sunningdale,' he said. 'But I didn't realise they did an amateur one. I thought I may as well.' He was tall, slim and steady-eyed, and his golf was arresting: he had spent the previous winter in Florida, and won four out of the five events he entered.

Griffiths was one of golf's coming things: a Wentworth scholar, well placed to make inroads into top golf. These scholarships were one of the best golf-improvement mechanisms available to young players. Aimed at talented non-members, the club offered sharp coaching, top-of-the-range practice, and help with junior tournaments. Its star graduate, Ross Fisher, had only that weekend been having a tilt at the US Open, missing putt after putt but still finishing fifth. 'It's amazing,' said Griffiths, standing by the clubhouse having his photo taken by the *Surrey*

Advertiser. 'A couple of weeks ago I was playing the Wentworth par-three course with Fisher, and there he was, practically winning the US Open.'

This is what golf skill can do. Griffiths was by far the youngest player here, and a lot of rivals glanced at him and wondered how come a boy who should have been doing his GCSEs was out here beating them. If he needed inspiration, he could look at the example of the 16-year-old Italian, Matteo Manassero, who at Formby, only a couple of days before, had become the youngest player ever to win a British Amateur Championship. Manassero would be the second-youngest player (after Tom Morris Jr) to play in the Open, unless Griffiths did something here.

Griffiths was an early starter – 7.11 a.m. – but he had devoted (the usual word is 'supportive') parents, who helped him out of Virginia Water at five o'clock, so he had time to warm up on the range and test the smooth, dawn-fresh greens. It was – a point in his favour – cool and still.

After nine holes he was two under par, and word was trickling back to the clubhouse. On the back nine, however, he was not able to reproduce the birdie rush that inspired his course record ('The putts just wouldn't go in') and when he stood on the 17th tee, a downhill par-five, he was still on minus-two. He tugged it into some links-style rough (knee-high straw) on the left, blasted out and then found the right-hand bunker. He splashed out, just missed the eight-footer for par – and suddenly his score was fragile.

At the last he played an iron off the tee to avoid the bunkers down the left, and middled his approach into the approved position right of the flag. His chip from the fringe had a chance, but didn't fall, and he tapped in for a one-under round of 70. Most of the world's golf fans would be ecstatic at such a score, but for the teenaged Griffiths it was a slight disappointment. He had no way of knowing whether it would be good enough.

Neither did Sweden's Jonas Enander Hedin. He was in the group behind Griffiths, and playing nicely. He too missed a putt at the last and settled for the exact same total: 70, one under par.

These were the two best scores so far, but that wasn't saying much; only nine players had finished. And there was no way – aside from unfounded, out-of-date rumours brought by word of mouth – of knowing what was going on out on the course. They were in for a long wait.

They were in luck, however. As the sun rose, so did the breeze. By mid-afternoon it was blowing steadily, and the into-the-wind par-fives were almost out of reach. Scoring would not be so easy.

Here came a Wentworth professional – Justin Evans – with a 67 to take the lead (it might have been embarrassing to have been beaten by an amateur, and a junior, from his own club). Tom Hayes did the same; Nicholas Redfern drove himself to a 68, and Paul Jones signed for a 69. No one else was ahead. Griffiths and Hedin were safe.

One of the last to go out was a local professional, Richard Edginton. He was all business, pulling his cart and scrubbing his irons with quick care. A couple of greenkeepers watched him belt a drive down the generous first fairway, and fell in beside him to wish him luck.

'I'd have caddied for you if I'd known,' said one.

'Couldn't afford it,' said the other. 'Not with our course knowledge.'

Edginton hit the green, rolled the putt close and pocketed a tidy opening birdie. At the second hole, 300 yards over the brow of a hill, he smote it up the left and let it bound out of sight down to the green. Another eagle missed; another birdie in the bag. Two-under after two – better than not bad. He crunched down to the next, ignored the lake – 'Danger! Deep water! Keep out!' – and blazed another drive up close to the green.

He missed birdie chances there and at the short 4th, but came to the 5th – the hardest hole on the course – with a spinnaker full of wind.

The same could not be said for his playing partner. To spare his blushes, let's call him Bud. Like everyone else at Effingham that day, he had swung out of bed imagining drives hanging in blue sky over fairways, arrowing approach shots thudding down on pins, putts that flowed into cups like water, and a final score of two or three under (let's not be greedy, even in fantasy). What befell him was the nightmarish opposite. He parred the first, but his second drive found the bunker on the right of the green, and it took four humiliating swishes to splash out.

Being stuck in a bunker was a golfing cliché, which made it even more humiliating. When at last he rolled the ball in for a three-over-par seven he, his caddie and a few passers-by looked as if they had seen a ghost. He had driven 290 yards on a 298-yard hole, and taken seven. After 20 minutes he was five shots behind Edginton – it was as good as over. On the next tee, trembling with dismay, he crashed a drive into some trees, hacked out, hustled the ball over the back edge and had to accept another triple bogey. He would play like a 16-handicapper for the rest of the day.

One of golf's more lethal charms is that improvement brings pleasure, but also an enhanced dismay. Each step forward lifts expectations, adjusts goalposts, raises the bar. A smothered six-iron that creeps on to the front of a green can leave novice golfers whistling with false modesty ('Nothing special, I just kept my hands forward and *punched* it'), but the same shot will haunt better players with lacerating self-doubt. It was obvious that Bud was better than this, but that was small comfort now.

He was still lucky to be here, though. Some players fell long before this first hurdle. One or two had been deterred by the ordinary routines of life – births, marriages, death; others saw that they would not be able to travel to Scotland even if they did get through, so had withdrawn. Others, well, everyone knows that luck plays a part. Scott Margetts, manager of a west London driving range, had been looking forward to Regional Qualifying all year. He was too calm and self-deprecating to boast about winning the Claret Jug, but he did want to take part ('It's the Open, isn't it?') and wanted to put his own game to the test, to aerate his life as a coach. 'It's good to put yourself through it,' he said. 'For me as a teacher to take on the challenge, to take it seriously, to practise, to do the best I can.'

And then, a few weeks before Regional Qualifying, he gashed his hand on the ball dispenser. A fiendish break. And you could bet your life that Ian bloody Poulter never had to fix a jammed ball machine.

He could not grip a club; he had no choice but to pull out.

Even this was not as agonising as the luck that befell Edginton after his bright start. The 5th was a longish par-four, with a fairway that tilted sharply and threw everything down to a thick wood. He knew better than anyone that the ball had to be aimed left, but it got away from him and plunged over the head of the kindly ball-spotter into the dense woodland.

The spotter did everything except spot. A gaggle of spectators helped search for the ball, but it refused to be found. Finally, with a heavy heart, the rules official had no option but to speak up.

'Five minutes, gentlemen,' he said, the studious politeness of the phrase failing to conceal the absolute cruelty of the judgement.

'Here it is!' cried a voice from the undergrowth. 'Titleist four?'

'That's it!' said Edginton. But he and everyone else knew that the cry had come too late.

'I did speak out just before you called time,' said the voice.

But golf is a stern taskmaster. The ball was deemed lost: the provisional was alive. Edginton had played three.

He hit a wonderful, steepling iron at the green, watched it curl around the familiar gradients above the flag, and strode after it. If he could trickle in a five-foot putt, he would escape with a bogey. But the ball refused to drop, and his bright start had evaporated.

He took a deep breath, carried on firing the ball at pins, and on the 13th tee was back to three under par, sitting on one of the day's best rounds.

This was the highest point of the course; the view was superb. But the players did not care. The main thing was: it was downhill from here.

Edginton's knowledge of the sunlit downs was an asset, but the breeze was beginning to ripple the long grass. It grabbed his tee shot and dropped it into a greenside bunker. Once again he was luckless: buried beneath the lip. It took two shots to get out. On the long par-four 15th he played a glorious approach to five feet and even though he missed the birdie he was still one-under with three holes to go – almost there.

Then – these damned par-threes! – he tripped up again. His tee shot fell four yards left; he fluffed a chip, overcooked the recovery and had a 12-footer for bogey. When he squatted behind his ball, he put his head in hands.

What had he done?

If he had holed that tiddler on the last, he would be minus-two; now, if he missed this, he would be plus-one.

This couldn't be happening.

It was. He missed. And there were only two holes to go.

He stormed to the 17th tee, expressionless, but swishing his driver.

His tee shot screamed into the wind and flew the best part of 300 yards. There was a buggy in the fairway with a rules official in it, and Edginton paused to see how things stood. The reply was guarded. It would not have been fair on the earlier starters, who lacked such information, to give him a detailed breakdown. But he knew there was no sense holding back. He hit a pure long-iron which rolled to the back of the green. That for eagle.

The first putt was a tremendous, snaking effort: the ball came to rest no more than two inches from the hole. But instead of a euphoric, Open-qualifying shout of joy, there was just a tap-in birdie, and a curt nod.

At the last he blitzed a driver over the bunker, hit a wedge to the green and missed the putt. Apart from a couple of costly mistakes, he had played brilliantly. He was round in 71, level par.

There was quite a gathering at the leaderboard by now. Curtis Griffiths was safe, and was standing in the sunshine with his parents, shaking hands with people he had never seen before and bracing himself for the weeks ahead: there was the boys' championship in Nottingham, and then it would be straight up to Ayrshire for Final Qualifying, where he would come up against players like José Maria Olazábal and Freddie Couples.

If only his teachers could see him now.

People were counting out the scores. There were eight on 70 or better, and only three (Edginton was one of them) on 71. With only six players on the course, it looked as though the level pars would be in a play-off.

Edginton was flooded with relief. As the home man, he knew the course better than anyone: he had a good chance of making it through.

His euphoria was short-lived. Ten minutes later, the penultimate group dragged their trolleys to the scorers' tent. Unbelievably, two of them had shot 70. The level pars were out.

Thank you. Maybe next year, eh?

Winning isn't everything. Down the field at Effingham was Guy McQuitty, the 46-year-old holder of an odd Open record: at Turnberry, back in 1986, he shot rounds of 95 and 87 for a 42-over-par total that nobody had ever exceeded. But his presence at Effingham was heroic. Two years ago he had required a kidney transplant and a heart pacemaker. He tried to come back in 2008, failed, but was giving it another go. His nine-over-par 80 was off the mark, but Lazarus-like; dozens did worse.

Two of the qualifiers were amateurs, but this was no surprise: they play more than busy club professionals, who struggle to maintain the standard they had when they turned pro. Up at Pleasington, one of Britain's most famous amateurs (the record points-scorer in the Walker Cup) was finding that out. Gary Wolstenholme had won the British Amateur twice and played two Opens, but was turning pro now because, aged 48, he fancied the Seniors Tour. Back in 1977 he had caddied for his late father Guy in the Duel in the Sun Open, and he ached for a sentimental return.

It wasn't going well. He had missed out at the European Tour qualifying school, and was finding it hard to keep his game tuned up.

'I've played only seven tournaments so far this year,' he said, 'whereas as an amateur I would have played about 19 by this stage.'

He was solid enough, even so, to get through with a round of 69.

There were similar tales – some happy, some sad – all across Britain. Alongside Wolstenholme at Pleasington, a 26-year-old assistant pro from Clitheroe, Ben Scott, confessed to being 'in shock' after also shooting 69 to make it through. 'I've been playing so poorly,' he said. 'But I only played about two bad shots, compared to my normal 30.'

In Coventry, Warren Bladon, a 42-year-old British Amateur champion (over the links of Turnberry, as it happened), was the top player of the day, far ahead of Gordon Strachan's son Craig, who shot 80 and missed.

At Ferndown, in Dorset, Martin Sell admitted he 'left it a bit late' before sinking the birdie at the last that earned him a spot. At Enville, another English amateur, Jon Gidney, birdied the last two to squeeze in. Level par on the last tee, he pulled his drive into the woods, resisted the urge to try a miracle recovery, chipped out sideways, hit an approach to 15 feet and nailed the birdie that put him in the next stage.

At a windy Gog Magog, Neil Lythgoe, Norfolk's number one,

fired in five birdies to amble through on four under par, while
at Abridge (Essex), an American professional called James
Doucettperry achieved the signal honour of posting the day's
worst score: he began with a car-wrecking nine, and ended up
taking 98 strokes; it could not have comforted him to learn that
this was nearly 30 more than a 15-year-old in Effingham.

As it happened, he was not even close to equalling the remarkable record set by Maurice Flitcroft in 1976, when he shot 121 –
49-over, in the qualifier at Formby. Unlike today's high-scorers,
Flitcroft was happy. He was a novice, a shipyard crane operator
from Barrow-in-Furness who, having no handicap, was posing as
a professional. He bought a half-set of clubs by mail order, did a
bit of homework by borrowing a Peter Alliss how-to manual
from the library, and hit some balls on the beach. His round did
not go well. His first shot went about four feet, a result his generous playing partner 'put down to nerves'. What followed was
'a blizzard of triple and quadruple bogeys ruined by a solitary
par'.

It was a scatty effort, which Flitcroft attributed to the fact that
he had left his four-wood in the car by mistake. The round, he
said, 'weren't a fair reflection' of his usual style. Predictably (even
then), he was a folk hero in the newspapers, which encouraged
him to become a serial gatecrasher. Two years later he posed as
an American professional, Gene Pacecki (he lasted only a few
holes), and in 1983, with dyed hair and a fancy-dress moustache,
he was Gerald Hoppy from Switzerland (this time he played nine
holes in 63 strokes). In 1990, as James Beau Jolley, he was 'looking at a par' on the 3rd when tight-lipped officials swept him
away.

Naturally the R&A was depicted as a spoilsport, harassing a
'harmless' intruder, but of course he was not harmless. To prevent such mockeries in the future (it was unfair on genuine
contenders to have to play with dunces), a convoluted new entry
form was devised. Every modern player who frowns over the

The Open Class of 1865, including Willie Park (left), Young Tom Morris
(second from left) with his arm on the shoulder of his father, Old Tom Morris.
SMG/Press Association

St Andrews, the early days. Golf grew up in bands of sandy hummocks
along a wild seashore. Empics

Duel in the Sun, 1977. Tom Watson and caddie, Alfie Fyle, lead Jack Nicklaus along the cliff path. 'Some of the kids playing today weren't even born then.'
S&G/Barratts/Empics

The Ailsa Course from the air. The course runs roughly clockwise: hole one from the starter's hut (centre) towards the cottages at the bottom, up and down the 2nd and 3rd, to the 4th tee in the bottom left corner. Players follow the coast to the lighthouse, turn inland and zig-zag back to the clubhouse. The disused runways make a fine Open car park. Air Images Ltd

Looking for the right line. Final Qualifying, Western Gailes. Getty Images

So few get through. England's Danny Willett strides towards the play-off at International Final Qualifying, Sunningdale.
Getty Images

Is this the way to Turnberry? Mark Cayeux (centre) on his way to Ayrshire in the Open's first qualifying tournament at Durban. Getty Images

Television cameras loom over Turnberry,
watching every move. Mike Egerton/Empics Sport

The hotel suggests a bygone
age. Greg Norman in practice.
Stephen Pond/Empics Sport

'I know if I can get into position, I can
win.' Padraig Harrington in the bunker.
Mike Egerton/Empics Sport

Few sporting galas begin with such a marked lack of fuss. Paul Broadhurst hits the Open's first shot at 6.30 a.m., Thursday, 16 July.

Hard going for Tiger in the first round.

Daniel Gaunt: 'On July 17th, Daniel was the best player in the world.' Mike Egerton/Empics Sport

Chris Wood: 'The dream of a lifetime.' Rebecca Naden/Press Association Images

Matthew Goggin: 'I've worked a lot on my short game, and that's the pointy end of the stick.' Stephen Pond/Empics Sport

Ross Fisher: 'I'm trying to put it to the back of my mind.' Stephen Pond/Empics Sport

Matteo Manassero: 'Don't change anything. You'll be there some day.'
Alastair Grant/Press Association Images

Sergio Garcia: a picture of dejection. Peter Morrison/Press Association Images

John Daly, in do-not-adjust-your-set clown's trousers. Lynne Cameron/Press Association Images

Padraig Harrington: going for a historic hat-trick. Alastair Grant/Press Association Images

Round two: Westwood tees off on the 7th. Getty Images

The magic of Turnberry. Watson birdies the 18th in his second round. Pete Fontaine/Corbis

form, with its need for detailed information, letters of commendation, proofs of identity and so on, has Flitcroft to thank.

The most exacting qualifier took place at Musselburgh, an authentic Open venue, right down to the thick fog. For a while it seemed that the event might produce a trio of Scottish brothers: Lloyd Saltman had already made the next stage, thanks to his showing on the Challenge Tour. Now his brothers Elliot and Zack were shaping up to join him. After missing the cut in a EuroPro event – the intermediate or satellite tour – the previous week, Elliot Saltman took himself to Padraig Harrington's coach, Bob Torrance, for emergency repairs. Then he went back to Musselburgh and shot a three-under-par 68.

'Bob said I wasn't leaving until we got it right. I ended up hitting balls for about three and a half hours, and though the feel and rhythm aren't quite there yet, I was able to grind out a score to get me through.'

The qualifier was also a grand homecoming for Andrew Gunson, a Scottish student at the University of California, whose father Brian was tournament director at Turnberry before emigrating to America in 2001.

'The family decided to come back for a holiday,' said Gunson, before securing a 68 of his own. 'Maybe we'll stay a little longer now.'

Three strokes ahead, dizzy after six birdies and an eagle, was another transatlantic expat, James Byrne. A 20-year-old student at Arizona State (alumni: Phil Mickelson, Paul Casey), he was fresh from making the last 16 in the British Amateur Championship. At the weekend, to warm up, he had shot two course records to win the Tennant Cup. He was happy with life.

'The way I'm playing,' he said. 'I just can't wait for Final Qualifying.'

Comments like these seemed rash, because well though he played, he did not win, and the most important truth about Final Qualifying is this: so few get through. Ahead of him, after an even fizzier 63, was his room-mate from Arizona, Scott Pinckney. Clad in toothpaste-white, the 20-year-old American shot the low score of the entire Open day.

'It was my best round ever,' he grinned, enjoying the irony. 'But I wouldn't be here if I wasn't a friend of James.'

If these happy amateurs (Michael Stewart, the Scottish boys' champion, was another to produce a sparkling round) had looked over their shoulder, they might have seen the tall, glum, figure of Gordon Sherry slinking to the car park. Back in 1995 he had been the toast of the non-professional world: he won the British Amateur and performed strongly in the Open, finishing ahead of the young Tiger Woods. His game then sprung a flat tyre – he went to Q-school six times without success – and here he was, struggling for a foothold. He didn't play badly – by most standards he played well – but his final tally of 73 was one miserable shot too many.

'I just didn't get it into the hole,' he sighed, echoing the anguished cry of disappointed golfers all over the world.

It was a good example of the way golf dreams crash as well as glow. In one of those melodramas that seem to pepper days like this, Ferndown produced a proper hard-luck story. Grant Slater, from Trevose, finished his round, assumed that his score of 70 was enough, and set off on the long drive back to Cornwall. But in a finale even more abrupt than the one at Effingham, four players in the last two groups came in on the number, and a play-off was required. There were five men involved, but only four spots available: the first to lose a hole would be out. Four were ready to put themselves through the mill, but Slater was on the road; by the time he reached the Atlantic it was too late.

One of the other contenders, Martyn Thompson, was not even sure he wanted to go to Scotland. He had played two

Opens, at St Andrews and Carnoustie, but was a family man now. 'If I had loads of money I would book my ticket,' he said. 'But it's a gamble. I've got to decide if it is worth the £600 it will cost.'

He too set off for home believing his score good enough. Luckily, he heard the news and was able to about-turn and present himself on time. When word came through that Grant Slater was a no-show, the four survivors shook hands: they were through.

A few days after Regional Qualifying, on a warm, grey Sunday afternoon at the end of June, two more golfers sneaked into Turnberry.

For a while it looked as though the BMW International in Munich was a German feelgood exercise; Bernhard Langer, watched by his mother, was making light of his 52 years to challenge for the title on a course just 45 minutes from home. But England's Nick Dougherty did what many had expected him to do since his days as a Faldo-sponsored junior, and played a blinding final round. After three early birdies he derailed himself on the 6th, when he dumped his second in a lake, but he rallied and (using a new putter he had picked up the week before) went on another birdie rampage. He was playing with Retief Goosen, who cut a sad figure as Dougherty's putts dinked into the cup, while his own did not.

'He's not doing anything wrong,' whispered Wayne Riley on TV. 'He's just getting smacked around the chops by Dougherty's putter.'

On the 15th green Dougherty was eight-under for the day, with a four-stroke lead, but before he could extend his advantage a big roar gushed from the stands and beer chalets at the 18th. Inspired by his effort at Sunningdale, Rafa Echenique had already had a fine day (one eagle, four birdies) and was in the serious prize money. The roar meant he had just smeared icing all over the cake by holing his second shot, a searing three-iron from 243 yards, for an amazing albatross. In as much time as it takes for sound to carry across three fairways, Dougherty had just had his lead cut to one.

It was a credit to his nerve that he parred the last three holes. And in claiming the title he put himself into an elite group of two (with Johan Edfors) who would qualify for Turnberry from the midsummer table. He was 16th in the European money list, and Edfors was 19th. It would have been odd to bar in-form stars like these from the Open.

It might have been dangerous to attribute Echenique's fine performance to post-Sunningdale glee, because Willett, after that bruising near miss in Berkshire, also stormed home in Germany to finish ninth. Golf has nothing in common with boxing, but it does require its combatants to take their hits and come back the next day. It tests the ability to recover from bad shots, bad luck, bad rounds, bad moods. As Bob Hope once said, it is a strange feature of the game that one afternoon you can top drives, miss greens, shank chips and yip putts, and the next day, without warning, your game just stinks.

The reverse is also true. Since the death of his mother, Dougherty's form had dipped. He was ranked 120 in the world. But now, as muggy evening fell over Munich, and insects whined up from the lake, he was back.

As for Edfors . . . after the horrors of Sunningdale he flew to New York for the US Open and battled valiantly through the rain to finish joint 27th. Now he had another major to look forward to.

That's golf: a game of ifs and buts – Kipling would have a poetic heart murmur. A few weeks earlier, Dougherty and Edfors had failed to qualify for Turnberry. Suddenly, they were a pair of snappy contenders. Football, it seemed, wasn't the only funny old game in town.

CHAPTER SEVEN

Final Qualifying

Some way below the peak of Mount Everest lies a rocky pillar known as the Hillary notch, after the great climber (Sir Edmund) who identified it as the route to the top. It is wild yet congested, both the way up and the way down, and frozen climbers have to stand in line, hearts thudding, like commuters letting passengers off a bus. In recent years the number of people at this tense junction has grown, and so, in turn, has the queue.

This is what Final Qualifying feels like to the golfers swarming at the foot of the Open proper. It is sometimes described as the last 'stage' of the entry process, but this makes it sound too straightforward, as if it were little more than a way station, a processing point where competitors must pause to have their tickets stamped. In truth it is a vicious bottleneck – a two-day, 72-hole mincer that will grind up almost the entire field.

A handful of well-known stars were welcomed with open arms: players such as the double Masters champion José Maria Olazábal, the 1999 runner-up Jean Van de Velde, the one-time European number one Ronan Rafferty, and American Ryder-Cuppers Fred Couples and Brad Faxon. The rest earned their places the hard way, by bashing their way through Regional Qualifying. From here on, however, the arithmetic was as bleak as the wind-whipped sea grass. Ten years earlier, 49 golfers had been rejected at this stage, but thanks to the new International Qualifying events the places up for grabs had been squeezed. There would be 288 golfers doing battle on the three chosen courses; only a dozen would line up against Woods and Harrington in a week's time. The majority, no matter how well they played, would have to swallow their pride, turn near-misses into amusing hard-luck stories, lick their wounds and trickle home.

The three host clubs were neighbours on the strip of links coast to the north of Troon. Glasgow Gailes dated back to 1787, though it owed its present form to Willie Park's design in 1892; Western Gailes, the other side of the railway line, was five years younger. Kilmarnock Barassie (1887) was the odd one out in that it was not quite so exposed. Tall stands of dark pine made some of the holes feel almost sheltered.

It is a strange and moving coastline partly because it is so beautiful, and partly because it is so ugly. The superb green fairways, the heart-stopping curve of smooth sand that embraces the slate-cold sea, and the low, wooded hills that rise above the misty shore are counterpointed by rain-spattered housing that looks like the work of a disillusioned (or vengeful) prison architect. It makes Coronation Street look like Wentworth, and that is another part of its charm. There is nothing bijou about these residences. The giant paper mill at Irvine towers above the pylons and satellite dishes, and the roar of aircraft lumbering to Prestwick competes with the clank and rattle of rusty goods trains on the Strathclyde line.

Golf often seems like the game of the managerial class, but its roots lie here in this half-dead coastal landscape criss-crossed by iron and steel. It is a child of the railway era – a golf course without a train is like chips without salt. It was railways that brought these wind-streaked links to smog-bound urban types happy to pay for a breath of fresh air.

Golf in Scotland followed the tracks down this wild Ayrshire coast and across to the even bleaker dunes of Fife. Its treasured spots were shaped by the railway hotels at Troon and Prestwick, St Andrews and Carnoustie. The same thing happened in Lancashire, where trains from Manchester and Liverpool ferried golfers to Lytham and Hoylake. And in the Home Counties. When Woking was founded in 1893 (by 'a few mad barristers'), it gave south-east England a new idea: theme-park Scotland. New courses sprang up: New Zealand (1895), Sunningdale (1901), Walton Heath (1904), West Hill (1909) and St George's Hill (1913). All were studious reproductions of misty-glen Scottish bliss: deep bunkers brought a heady coastal flavour to trim rhododendron suburbs.

The Claret Jug, or one of the replicas, was on display at Western Gailes, right next to the practice putting green. In 1927, when Bobby Jones took the jug to America, an alarmed committee voted to commission a copy, just in case, so when Walter Hagen won the following year he was not given the real thing. The original became a museum piece, and soon other versions were added, making six in all – enough for quite a dinner party.

The coffee was put on to warm as soon as the sky grew pale. But when the time came, the eastern sky never brightened: it just went grey and damp. Rain dripped on the moist scenery, on the fields and hedgerows, the horses and sheep; it gushed from soaked trees and rooves, splashed in brown roadside puddles, formed pools in bunkers and wormed its way down necks and up sleeves. Wet flags hung limp from poles, crows and starlings sat hunched on wires, car wheels skidded in soft mud.

On the practice tee – in normal life a picturesque par-four – there was a bucket of water for wiping clubs and balls, next to a grim sign: 'Practice balls are the property of the R&A. Theft will lead to prosecution.'

Was this the five-star world of top golf? Was it for this that José Maria Olazábal had hired a private jet (costing £6000) to ferry him from Paris, just so he could submit to probable humiliation the next day?

'The Open represents the game's tradition,' he said, and one of its traditions was that it was not willing to pay for such praise. Olazábal was the star attraction, especially when many of the notable Americans pulled out, but that didn't mean that he could expect special favours.

Olazábal forked out for the jet because he was playing in the French Open, outside Paris, on the day before Final Qualifying. He was kind enough to offer a couple of fellow players, Barry Lane and Jean Van de Velde, a lift to Scotland, and while Lane was delighted, Van de Velde was already racing for his Ryanair flight to Prestwick, and had to decline.

The private jet made good time to Prestwick Airport, so Olazábal and Lane arrived at Kilmarnock Barassie in time to acquaint themselves with the course. Most of the field had been there all day, playing and putting, getting to know their caddies, figuring where to place their drives, finding the dips and hollows that needed to be avoided. But Olazábal and Lane, despite a willingness to risk their own hard-won seniority against ambitious teenagers, were informed primly that they were too late.

It is the presence of international players such as these that ensures newspaper inches and gilds the idea of the Open as a genuine sporting meritocracy. But rules were rules. Sorry, gentlemen: the course is closed.

It was tough love, to say the least. But it is worth remembering, at times like these, that if the R&A can be as stiff as an old thistle, it is also true that the voices clamouring to relieve it of its prestigious responsibility are often merely angling for a piece of the action themselves. The R&A is often dismissed as anachronistic or 'amateur' – the word 'bumbling' is rarely far away – but

amateurs, at least, do it for love rather than money. Commercial
management could hardly mobilise the necessary army of kindly
volunteers, and even the R&A's fustiest manner may be preferable to the corporate smarm that would otherwise (for the 'good
of the game', of course) better exploit the rich possibilities of the
Open as a brand.

Before playing in this qualifier, Curtis Griffiths, the young
Effingham qualifier, had to consider the small matter of the
McGregor Trophy: England's Under-16 Amateur Championship
was being held at Radcliffe-on-Trent, near Nottingham. He
played tidily in the first round, brilliantly in the second, and at the
halfway point was in third place, a stroke behind the joint leaders. He could not accelerate, and finished tenth, four short of the
five-man play-off, but this was fine form. His parents booked a
hotel room in Irvine and aimed their car at the nine-hour drive
to Scotland. They had 'asked around' about caddies, and secured
a tall, relaxed, helpful youngster who was a one-handicap golfer
himself on these very greens.

On the Monday morning Griffiths hit a few chips, then parked
his bag at one end of the range and began to warm up. It was
hard not to gulp when he looked along the row of flashing steel
shafts. He was due to play in the group ahead of José Maria
Olazábal, Markus Brier and Barry Lane, and there, for goodness
sake, was Olazábal, stock-still over his irons, zinging them away
like javelins before sighing at some invisible imperfection.

Brier, slim as a jockey, and Lane, supertanned after a long and
sunny golf career, were chatting about Paris. 'I actually played all
right,' Lane was saying – a curious description of a round that saw
him leak seven shots on the last four holes. He too had obtained
the services of a local caddie, in his case a 13-year-old boy. Lane
was a fine player, but this youngster, aside from lugging a very
heavy bag, would have to learn where the cigarettes were stowed,
and keep a lighter handy.

While Olazábal was talking to Spanish television, Curtis Griffiths was waiting on the tee. In truth, he might not have been so in awe of Olazábal as the spectators. The man was old enough to be his father, after all.

So far only one good score had been posted: a two-under 69 by a Scottish amateur from Carnoustie in the first group of the day. The rainy start was bad luck on the early players: soft greens did not quite make up for wet grips. It was possible that this 69 was worth more than a 66 in sunshine, but golf's supple handicap system does not extend to the weather. This is why records are sketchy indicators of quality; par in a gale is far better than the same score on a calm evening (some courses – the Berkshire, for example – decline to keep records for precisely this reason). It was certain that a new record would be posted today at Barassie, however, because the course had been altered to embrace a run of new holes. As the rain eased, it looked as though low scoring was, as they say, on the cards.

The railway line ran up the right-hand side, and the players watched as a long, slow freight train ground past. When his turn came, Griffiths drove into the gentle rough on the right, steered himself safely up the left, guided a wedge in close to the pin, and holed for an opening birdie.

Who said links golf was tough?

Retribution was swift. By the time his threesome made it to the second tee, the gallery following the more famous group behind was swarming around the back of the first green, feet crunching on the white-shell path.

Griffiths was wearing a red sweater over regulation golf gear that made him look older than his tender years, but he had the slim arms of a youth, and wasn't used to a crowd of this size and volume. His tee shot at the 2nd found one of the bunkers on the right. A wide ditch crossed the fairway up ahead – no sense flirting with that – so he took his medicine, splashed out sideways and . . . what the hell? His ball flopped and died. 'There was just so much sand,' he said. 'My club disappeared.' He faced the same shot again, and heaved the ball out, but his wedge to the green was short, his chip left him a slippery one for bogey, and he missed.

That is how easy it is to leak strokes. When you are middling the ball, even tough courses feel easy. But on championship set-ups the penalty for errors, however minor, is severe. On the 3rd, Griffiths was last to play, and by the time he stood over his ball the Olazábal–Brier–Lane gallery was on the move. It wasn't an easy drive at the best of times, with a low out-of-bounds wall on the right, and something told him that these people – some pausing to let him hit, others crunching along without a care – had an unsettling thought on the tip of their tongues: Who on earth is that?

Self-consciousness is a swing-wrecker, but it isn't easy to keep calm, so it was no surprise when Griffiths shoved his ball high to the right and watched aghast as the breeze threw it over the wall and out of bounds.

A few of the spectators turned, curious, to watch him have another go.

'Anyone know who that is?'

'Young fellow from Wentworth, I believe. Useful, apparently.'

'Poor chap.'

Griffiths's mother and father were striding out ahead beneath umbrellas, as volunteer ball-spotters, but there was nothing anyone could do to help.

Second time around, he found the centre of the fairway. But there was no remedy for that lost ball. Five minutes later he had a triple bogey to his name, and after three holes, and a birdie at the first, was three over par.

This was not how he had imagined Final Qualifying, not at all.

And he did not know it, but he was already six strokes behind Markus Brier, who had nailed three birdies in a row. It was hard to see how the man could fail to win one of the Open qualifying spots: he was lancing it up the middle, tossing it at the flag, and draining putts – what could possibly go wrong?

It is a feature of golf that the same quirky terrain can offer, given only a marginal variation here or there, dramatically different outcomes. For Brier this was a pleasant ramble on smooth lawns spread between wheat-coloured fringes, yellow swirls of dandelion, mauve harebells and spongy heather; for Griffiths it was a military gauntlet, an intimidating wilderness of hag-bent gorse, harsh stone boundaries and deep, frightening sandpits.

It would have been easy to surrender, or press too hard, but he did the opposite. He teased home two birdies to put a smile back on his face, and by the sixth was back on track.

'The good news is that Curtis has had three birdies,' said his father. 'The bad news is, he's one over par.'

At the par-five 8th he retrieved another stroke by getting up and down from a greenside bunker and at last was back where he began. If only he had not found that bunker at the 2nd, or cleared that wall at the 3rd – he should be three- or four-under by now, and right up there with the leaders.

But anyone can play if-only. He might just as easily have thinned the sand shot into the thicket over the green, lost it, taken another triple bogey, and be wondering what music to listen to on the M6.

Most of the games had a tiny handful of people watching; only the group behind Griffiths had a tournament-sized gallery. The course was not roped, so spectators were free to wander the fairways behind the players. Sometimes they ambled ahead, forcing them to squeeze through.

It seemed to suit Brier; he would just smile, pick a club, brace those skier's knees, smack the ball at the target, smile again and march on.

At the 10th, where most of the players were laying up, Barry Lane's 13-year-old caddie whispered that if he snapped a driver over the corner he would be as good as on the green. Lane took the hint, crushed it over the dog-leg, chipped close and snared a birdie. Brier followed suit, and then, at the short 11th (398 yards), repeated the trick and nabbed another one.

Up ahead, Griffiths had found the green on the par-three 14th and stood over a makeable downhill putt. His mother turned her back and looked away at the black bushes and grim rooftops opposite: few sports are so taxing on a parent's nerves. But she knew from the clatter of applause that he had found the hole and put himself back below par. And you did not have to be his mum to be impressed by the way he had recovered from the blows he took on the first few holes. On the 4th tee he was four over par; it had been a sterling effort to pick up five strokes from there. There were nearly 300 excellent players in this part of Scotland, all trying to clamber their way to the game's top rung. Griffiths had youth on his side, but, even more important, he seemed to be made of the right stuff too.

It is not easy – in fact it is not quite possible – to follow Final Qualifying as a whole. Spectators can follow a single group, and enjoy watching expert players play their way round 18 holes; but the big picture is not visible until the end. Each of the three courses had a small leaderboard near the clubhouse, and this was where players who had finished hung about with their caddies and friends, but information was patchy, and it was never possible to know what was unfolding out on the course itself.

By the practice green at Kilmarnock Barassie, heads turned when the scorers reached for the box of names and numbers. Manuel Quiros, from Spain, had set a bold new target with a six-under-par round of 67, and now one of the Scottish hopes, Gavin Dear, inspired a rumble of appreciative applause when he signed for the same score. All three of the par-fives were reachable, and Dear had taken full advantage by securing two eagles. On the sweeping 8th he was two over par, after a jittery start, but his second shot, a four-iron, curled in to 15 feet and he holed it to ignite a burst of better scoring. Three birdies later, he did the same again at the 491-yard 16th (this time with a nine-iron) and leaped into forceful contention.

Half an hour after that another Scot, Lloyd Saltman, went one better: 66. Saltman had some good Open form to his name. At St Andrews in 2005 he came 15th and won the silver medal for the best-performing amateur, and though he had not been able to 'kick on', as they say, he looked a winner-in-waiting. This was his best round of the year (eight birdies) and it came at a good time. Late in the day he was boosted by the arrival of his older brother Elliot, who had helped himself to a four-under-par round of 67 at Glasgow Gailes to seize the first-round lead.

Two Scots in the van: was the Open coming home?

Lloyd Saltman was by no means the only one to find it hard to convert a brilliant amateur career into professional success. The Australian Daniel Gaunt was in a similar boat. In his Victorian youth he considered professional tennis, but chose golf when it became clear that he would not reach six foot five. In 2004 he qualified in style for the European Tour, but since then had been groping for both form and finance. He was a family man now, with a mortgage, a wife and two small children, and could no longer afford to be merely promising. He was working two days a week at a golf discount store in Esher, Surrey, to scrape together entry fees to professional events, but he was not earning enough to live this way for long. He was ranked 1212 in the world.

He too had a brother attempting to qualify at Glasgow Gailes – Chris Gaunt had flown over from Australia and would be teeing off an hour after him. If nothing else this was a stirring family trip, which inspired echoes of their Melbourne boyhood. 'It's one of the tournaments I won't miss,' said Daniel, 'whether I'm playing golf or working. I don't know why, but I actually prefer it to Sunningdale, even though that's only down the road from me. I think it's just the buzz of being up here in Scotland. It feels like part of the Open.' This year, however, the pressure was on. He was not in the best form ('angry with my game') and was having to face the prospect of quitting. 'I'm giving myself three weeks to earn enough money to keep going,' he said. His employer had offered him a full-time post which, barring a successful end to the summer, he planned to take.

There was no clearer evidence that, in golf, the winner takes it all.

He was supposed to be playing in the group behind Lloyd Saltman alongside the Welsh Ryder Cup hero Philip Price ('The R&A usually look after me – last year I played with Scott Dunlap'). In the event, Price withdrew, but Gaunt rose to the occasion by firing a four-under-par 69. His name looked nice on the leaderboard, up in joint third place, but ten minutes later he had been knocked back a place by Markus Brier, whose stunning 64 (an imposing new course record) was now the score to beat.

It had not been the best day of Olazábal's life, but he battled his way to a three-under-par 70, not out of things, by any means. Curtis Griffiths, meanwhile, finished two shots further back on 72, level with Barry Lane and the hot American amateur Scott Pinckney. Though he was well in the top half of a strong field – only Brier was out of sight – he wasn't sure how to feel about it. 'I'm pleased about the way I came back,' he said. 'But I'm sad too; if I'd just played my normal game I could have been up there.'

At Glasgow Gailes the better-known players – Emanuele Canonica, Scott Dunlap, Ronan Rafferty, Patrick Sjöland and Jean Van de Velde – were struggling to keep up with impressive youngsters like the South African Thomas Aiken, who struck the ball neatly through the drizzle to join Chris Gaunt, and the group behind Elliot Saltman, on 69. It seemed that Van de Velde – an Open hero for the last-ditch antics that cost him victory at Carnoustie in 1999 (when he threw away a three-shot lead on the final hole) – had not recovered from his late-night flight. Like Griffiths, he dropped four shots on the first four holes, but he could not find a way back, and finished five over par, his Open as good as over.

Some 25 players were bunched behind Saltman, so nothing was settled; the Turnberry invites would go to those who shot low the next day.

At Western Gailes, where the wind was whipping the flags, the Scottish amateur James Byrne was following up his dizzy form in Regional Qualifying by flashing round in 68. Spain's Carlos Balmaceda was a shot behind, and there were ten more players on the shoulder of the leaders. One of these was Martyn Thompson, who had come through Regional Qualifying in Dorset without knowing whether he could afford this northern golf break. He shot 70, and was two off the lead.

The Saltman brothers celebrated their joint success by driving down to Turnberry (a touch prematurely, some said) for a look at the course – but also to inspire themselves. Lloyd Saltman soon ran into an old comrade from his amateur days, Rory McIlroy, who had nipped by helicopter from Northern Ireland to sneak in a practice round with Graeme McDowell.

'I said to Lloyd that I hoped to get in a practice round with him too,' said McIlroy, ignoring the huge disparity in their golfing stature that had opened up in the last two years. 'I actually took inspiration from him in 2005. And it wasn't winning the silver medal at St Andrews – it was finishing 15th. That was some achievement. He is a very, very good player, and I'm sure his game is suited to links courses.'

If that didn't make Saltman feel better about his task next day, what would?

As the McIlroy–McDowell chopper whirled over the Irish Sea, a dashing emblem of top-level golf, Curtis Griffiths was taken to Pizza Hut by his parents for what Curtis's father called some 'high-fibre nutrition'. The road to Turnberry really is twisting, with many alternative routes.

On the second morning it was not raining, but it looked as if it might start at any moment. On the driving range Markus Brier was picking wedges off the turf and landing them by the 50-yard marker post with a bored glance, as if this were far too easy. Olazábal, meanwhile, was glowering over his tee shots, as he had been for a couple of decades, it seemed. He teed the ball low, cracked it away, shook his head, and bent down for another ball.

Curtis Griffiths made a solid start, parring the first four. But then he let shots go at the 5th and 8th, where his par putts shaved the hole. At the 10th he tried to play safe and suffered, if anything, from too much course management, laying up short of the dog-leg but missing the green to the left. Up ahead, Lloyd Saltman had carried this green with his driver, and then done the same at the 11th, knowing that attack, sometimes, was the best form of defence. Griffiths was playing better than he was scoring, but who cared? It was the score that would be handed in, not the swing.

When he prepared to drive from the 12th tee, a yelp erupted behind him. About 50 yards away, on the 8th fairway, a blond golfer in grey trousers and a white shirt had his arms in the air. He had just holed his second shot (a six-iron) on the par-five for an improbable and rare albatross. At most tournaments players are accompanied by volunteers with boards showing up-to-date scores, but here it was unclear to which group that lucky golfer belonged. Counting backwards, it looked like someone three groups behind Griffiths – most likely Kevin Na, the American – and since no one in that three-ball was among the leaders, that albatross might count for nothing.

Up ahead, Lloyd Saltman was holding his game together to shoot minus-three, giving him a two-day total of 136, ten-under, the first challenging number. But such was the intensity of the contest that his position was far from secure. The word from the course suggested that Markus Brier was going well again. Yet Saltman had been looking good ever since that birdie at the first. As an early finisher, it was his turn to hop round to Glasgow Gailes, to see if his brother could complete the story.

One group behind, Daniel Gaunt was also driving the ball well, leaving easy irons into generous greens, and enjoying himself. He hadn't played like this in quite a while (not since winning a EuroPro Tour event the previous autumn), but his racy 67 put him alongside Saltman at the top of the list. He was beginning to regret those bad-tempered remarks about his own game, but facts were facts. 'I don't want to quit,' he said. 'But I have a wife and two kids to support.' Qualifying for the Open would be one of the highlights of his golfing career, but he wanted it to be the start of something, not the end. Above all, he hoped that his brother Chris would qualify too. 'It's like my brother says, we've been doing this for years and years,' he said. 'It's just a question of turning it up on the big stage.'

As expected, Markus Brier soon seized the day. He followed his course record with a barely less impressive 66, and had a cool six-shot lead. He had, he declared ominously, a special fondness for Turnberry, a course he had played with a clutch of fellow Austrians many years earlier.

Brier had an Alpine temperament too: golf was not a sunny game. 'Links golf is in my body,' he said. 'I've loved it from when I was a teenager.'

Quite a few onlookers began to wonder about his chances in the main event. He had not played at Birkdale but at Carnoustie, in 2007, he had come 12th. What was that saying about horses and courses?

'The Open is the biggest tournament we have, and I love it,' he said. 'Do I have a chance? If I play like the past two days, of course.'

Twenty minutes later, a third player joined Saltman and Gaunt on 136: a young Dane, Peter Ellebye. In one sense he was lucky to be here at all. In the regional qualifier at Royal County Down he had fallen one short of passing through, but had been called up as a late reserve. He was such a last-gasp entry that he was not even listed in the order of play, and it had taken an emergency dash from Denmark to get to the first tee. But he was playing well, and produced a second 68 to catapult him into the group in second place. He could solve another mystery too: that albatross at the 8th had been his. Nothing much had happened in the first hour, but by snatching three strokes on one hole he found himself in good shape. 'Trouble is, I bogeyed the very next hole,' Ellebye said. But he did manage to find two more birdies on the back nine to give himself a good chance of earning a place in the Open. He might have to race back to Denmark to cancel his life for a week.

There were still 60 players on the links, and since it was almost certain that someone would have a day to remember, those three players on 136 would probably be involved in a play-off. There was nothing for it but to have lunch in the clubhouse and wait to see what developed.

Their fate, it turned out, ended up resting in the hands of Ricky Lee, a 23-year-old professional from Tyneside. After a stunning chip-in at the 16th (for an eagle three), he came to the 18th knowing that a birdie would force a play-off, and he was feeling pretty good. His ten-footer for birdie at 17 had shaved the hole and not fallen, but it was still all to play for. He didn't mind hearing that one of the trio on minus-ten was Lloyd Saltman, because it was Saltman who had pushed Lee out of the Open two years before, at Final Qualifying for Carnoustie. 'I was looking at being in the play-off,' he said, 'and in came Saltman in the last group to knock me out.' Revenge wouldn't exactly be sweet, but it wouldn't be sour either, and the 18th was a short par-four: a drive and a wedge would get him there.

But the green was a heartbreaker – a fluent expanse of delicate inclines; a single putt could break three or four ways. And the pin was on a sharp slope that fed balls to the back of the green. There'd been a barrage of three-putts in two days, and only a handful of birdies.

Lee's drive found the wispy rough on the outside of the curving fairway, but the grass, though long, was no longer wet. He punched his ball forward on to the green and marched after it, breathing deeply. He had a putt of 20 feet to qualify for the Open – a shot he had holed often enough in dreams. But this was real, and as he neared his ball the putt began to grow in length: it was 25 feet – maybe even 30 – and it was anything but easy.

Don't leave it short, he told himself. He stalked the borrows, tried to stay in his usual routine, and set the ball rolling. It ran close, then closer . . . and drifted by. And that was the end of that.

If you are going to miss by one you might as well miss by two. Deflated, Lee missed the return as well.

Lloyd Saltman's brother Elliot was involved in an exciting finish of his own. Thomas Aiken had blazed the trail with an excellent 67 to give him a total of 136, and Peter Baker looked safe in second, two shots back. As things stood there was one player alone in third place, the young Irishman David Higgins, so there was room at the top. But Elliot Saltman had been leaking shots all day, and on the 16th, under a sudden blue sky, he was one over par – level with Higgins and one ahead of four players on 140. If he gained a shot he would go joint second; if he dropped one he would be part of a five-man group playing off for the final slot. But on the 16th green he drained a 30-foot putt for birdie that took him to level par, and had a breathing space: he could afford to drop a shot and still qualify. At the uphill 17th he dragged his drive left into the rough and could only chop his ball up to the bottom right edge of the green. The route to the hole led up and over a steep bulge. Saltman tried to chip the ball up to the top, but failed to make it. He now faced a treacherous up-and-down putt, and left himself a nasty one for bogey. That went in.

This was what it came down to. Par at the last.

Once again he tugged his drive into the left-hand rough, but it was not far to the green from here, and he forced it high to the back fringe. Two putts for Turnberry. He coaxed his lag to the side of the hole, and at last the Saltman family could pop the champagne. They were the first pair of brothers to qualify for the

Open since Seve and Manuel Ballesteros, or was that Jumbo and Joe Ozaki?

'Wow,' said Lloyd. 'It's just fantastic that both of us are going.'

What golf gives with one hand, though, it takes with the other, and Elliot's finish drove a nail through the hopes of another pair of brothers. Daniel Gaunt was in a good position behind Markus Brier, but his brother Chris Gaunt was one of the four at Glasgow Gailes pushed out by Elliot Saltman. A regular on the Australasian tour, he once sold a construction business to finance his golf aspirations, and now had flown across the world for these two days of wet-weather golf. He played very well, but was one putt short of joining his brother at Turnberry. On the long flight home, he would be able to imagine just one more putt falling.

Daniel Gaunt, like Lloyd Saltman, had dashed across to the neighbouring course to see how his brother was faring – unlike the Saltmans, the Gaunts were far from home, and did not enjoy much support. 'I could see it was going to be close,' he said. 'But I had to go back to Barassie and get stressed about every score that went on the board. It's a tough day, because you don't know what is going on, and there were a few late groups that had a chance to do well. I hit some balls in case there was a play-off, but I was praying there wouldn't be, because to be so close and then fail would have been tough. When I realised I was in I didn't move. I just froze.'

He made it; his brother did not, and several others shared the pain of the near-miss. The moment Brier's score went up, Gavin Dear, Gordon Brand and Kenneth Ferrie had to face the fact that they were out. It was especially cruel in Ferrie's case because he seemed, when he won the European Open back in 2005, to have claimed a seat at the top of the game. His ranking had slipped, however, so he could not skip this exam. After a so-so first sally of 71 (two under par), he knew he needed a spectacular second round, and by most standards he got one, opening with a birdie, picking up two more at the 8th and 10th, and nailing his approach on the par-five 12th to just six feet for an easy eagle.

Two further birdies at the 14th and 16th got his pulse racing, but even a birdie at the last would not have been enough. Ferrie, like Lee, three-putted that deceptive final green, and he made no effort to hide his feelings about the 'horrific' pin placement. 'My putt had four different breaks in 25 feet,' he said. 'It's ridiculous. Open qualifying should be about the best players over the two days, and not because of flags like that. It's just a farce.'

It would not have been polite to point out that the 18th was only 380 yards long – chicken feed for a player like Ferrie. That dimpled green was the hole's one defence; it was greedy to resent it. But Ferrie's chagrin was understandable: what a week! On Sunday, in Paris, he had finished with a blistering 67 to sweep into joint sixth and scoop £100,000 (enough to cheer a fellow up, one might think). And of course he was thrilled, after a fallow period, to have found form at last. But he was vexed to discover that even this impressive effort left him one shot shy of a berth in the Open. Just one more birdie – and he could think of several that burned the lip – and he could have skipped this qualifying swamp, but here he was. In few other sports is a miss so clearly as good as a mile.

Ferrie had flown home from Paris to Newcastle, downed a cup of tea, and driven across the Borders to Ayr. Now, after two days of pressing, he had missed by the same wafer-thin margin. Nor could he take a breather. When he eased out of the small car park at Barassie, he headed for Loch Lomond and the Scottish Open. He had only one day to practise, but he could still make it to Turnberry if he finished in the top five.

What he really needed, though, was bug repellent. The mosquitoes bit like bastards around that damn lake. It looked gorgeous on television, or from a car, but out on the golf course it was, quite literally, a fleapit.

When all the dust, and the rain, settled, the winners couldn't stop smiling. There was no great media presence at any of the three courses, but a few reporters hung on to record the success stories.

Steve Surry, a Wiltshire professional playing on the EuroPro Tour, had played well (though not well enough) on the first day – there were 23 players ahead of him. But he practised in the afternoon, and something clicked. His second-round 66 was a course record, and included nine birdies. He too had to endure a long wait before qualification was guaranteed, but he was two shots clear of Didsbury pro Daniel Wardrop, so had some cushion, at least.

David Higgins was another. He had been there, done that, and tripped up. He grew up on links golf at Waterville in south-west Ireland (one of Tiger Woods's favourite Open testing grounds), but had lost his tour card two years earlier. On the par-four 9th he drove close and chipped in for an eagle, but shot himself in the foot with a double bogey at the 12th, for the second day in a row. His response was to birdie the 13th and 14th and par his way in, no mean feat in that fierce grey wind. Two hours later, Scott Dunlap of the US came in one shot behind, and Higgins was through.

'I'm delighted,' he said. 'It couldn't have come at a better time.'

Peter Baker had enjoyed plenty of high points in a long career, but even by his own standards the last few days were memorable. On Sunday he won a second-tier tournament, the Credit Suisse Challenge, and dashed to Scotland to try his luck on a course he had never played before. Now he had qualified for Turnberry. He was one of the few who had played an Open there (in 1994). 'I can't remember the course that well,' he said. 'But for me it is the best event in the world, and I just want to enjoy it.'

It had been hard. After winning in Switzerland he flew from Basle to Heathrow, transferred to Glasgow and arrived at his hotel just before midnight. The R&A kindly gave him a 10.46 a.m. tee-time, and he made the most of it. He had no explanation for his sudden form. If it were easily explained, it would be easily retained. 'Things went my way,' he said.

Western Gailes was the toughest of the three venues. The sea breeze rippled across the exposed dunes, and there was not a dram of shelter. Sweden's Fredrik Andersson Hed didn't seem to mind, and followed his first-round 70 with a 67 to leave him a stroke clear of Steve Surry. 'Getting into any major is special,' he said. 'But the Open is the one.' On his website he was encouraging fans to buy a pixel for 50 pence each to sponsor his golf dream, and now, at 138 strokes, a little piece of it had come true.

Beneath the leaderboard by the practice green, Daniel Wardrop's father was pacing in a lather of nervous anxiety. His son had been to Florida to see his coach, who now worked at the David Leadbetter school, and had also seen the guru himself. The result? One of the rounds of his life – a 68 – to join Thomas Haylock in joint third place. He was sitting in the bar keeping warm while his father walked in circles outside.

'I think this is the worst I've ever felt,' he said.

Neither knew what was happening on the course, and no one would say.

'It wouldn't be fair to pass on the scores,' said the R&A rules official, up on a dune, scanning the links with his binoculars. 'It would be too big an advantage for the late players if they knew what they needed to do.'

Group after group came to the final green, shook hands, sighed, climbed the steps to the recorder's hut, and trudged away towards the car park. As the skies brightened and dirty gulls began to wheel and screech over the emptying links, some very good players were coming and going: Zane Scotland, the youngest qualifier at an Open when he made it, aged 16, to Carnoustie in 1999; James Byrne, Scottish boys' champion; Hennie Otto, winner of the Italian Open in 2008; Wade Ormsby, joint second in the New Zealand Open of 2007; David

Carter, a World Cup winner; James Heath, England Amateur champion. Players like this take a bit of beating. But the leaderboard never moved. Haylock and Wardrop were both in.

In a way it is artificial to concentrate on winners, because there are many more losers: defeat is the usual experience. There were 12 qualifiers, but a dozen more missed by a single stroke. James Byrne, the halfway leader at Western Gailes, stepped on a rake (figuratively) at the 4th hole and suffered a triple-bogey seven. He rallied bravely with birdies at 9 and 14, but a dropped shot at 16 stopped him dead. At the 17th he went for broke, as he had to, and landed his three-iron approach 25 feet from the pin. But his first putt was too strong, his second too weak, and Byrne would have to wait another year.

'After that bogey at 16, I thought I would need to birdie the last two to have a chance,' he said. 'I had a go at 17 but it was a disappointing end.'

Nor could Martyn Thompson repeat his fine form of the first day. He shot 75 to finish five behind Wardrop at Glasgow Gailes.

All of the also-rans were in good company, because Olazábal fell short too. After his three-under-par 70 in the first round, some old-style sharp-shooting could have put him back in the frame, even if he had little chance of overhauling Brier. His start was poor, however. He banged his first drive at the railway line – it looked as though the 8.53 to Prestwick was going to be delayed by wet balata on the line – and battered his second attempt in the same haphazard direction. He sulked off into the right-hand rough, shaking his head.

In the event he found his first ball, dropped it out, thrashed it to the edge of the green and two-putted for a fortunate bogey. But no sooner had he sighed with relief than he did the same thing at the third hole, pushing his drive over that low stone wall on the right. This time he would not escape so easily. He made a triple-bogey seven, which left him four over on the 4th tee, on a day when he needed to shoot half a dozen under to have a chance.

'It was doom and gloom after that,' he said.

There are many ways to lose in golf, however, and Olazábal had at least won the admiration and respect of those he met and entertained. And Curtis Griffiths, 28 years his junior, won something even more tangible: experience. When he climbed into the car with his mum and dad for the draining drive back to Surrey, he knew he could hold his own at this level of golf: not a bad discovery for a schoolboy. There was work to be done, but a bright future was on the cards, if not in the stars.

It was a long way to Virginia Water, though, and he would not arrive till dawn. He would have to sleep in the car.

'I've got a lesson tomorrow at two,' he said.

The winners meant business: they knew that a decade earlier someone just like them, Paul Lawrie, had come out of Final Qualifying and won the Claret Jug at Carnoustie. But they faced an immediate problem: where to stay. The R&A is not a travel agent, and offers surprisingly little help to these eleventh-hour qualifiers who are left to forage for beds in what is suddenly, and temporarily, one of the priciest places in the world. Hotel prices were spiralling. The normal rate at Ayr's Swallow Station Hotel was £40 a night; for late-bookers in Open week it was £500, the same as the Holiday Inn, a utilitarian tower block on a roundabout by the dual carriageway. These were typical adjustments. Even bed and breakfasts, usually less than £40 a night, were going for five or six times that.

The R&A does block-book rooms in the Turnberry hotel, but if the cost – £375 per night, for a minimum of seven nights – might not move the needle on Greg Norman's financial planner, it is steep enough to make these qualifiers turn white: a week would cost over £2500. And it would be mean not to look after the caddie, so the cost of the hotel would be . . . well, anyone could do the sums.

Players who did not make the cut would win prizes ranging from £3100 down to £2100, so a couple of bad lies in a bunker could make it a costly week. And these were career golfers: it was not possible for them to look on it as a fabulous cheap holiday.

The alternatives were not practical. The Orient-Express Northern Belle was offering a 'luxury package' which put 'guests' in the Gleneagles Hotel (venue for the 2014 Ryder Cup), and on a 7 a.m. train for a full Scottish breakfast – similar to full English or full Welsh, though served with the same (Polish) accent – with a 'Champagne Bellini'. They would arrive at Maybole at 11.20 a.m., take a 15-minute coach ride to the course, and return at 6.30 p.m. for the onboard dining experience – haggis, asparagus terrine and 'Frivolity of Highland Beef'. The cost had been slashed to 'only' £399, but it still did not fit with a 6.52 a.m. tee-off time.

There was scary news from the Gulf too. Leisurecorp's chief executive David Spencer had been replaced ('glandular fever') and the business had been taken in-house by the parent company, Nakheel. The Dubai property market was in freefall, and the Leisurecorp model suddenly seemed as vulnerable to the downturn as a golf ball in a Hebridean gale. According to the new chief executive, Colin Smith (a former UEFA executive), the majority of 'homes' had been sold off-plan, with final payments due when the houses were complete, but many of these early investors would be looking (in vain) to sell. It didn't look good, and it didn't sound good so far as the Ailsa was concerned when Smith added that he would, naturally, be in conversation with South Ayrshire Council about building houses 'in the area of Turnberry'.

This, of course, was the prospect that had alarmed local diehards all along. Was Turnberry set to be one of those idyllic, brochure-beaten golf-spa-villa destinations that the magazines were full of these days – part of the groomed, affluent residential fantasy that lies 'beyond imagination'?

If so, one thing was (almost) certain: whatever happened there next week, it could say farewell to the Open.

CHAPTER EIGHT

The Road to Turnberry

The Open may be a special week, but it has only seven days, and since many contestants compete over the previous weekend, they arrive in dribs and drabs.

Some came early. Jeremy Kavanagh, the English qualifier from Durban, had been planning this since February, and didn't want to miss out on a single thing, so he rented a house, filled it with family and friends, and started hitting balls.

'I tried to keep expectations down,' he said. 'But I've had six months to get excited because, to be honest, just getting in gave me a lifeline.'

Luke Donald, a thousand places higher in the world rankings, also wanted to 'practise, practise, practise' – he, like Tiger Woods, was working his way back from an injury (a wrenched wrist). In the spring, in Arizona, he had pulled out when a tendon creaked during a tight match against Ernie Els. 'I panicked a bit. I had visions of missing half a season again.' His doctors gave him the all-clear, however, and since his record in the Open was 'poor', in his words, he was spending time before the Open playing links golf at Troon, Dundonald and Western Gailes with his brother. 'If it's raining I'll be out there, getting used to playing in the wet,' he said.

Some players – Greg Norman and Justin Rose – also chose to play bad-weather golf on the west coast of Ireland to acclimatise themselves to the Open wind. Stewart Cink took his family to Doonbeg, a Greg Norman resort in County Clare, acclimatised himself to Guinness and rain, and in three or four rounds of links golf never came close to breaking par.

'It was blowing like crazy,' he said. 'I made some bad numbers.'

The road south from Ayr might have been improved, but it was still full of police cones, and the street that curved down the hill towards the village was not designed for traffic. Turnberry itself was not even a village: it had no church, no pub, no school, no shop, no post office. It was simply a lane that led to a golf course designed to be reached by train.

The historic resort was the gilded child of the Victorian Light Railway (the 'Golfers' Line') that pushed south from Ayr to Girvan. The Glasgow and South Western Railway (GSWR) had been running to Prestwick and Troon for years, but in 1896 the directors resolved to extend it. A decade later, Turnberry opened its doors as the first and grandest golfing oasis in the kingdom. The man behind the scheme was the Third Marquess of Ailsa, a local grandee and director of the railway. Willie Fernie of Troon, who won the Open in 1883 and had come second three times, was hired to lay out the holes.

The land the Marquess proposed for the golf course was his own (he had 76,000 acres in these parts), but it was exceptional: a spectacular coastal sweep that included a homely lighthouse built, in 1873, by David and Thomas Stevenson, relatives of Robert Louis (the beacon flashes four times per minute, to distinguish it from the faster beams at Corsewall and Davaar). The rocky shore also held the ruins of the castle where Robert the Bruce was said to have been born – possibly, plausibly, maybe. Nothing was certain (that's links history), but it was nice to imagine that it was to this salt-blown cave that Bruce retired to contemplate his spider and develop the mantra – try, try and try again – that became the cry of golfers down the ages.

The name Turnberry suggests a castle (from the Old English *byrig*, meaning 'fort') of tournaments (from the Norman *tournei*), so it was possible that these open grounds had seen sporting contests for many centuries. A tall, proud fortress with a portcullis for boats stood here in the 12th century. Now it was the 10th tee. How were the mighty fallen.

The course opened in 1901, and *Golf Illustrated* reckoned it 'among the finest in the world'. Five years later, in May 1906, the dedication speech at the opening praised the happy chance that led the game to this blessed plot – 'a glorious combination of picturesque grandeur'. There were no roads; the station was linked by 'covered way' to the hotel lobby. Like the Greenbrier in West Virginia, it was a splendid new feature in the social whirl, a place where the affluent could flee smoky cities and enjoy ice-fresh air, with whist drives and billiards after the salmon-en-croute. It was, said the literature, 'comfortable and complete', with 'perfect heating, ventilation and sanitation' – those glamorous turn-of-the-century equivalents to our own air-conditioning, in-room iPod, and wi-fi internet access. 'The climate,' ran the brochure a trifle optimistically (this wasn't Switzerland) was 'mild, pleasant and recuperative'.

In London, art-deco posters showed ladies in gowns wielding putters and parasols on sun-kissed lawns, and shouted the merits of the fresh air and freedom up north. 'Leave Marylebone tonight,' they said. 'Be in glorious Turnberry by morning!' Leave St Pancras at breakfast and walk into the hotel in time for a dram at sunset. The resort had a golf green, a garage, and – wonder of wonders – 'electric lifts'. Fetch the car, Jeeves!

Not everyone jumped for joy, especially when it was proposed that play be permitted on Sundays. In 1908 the GSWR received a petition which ran as follows: 'We the undersigned, being permanent dwellers of the district contiguous to Turnberry golf course, desire to make known our strong conviction that the practice, recently introduced, of playing golf on Sundays is not only contrary to the tradition of the parish, but a grave encroachment on the sentiment and sacredness of the Lord's day.'

The Duel in the Sun an encroachment? Talk about sacrilege!

There were 157 signatories. As coincidence would have it, the last, in very faint ink, said: T Watson.

There are still vestiges of the jolly old, good old days. The two roads down to the golf course pass between rusty reminders of the age of steam, in the form of crumbling brick bridges. The whole appearance of the hotel, too, like a luxurious, beached ocean liner, suggests a bygone age. If you closed your eyes, you could still hear the merry tinkle of a jazz ensemble, the rustle of ladies' silks and the whiff of saddle leather and cigars. This is where Bertie Wooster might have run into Jay Gatsby in the snooker room, or lent his smoking jacket to a chap named Cunard, while their butlers and maids made themselves rum and cocoa in the pantry.

It was a long way from the frontline, but Turnberry felt the full force of both world wars. In 1916 it was requisitioned as a flying school and an aerial gunnery centre, and the rooms soon filled up with wounded and shell-shocked troops from Flanders. Between the wars the courses were rescued, and even tweaked by James Braid, but in 1941 the whole place was requisitioned again. This time the golf course was destroyed. First World War aircraft could land on grass; the Second World War had heavier machinery. A triangle of runways and concrete bays was laid over the fairways; wind socks replaced flags; hangars rose above bunkers. Turnberry became a base for Air Sea Rescue and Coastal Command (Beauforts and Wellingtons flew out over the North Atlantic sea lanes, looking for U-boats), while the hotel was used as a hospital and as a (pretty nice) prisoner-of-war camp.

The golf course was ruined. Thousands of tons of concrete were poured across the idyllic greens and swales, and after the war the hotel fell under the ownership of the newly nationalised British Rail, which delegated it to a subsidiary, British Transport Hotels. Who knew what might happen? It might become a conference centre for high-level signalmen and area managers. But Suttons, the seed merchant, was invited to restore the grass, and they invited (nowadays people would say 'tasked') Philip Mackenzie Ross to attempt a restoration. It looked impossible: the runway foundations were four feet deep, capped with nearly a foot of cement. Somehow, two years later, a golf course emerged from beneath the oil-stained rubble.

Is it ironic that a course which seems a byword for the old, weather-worn pastures on which golf was born was in fact the fruit of much excavation and change? Maybe. That 'natural' look was created by mechanical diggers. But the result, in the days before the 2009 Open, looked spot on. The grandstands stood tall in the sunshine, and the fairways shone a vivid emerald. It had been a warm, wet summer, and there was a bumper harvest of rough; so the R&A decided to cut the players some slack by widening the mown strip. 'We don't doctor the rough,' said Peter Dawson. 'We take what we get.' When the revised course opened for members, however, nearly 500 balls were lost in the tangled grass that flanked the green carpet. 'We took the decision to widen the fairways,' said Dawson. 'We don't want to get the reputation that the Open is all about hacking out of the rough. We widened the cut sections a bit on either side.'

Getting the course just so – not too easy, but not too harsh – is a delicate balancing act, and it would have been easy for an incoming golf architect to trample on historic sensitivities. In estates manager George Brown, however, Turnberry had a curator with 23 years of local knowledge, so it wasn't as if Martin Ebert had been given a free tilt at a classic. 'I'm a traditionalist,' said Brown. 'And I think the R&A – we're all in the same boat: we want to keep links traditional. We don't want to change the character. But the players seem to hit the ball further every year, and we felt we had to lengthen the golf course – not dramatically, but enough. I think what we've done this year will bring back skill into the game.'

The bunkers were 'quite penal: the players won't like them' and the great imponderable, as always, was the weather. 'The man upstairs has an awful lot to do with it.' There had been several unkind predictions that the course would play too easy, that the true par was 65, but Watson and Nicklaus would not have shot 65 and 66 in their final rounds if the sun hadn't shone; in wind and rain, the Ailsa could cut up rough.

Brown was aware of the pressure. 'There are new owners of the hotel, a lot of money is going in, so my head is in a noose.' He was 70 years old and was saying his farewells after the Open. But he knew the course was in fine shape. 'We have all the ingredients in the stove,' he said.

The hotel was ready, too. It opened for business just in time to greet the first arrivals on the Saturday before the tournament started. In golfing terms, it was a bit like needing a birdie at the last: possible in theory. The manager, Stewart Selbie, had been sweating. Nobody took a day off for weeks: they were dotting i's and crossing t's right up to D-Day. 'We knew it would be tight, and it was even tighter than we thought, but . . .' He broke off. For a moment I thought he was going to say '. . . that's links golf'. But he didn't.

The restoration gobbled up £43 million, and there had been hiccups along the way, yet the contractors had pulled it off. One set of rooms was not complete, but it was never in the plan that they be ready: they were being turned to face the sea rather than the kitchen roof, which involved moving a corridor, a job too heavy for the time frame. The finished rooms were stunning, all cool, retro chic.

Workmen had been prowling the site as the clock ticked down, egged on by anxious executives. Furniture was lugged in

(4000 new pieces were designed and made) and last licks of paint
were applied; wiring was stowed out of sight; glasses were polished. There was a modern, eco-friendly heating plant, and new
plumbing, electric and light systems. There were fresh tiles on the
famous fountain forecourt, and the gardens had been re-land-
scaped. The first-floor bedrooms had been ripped out, and there
was a swanky new kitchen, with nods to both fine art and grunt
work: the sous-vide oven was near the spud-peeling room.

Although the hotel stood proudly on the hill overlooking the
golf course, the sea and the shining Ailsa Craig (the superb
granite island after which the course is named), the old
staterooms did not quite taken advantage of the fact. In a way the
hotel was the wrong way round: the front entrance was at the rear
(sheltered) side, and interior panelled walls screened off the sea
view. All that had changed. New arrivals now came straight into
an immense lounge, the Grand Tea Room, with huge views
down the slope. Rare teas – Gunpowder Green, Butterfly in
Love, Taiwanese High Mountain Oolong, even a Russian camel-
train leaf that promised the 'aroma of travellers' campfires' –
waited beneath fabulous sprays of white orchids, giving the room
an appropriate Empire feeling – port out, starboard home, what?
The enormous room lounged between pillars that had lain
hidden for years, and there was a huge fireplace at one end of the
room where log fires could burn through the winter.

'It's always been a great place to arrive,' said Selbie. 'But the old
entrance left something to be desired. The whole thing's been a
bit like restoring a painting – we had to be careful to reveal the
original without erasing it. Because we didn't just want to put it
back to what it was, we wanted to make it better than it was,
while keeping that same feel. We wanted to make it more like it
was originally, if that makes sense.'

Now the first impression had been opened up and aerated
(even here, openness was a theme), guests could feel luxuriously
ushered back in time, back to the *fin-de-siècle*, Queen-of-the-

oceans aesthetic of the original James Miller design. The plain wooden seat in the new reception area echoed the benches in a railway station waiting room. The colour scheme was olive-cream; it was like *Brief Encounter* with a five-star buffet.

This is where the players and their families would stay, nibbling on chicken wings or the 'finger' sandwiches (£11.50). R&A officials and their guests would be in the cottages at the base of the hill, the other side of a sweet little pitch-and-putt area below the trees.

One thing was obvious: they would be pampered. But the transaction went both ways. Not many tourist hotels ever had a relaunch party quite like this. There were no passing visitors, but Leisurecorp ran a preferred guest scheme that gave its most privileged members experiences that 'money couldn't buy' (though this alone was proof that, in fact, it could), so one or two frequent stayers got to have their morning orange juice alongside Vijay Singh, Greg Norman or Nick – sorry, Sir Nick – Faldo.

One of the most senior guests was Sultan Ahmed bin Sulayem, chairman of Nakheel. He now owned this famous hillside, and was anxious to allay fears that the well-documented financial squall in Dubai would not affect his £100 million investment (over ten years) in European golf. 'We stand by our commitment,' he said. 'And we hope that by standing by golf in the hard times, the game will remember us when times improve.'

For some players, the Open adventure was already over. In the week before the tournament, four players formally withdrew. Phil Mickelson (the world number two) was staying in America to support his cancer-stricken wife and mother, while Trevor Immelman (wrist) and Robert Karlsson (eye) had also been forced to pull out. Tim Wilkinson, having qualified the hard way by finishing in the top ten in Texas, was missing the entire summer after surgery on a wounded thumb; Dudley Hart had a bad back; and now, only days before the first ball was struck, Shingo Katayama's back was also telling him that he could not compete.

At this late stage, replacements are taken from the world rankings, and the happy recipient of this spot was the American Steve
Marino. He was playing at the John Deere Classic in Illinois, a
tournament that turned out to be vexing for those who were
itching to get over to Scotland. Stormy weather meant that the
last two rounds were both played on the Sunday, which made for
a late finish. Luckily, the tournament had generously laid on a
private charter plane, and this was no emergency measure: it was
designed to entice Open-exempt players who might otherwise
have skipped Illinois and gone to warm up (or cool down) in
Scotland.

Steve Stricker shot a course record, ten-under 61 (holing out
twice from the fairway, which helped), and won by three shots
from Zach Johnson, Brandt Snedeker and Brett Quigley. He was
thus the last man to scoot away to catch the transatlantic journey.
The luckiest man in the field, however, was Marino. When he
heard he was in the Open he was thrilled, but there was a snag:
his passport was in Florida. He had to persuade his father to fly
down from Virginia, find the damn thing (in a bedside table) and
courier it up to him in Illinois.

'He had keys,' said Marino. 'He didn't have to break any win-
dows.'

By all accounts, this was typical Marino. His father, a low-
handicapper, was an Air Force man who now worked for
Lockheed-Martin. Marino had what the American journalists
called a 'loose-fitting attitude', but also a steely eye for the main
chance. Since shooting 62 to burst through qualifying school three
years earlier, he had won nearly $5 million, with a dozen top-ten
finishes. The 1989 Open champion, Mark Calcavecchia, was
impressed. 'He lets it rip. He likes to go out there and scratch and
claw.' Marino still didn't have any waterproofs, but in other
respects he was ready to give this unexpected chance his best shot.

Some get lucky; others don't. When the plane took off,
Australia's John Senden could only sigh. He was back in Dallas;

thanks to the weather, the tournament had imposed an extra cut, and since he was not playing on the final day, he went home. He believed himself to be the fourth 'alternate' in the list, and had not expected so many to drop out. But now he learned that Brett Quigley had decided not to take up the Open slot he had earned by coming in the top five. Quigley had decided to play in Milwaukee. 'My heart is not into it,' he said. He had a funeral on the Tuesday, and did not have his passport with him in Chicago – he would have had to travel to Scotland via Florida. 'I know I'll catch some heat for it,' he said, 'but it's the right decision. I would get over there and be rushed and just not be excited to play. There's a million reasons to go – I just feel like it's gonna be better for me to go to Milwaukee.'

Quigley wasn't going to catch any heat from Thomas Levet, far from it. Having been disqualified in that fiasco at Sunningdale six weeks before, the multilingual Levet, one of the most popular guys on tour, and who had lost an Open play-off to Ernie Els back in 2002, was on his way to Scotland.

And thanks to various other last-minute commotions John Senden was now the first alternate. Since Jeev Milkha Singh was giving himself only a 70 per cent chance of competing, there was a fair chance that Senden could play the Open after all. He took a swift decision: he would travel to Scotland right away, on the off chance, with all his fingers crossed. There was a flight at lunchtime: it had to be worth the gamble.

It is not all milk and honey, the golfing life.

Europe's golfers had a much easier time. Most of them, and a good few international names besides, were playing in the Scottish Open at Loch Lomond, only a slow bagpipe march north of the Ayrshire coast. Martin Kaymer was busy winning his second tournament in a row to confirm that he was a major-winner in waiting, but he downplayed his chances of a hat-trick with a calm confession: 'I'm not a great fan of links courses.'

There were other strong finishes from Spain's Gonzalo Fernández-Castaño, France's Raphaël Jacquelin, Denmark's Søren Kjeldsen and Australia's Adam Scott. Any one of these was good enough, and playing well enough to win the Open in a few days' time: that was the whole fun of it. It was like a blue-riband horse race, all the runners had a chance. You wouldn't expect a novice qualifier to win (though it had happened) and some of the old-timers – Lyle, Norman, Faldo, Watson – were hardly worth a bet, but everyone else had the game to win, and after Norman's performance in 2008, even the seniors couldn't entirely be ruled out.

No one could help looking at Loch Lomond for clues. Retief Goosen might well have won if he had not forgotten what to do with his putter in the middle of the last round. He three-putted the 7th and 8th, four-putted the 10th and then three-putted the 11th as well. That was half a dozen dropped shots, a horrible lapse. He ended up four strokes behind the leader.

Lee Westwood wished at first that he hadn't even entered. After losing the French Open play-off in Paris he flew to Scotland, caught a chest infection and had a sleepless night before shooting 73, two over par and nine off the lead. But in the third round, after a solid sleep, he nailed nine birdies in 12 holes to make a barnstorming run; he was still in prime form.

Rod Pampling, on the other hand, felt like celebrating, even though he came 20th. There are different ways to win at golf, and he found himself summoned to the Open on the grounds that no non-exempt player had finished in the top five. He had come to Scotland chiefly in order to try and qualify by finishing that high, but missed out; now he saw that the leaderboard was full of already-exempt players. 'I wasn't too sure about Jacquelin,' he said. 'But then I found out he was already in.'

Pampling was lucky, but he had also been smart. There were four golfers ahead of him in the rankings – his fellow-Australian Aaron Baddeley and the Americans Pat Perez, Kevin Na and

Mark Wilson – who would have been eligible for the vacant place if they had filed forms. 'Thankfully, I entered,' said Pampling. 'Maybe some other guys didn't know the rules.'

The Open was glad to have him, because he owned a little piece of its history. In 1999, at Carnoustie, he was the leader after the first round, with a sharp 71, but missed the cut by tumbling to an erratic 86 in round two. The only first-round leader ever to miss the halfway cut, Pampling embodied the caprices of golf as well as anyone, and just think: if Raphaël Jacquelin had missed a putt or two back in the qualifier at Sunningdale, the Australian would not have been teeing it up at Turnberry. Such is life.

One more thing came out of Loch Lomond: trousers. Ian Poulter, Rory McIlroy and John Daly had turned the bonnie, bonnie banks into a kitsch fashion shoot by modelling extravagantly patterned strides. Poulter and McIlroy both chose sycophant-tartan, but Daly, not an obvious clothes horse, wore a multi-coloured polka-dot clown costume. If this was a trial run for the Open, people needed to be warned not to adjust their TV sets. Not surprisingly, the tabloids lapped it up, and produced obliging photo-spreads as if they were mere observers of this strange behaviour, rather than eager collaborators in a marketing stunt. It was rebel-golf imagery aimed at those who find the sport too tame for their own flamboyant natures.

The toughest slog to the Open was the one endured by Lee Westwood's caddie, Billy Foster. For him, the end of Loch Lomond was only the beginning of a long route march, thanks to his promise, on behalf of Darren Clarke's breast cancer foundation (Clarke's wife died from the disease three years earlier) and a children's cancer unit in Leeds, to lug his master's tour bag to Turnberry on foot. It was nearly 90 miles, and he felt every one of them. At one point he decided to cut across a field and found himself in a bog, which cost him a three-mile detour, but otherwise all went well. It took four days, and he stayed at golf clubs en route, where he topped up both his stomach and his begging bowl. When he arrived, blistered and sore, at the Turnberry hotel, he had raised £135,000 for his charities (golfers are good people to touch for a donation).

'I actually enjoyed the walk,' he said. He had 'a couple of good blisters and a stiff neck', but it was worth it. 'The support was incredible. People were stopping their cars to give me money.' Darren Clarke was more than grateful. 'He was on my bag for 12 years,' he said, 'so he knew the whole story. It is people like Billy that make the foundation special.'

One man keen to make a rapid getaway was Ross Fisher. He had enjoyed a remarkable year; in the course of a highly successful summer he had become a major force. He missed out on a win in the BMW at Wentworth (where he had won a scholarship and acquired his excellent game) by a single shot, and then came within a putt or two of winning the US Open. It was a brilliant performance, rendered even better when he described it as 'a bit deflating'. He had come close, while putting poorly. 'I know it sounds stupid,' he mused, 'but if I had putted half-decent . . .' The message was clear. If his putter glowed, he would be a hard man to catch.

After Loch Lomond he rushed to Surrey to see his wife, pregnant with their first child; the due date was only days off (the middle of the Open) and he was determined not to miss it. 'It doesn't matter if I'm six shots clear. There's a baby fish on the way. If my pager goes, I'm off.'

Was there, as sport likes to say, a 'little omen there'? When Mark Calcavecchia came to Troon (half an hour north) in 1989, he too had a baby on the way, and announced that he would go home the moment anything happened. In the event, the baby did not come for three weeks, but an inspired Calcavecchia fought his way into a play-off, and won it. This year, his wife had a somewhat different role. She was his caddie, and would lug his heavy bag around the seaside for the next four days.

Calcavecchia was a popular visitor, not least because he had few of the self-important airs and graces that seemed to come quite naturally to some of his younger, more serious co-workers. When asked whether his 'experience' (i.e. his age) would give him an advantage, he was dismissive. 'Experience just means I've hit more bad shots than the other guys.' He had a dodgy back too, but he thought the Duel in the Sun bar had just the cure: several pints of the local St Mungo's every evening.

The Open didn't begin well for Ian Poulter. He arrived with great hopes of being 'in the mix', but when he wandered out at ten o'clock on the Sunday evening to have a look at the 18th green, a security guard politely told him to 'clear off'. Other than that, things were going well. 'Life could hardly be better,' he said. His wife had recently given birth to a third child; he was in tip-top form, and his clothing company was 'doing great' (the *Sun*, no less, was offering his 'clobber' as a prize). There was 'lots more' to come, after his sterling effort to bag second place in 2008.

At the end of his practice round he was thrilled to see his name on top of the great yellow leaderboard; the operators were having a rehearsal. 'That looks great,' he called out, when he saw Peter Dawson behind the green. 'Can you organise it for me that way next Sunday?'

No matter where they came from or how they had come, the players knew they had arrived at a fountainhead of golf as soon as they walked into the clubhouse. It mimicked the lines and colouring – white walls, snug red roof – of the giant hotel on the hill, and the interior was a plush courtyard, crowned by galleries stuffed with mementoes from golf's early days. Downstairs there were marvellous old clubs: smooth-faced lofting mashies, curved anti-shank devices, strange spoons, neat cleeks, strong baffies and chirpy niblicks. Upstairs there were pictures of past Open winners, glimpses of the beautiful people who brought a touch of

Henley and Ascot to the pre-war links, and sobering reminders of the dark days. In May 1918, with the end of hostilities almost in sight, First Lieutenant Squires circled the airfield, came in low and crashed just two miles from the runway. Death, it was said, was 'practically instantaneous'.

Calm frames told the story. One RAF record related a near miss: 'On 9th of November 1942, Anson N9722, Pilot Sgt WALTERS, experienced engine trouble near Ailsa Craig. Machine had to be ditched. Crew of six took to dinghy and were picked up by the motor vessel FRUGALITY.'

Some were not so fortunate. Just two nights earlier, this happened: 'Beaufort L9865 Pilot Sgt SUTTON crashed into sea soon after take off on local night flying. Cause of accident unknown. Although search was made two occupants, composing crew, could not be found.'

On one wall there was a torn chunk of aero-metal, next to a picture of the crashed plane, nose down on the golf course somewhere.

Yet even the war years could carry the whiff of a more innocent time. One letter from the commandant of the aerial gunnery school, in 1917, spoke of his 'surprise and delight' to have landed such a wonderful assignment. 'The General evidently took a fancy to me, and here I am,' he wrote. 'There's nothing here except the Station Hotel. Kitty and two other wives will be the only two ladies in the neighbourhood.'

Although Turnberry did not hold an Open until 1977, it was always a popular venue for other tournaments. If nothing else, the combatants could count on eating well. The menu for the 1933 Scottish Ladies Championship ran: 'Melon Cocktail – Cream of Asparagus – Suprême de Turbot Véronique – Roast Poussin – Bombe Alhambra – Delices-de-Dames'.

Tiger Woods flew in his own jet to Prestwick Airport on the Sunday and headed straight for the course. Peter Dawson was there to welcome him, wish him well, and accompany him down the first couple of holes – not an honour the R&A man extends to all the players, but one he is almost obliged to bestow on the week's star attraction – along with the two policemen assigned to keep the curious crowd at long-arm's length. Woods didn't bother to warm up at the range: he simply knocked a ball off the first tee and marched off after it. He was inspecting the course, not his game, and when he blazed his tee shot at the second a mile wide, he simply dropped a spare without a second thought. He did seem wary of the thigh-high rough, however: he only tried his driver on two tees. Instead he spent hours dropping balls on greens, often putting one-handed to spots likely to hold pins when the time came. On the second green, according to some reckonings, he hit more than 50 putts. No wonder Peter Dawson took the opportunity to peel off back to the clubhouse.

The next morning, Woods strode in with the dawn, as was his habit (Camilo Villegas met his caddie at 6.10 a.m., hoping to be the first out on to an empty course, but was pipped by Woods and Michael Campbell), and seemed to find little in the task ahead to make him smile. By his own unique standards he was virtually alone; only a few policemen, a couple of bodyguards and a smattering of fortunate early-risers followed him out. It was not his first glimpse of the course, but he didn't seem pleased by what he saw. He kept his hands in his pockets and his head down, giving him an icy fume of don't-bug-me prickliness. It was impressive in one sense: he was working, not merely enjoying a round of golf. But it is possible to enjoy one's work, and as he dropped balls on greens, sometimes spending 20 minutes sizing up the borrows hidden in the gentle folds, he looked less a sports-man than a law student cramming for the bar exam. It was hard not to think back to those heady days when he dazzled his way to trophy after trophy with a broad grin, when *joie de vivre* seemed to be the best club in his bag.

Still, he was the scorching-hot favourite. Most bookmakers priced him at 2–1, silly odds in so unpredictable a contest, with Garcia, Harrington and Westwood at 20–1 or better (the US Open winner, Lucas Glover, was 100–1, along with former winners Justin Leonard and David Duval).

An hour later, the gallery had grown somewhat; the grapevine hums hot when Tiger is out of his cage. For the most part people were quiet, but when he blazed a three-wood off the 8th tee, one brave boy ventured a comment.

'Good shot,' he said.

'Thank you,' said Woods.

There was a comic skirmish at the 10th tee, when Tiger needed relief ('My teeth are falling out of my head'), but the halfway restroom was locked, and there was an embarrassing search for the man with the key.

Once again, Woods barely used his driver. On the par-five 7th he dragged the ball left into waist-high dune grass, shrugged, and relied instead on bristling long irons and raking three-woods. He barely missed another shot. On the 17th he risked his driver again – the tee had been pulled back some 61 yards, so this was his only chance to reach the green in two, and a man who has spun legends out of his ability to eagle the par-fives could hardly duck the challenge. He still needed a three-wood to carry the ball up the hill.

Woods wasn't proposing to speak to the press, but his verdict on the course would be decisive, so several newspapermen tracked him through the car park. Over his shoulder he confided that it was in 'great shape'. Rarely have two words brought such swift comfort to the golf world. Woods's verdict would reverberate around the world within hours, and set the tone for all discussions about Turnberry's eligibility as an Open venue. All of that thoughtful remodelling, all those anxieties about the weather and the hotel, all the concerns about the density of the rough, not to mention all those remarks about 'resort' golf – the whole lot could dissolve into the grey sky. Tiger Woods said the course was in great shape. A Papal blessing could not have wrought such rich absolution.

Did it matter that Woods might well leave his driver in the car? Two years earlier, at Hoylake, he had eschewed the big stick, kept the ball in play and his emotions in check, shot 18-under and won the first Open since the death of his father. Was that the way to tackle Turnberry too? It was all very well complaining about the distance a top golfer could achieve with modern clubs, but this might have toppled the risk-reward too far in the direction of caution. Spectators like seeing the world's best players hit a driver; it's like watching fast bowlers throw down a bouncer. It is one of the few areas of the game where an amateur cannot conceive of matching a professional effort; any old weekend idler can hole a long putt from time to time (luck does have a role to play), but the drive that pierces the clouds and flies the bunker – that is the stuff of dreams.

On the other hand, it seemed the pragmatic option. A good part of the modern game was predicated on big hitters being able to wedge the ball out of the rough on to holding greens, but Turnberry would not permit any such latitude. Errant play would be punished; length was of little value in itself. 'I think he realised what is obvious to a blind man,' said Dawson. 'You have to keep your ball on the short grass.'

To say that accuracy was important was like saying that runs mattered in cricket, or that running was important in rugby. Tom Watson had once hit only seven greens in an Open, and still shot 70. But the rough and the bunkers were undoubtedly punitive here. Apart from anything else, you had to find your ball. Professionals have a distinct edge here. There are marshals and spotters watching every shot, and even their wild efforts rarely land more than a few yards from a spectator who is only too glad (I'm on telly!) to throw his cap on it, or mark the spot with an umbrella.

Still, you never know. At Muirfield in 1966 the rough was so long that one caddie put his player's bag down while he looked for his man's ball, found the ball, and lost the bag. The only thing anyone could compete for here, said Jack Nicklaus, shortly before winning his first Open that same year, 'is a harvesting championship'.

Pushing back the rough to give the players more room was smart as well as kind. Viewers love watching players struggle to make par: it reassures them that the game is not easy. But seeing them hack about in the rough or search in vain for lost balls is not inspiring television, and that, in the end, is what this was about. There were 45 national TV companies taking pictures from this groomed shore. If the weather were kind, that was four days of dramatic wall-to-wall coverage, right across the world. Whatever it was costing Leisurecorp to host the event, it was cheap.

Where Tiger led, others followed. The verdict on the course was united; the players were happy. The word 'awesome' was used more than once. But David Howell spoke for a few when, in praising the set-up, he pulled an amused face. 'You stand on the tee and all you can see is hay,' he said. 'It's proper difficult. I'm really looking forward to it.'

CHAPTER NINE

Finishing Touches

The practice days in Open week are a bit like the day before a wedding. Expectation haunts the white pavilions of the tented village, and the air hums with soft-spoken excitement and the grassy smell of fresh matting. Players linger at microphones to emphasise that this is just another tournament, but even before a ball (or spectator) has been struck in anger, this is clearly not true. Not all tournaments are equal. The majors are different because posterity is watching, and at the Open – or British Open, as it is known abroad – it has been watching for the longest time.

There it is, up in the looming television cranes that rear over the vacant course like dinosaurs, while mowers fuss at the grass. Water drips from fairway ropes, sudden bursts of sunshine light up the flags, and a sharp sea breeze frets the pins as players drop balls into hollows and fine-tune their ball-turf contacts. It feels like a backstage reunion; almost everyone is in a good mood. It is not as casual as it appears, however. Lists are pinned in the locker room; players write their names down. Daniel Gaunt, anxious to make the most of it, chalked himself up for a Monday practice round with the greatest Open champion in the field, Tom Watson.

'He gave me some great advice,' he said. 'And he told us a lot about the course, stories about when he played Jack. He doesn't forget a shot, he knew what club he played, and where he hit it. It was fantastic. He knew how to deal with the cameras and everything. I asked a lot of questions, not as many as I wanted, I didn't want to hassle him that much.'

Advice from Watson was welcome, but he also gave a sharp masterclass in how it's done. That night, after watching Watson drill it over the dunes, Gaunt went back to the crowded house in which he was staying and said, contradicting the received wisdom somewhat, 'He's definitely got a chance of winning. He doesn't hit it short, he was getting a lot past me. And he doesn't change his swing for anything, he just works with the wind, doesn't fight it.'

On the following day, the Tuesday, Jeremy Kavanagh did the same thing. At the allotted time he bounded on to the 1st tee to join Watson and his fellow senior, Greg Norman.

'Hope you don't mind,' he said.

Watson and Norman shook his hand. Of course. No problem. They gestured him to go ahead. Perhaps he would care to show them the way.

Talk about nerve-racking. Kavanagh took a deep breath, an extra firm grip, and carved his first shot miles to the right.

'That's all right,' said Watson. 'It's a practice round.'

Three Japanese players, Koumei Oda, Azuma Yano and Kenichi Kuboya, wrote themselves down to play together. There were all-Swedish groups, American groups, South African groups and Australian groups. The pairings were listed on screens and leaderboards across the site, and one glance was enough to reveal a very singular pairing: Holmes and Watson. This was J. B. Holmes and Bubba Watson, a pair of heavy hitters, but just for a moment it was tempting to imagine Conan Doyle's hero striding the links. He would naturally have been rapier-like off the tee and a frosty holer-out, but easily bored, perhaps. Indeed, Watson, a most predictable pastime – though not without certain points of interest.

'Hi Sean,' said Davis Love to a ginger-haired under-eleven as he walked past. 'Want to walk a few holes?' He lifted the rope, and a young boy darted through. Todd Hamilton was like the pied piper: he had gaggles of children in tow. And here came Harrington, with that waggle-shoulder walk, signing caps and grinning that bashful, lop-sided smile of his. Thomas Levet chunked a ball out of the sand and almost knocked Markus Brier's caddie's cap off. There he went again, spotting Garcia up ahead, grabbing a pen and pleading, with a naughty-boy grin, for an autograph. Here came Westwood, marching through the car park, holding a child by the hand ('I think we can get out this way'). There! Gary Lineker, chatting away to Butch Harmon by the putting green; that must have been John Daly, with his glaring trousers to match his girlfriend's skirt.

On the putting green by the entrance, or at the driving range on the far side of the tented village, equipment suppliers laid out their wares: trying to tempt players into using this putter or that wedge. Links golf inspires subtle alterations, and you could hear the machines growling in the tool-shop trucks, as engineers ground the soles of irons in search of a nippier contact, or lowered the loft on a driver. Five-wood or two-iron? If it were calm, then a higher flight might actually be helpful. Padraig Harrington had fallen in love with a customised hybrid de-lofted to tear off like a two-iron. He had used it a good deal in his win at Birkdale the previous year: it was rock-solid for 265 yards. But there were big choices to be made here. If the wind did blow, the players would need different clubs into and against the breeze. And if they played a two-iron off the tee, they might face more than 200 yards to the green, and then they would dearly love a five-wood to land it softly. But they could take both these clubs only if they left out a wedge, and with firm greens and a wind they would probably be doing a lot of chipping.

Hmmm. Stick or twist.

It was bemusing for those unused to links golf, who suddenly found themselves hitting with-the-wind three-irons 280 yards. They didn't know whether to blame the porridge, the course or the three-movie flight. The American player James Driscoll (from Brookline, Massachusetts) was doubling up as a columnist for the *Boston Globe*, and confessed to some bemusement with the conditions: 'I took my umbrella out six or eight times, and every time I did the rain stopped within a minute.'

As they practised, players looked for patches of rough mild enough to be worth aiming for: if they could fly bunkers and still get a decent lie, that might be preferable to aiming at the green from long distance.

The bad news was: none of the rough looked inviting.

There are few sports that permit fans to get so close – you'd put them off if you coughed. Look: there went Watson and Norman, this time in the company of Kavanagh, taking aim at the 4th green with a nine-iron. Watson was happy to chat about the clubs he took back in 1977, and recalled that during the Duel in the Sun he needed a four-iron for this shot.

'Four-iron?' His playing partners were surprised. 'Into this thing?'

'I hit it to about six feet. Of course, Jack made his 25-footer, and I missed mine, so he went three up.'

Oh, but it was a smile to look back. Among other things, the Open was a reunion, and in a pre-Open press conference, Watson, in his capacity as benign former champion, retold his favourite Arnold Palmer stories and smiled at the memory of the time he and Jack hid from lightning in the rocks by the 8th hole; he also mentioned the time he nipped out with Ben Crenshaw to play a couple of holes with hickory clubs and an old gutty ball, and spoke warmly of his reverence for Scotland, about that first win at Carnoustie when a little girl gave him a sprig of white heather for luck.

Everyone wanted him to proclaim once and for all that Turnberry 1977 was the greatest day of his life (partly so they could hang his words on the tourist banners), but Watson was reluctant to put it ahead of Pebble Beach 1982 (when he chipped in to win the US Open) or the Kansas City Men's Match Play he won when he was only 14. 'It's not for me to write about,' was all he would say. 'It was pretty good. It was pretty good theatre.'

Amid these nostalgic souvenirs were bright glimmerings that Watson was not, in fact, here only to wave at the ghost of his former self.

'The experience of playing in different winds, that's the key,' he said, suddenly serious. 'We're going to get some different crosswinds, and with the rookies out here who haven't played this before . . .'

He was trying to work up the bravado to say that he had an actual chance, and when someone asked him precisely this, he was ready.

Was this a course where he felt he could come back and do well?

'Yes, it is. The quick answer is yes.'

He had planned his campaign in detail. He knew which holes needed which clubs, which greens needed to be approached from which angle.

'The one hole that is disappointing is 17,' he said. 'They moved the tee back so far it's going to be a very boring hole, unless you get a wind from the north. It's going to play driver or three-wood off the tee, eight-iron lay-up, wedge or nine-iron third shot for 95 per cent of the field. And there's going to be a whole lot of divots right down there just short of that bunker . . .'

Watson looked as though he would have been happy to discuss every shot on the course. But soon he was being asked about his age, and how long he thought he would continue. He said without pleasure that thanks to the age limit this would be his penultimate Open – 'unless I play well and maybe have a sixth championship under my belt on Sunday'.

The room smiled at the thought, silly though it was, as did Watson.

'Now that would be a story, wouldn't it?' he said.

Everyone enjoyed the joke. As if.

That day the 17th was playing into the breeze and was, as Watson said, hard to reach in two. Luke Donald, playing with his friend Sergio Garcia, was trying to force it up the hill with a three-wood, but his ball staggered on the slope. He tried again, and this time tipped it right into a deep bunker.

Lee Westwood had attempted the same shot with his driver and didn't make it. But Garcia's fingers were fluttering on his club like someone tickling a trout. He blazed it all the way up the hill to the putting surface.

As everyone kept saying, length did matter.

Over at the practice area Søren Hansen was working with his short-game guru, Mark Roe.

Ever wondered what gurus get paid for? Praise.

'Lovely,' Roe was saying. 'Perfect angles ... Lovely ... Brilliant! And ... one more ... there you go.'

Fans clustered close, eager for a free lesson. Of course, it does help if you can, like Hansen, chip it close, and then closer. Roe might have needed a different vocabulary had some of the onlookers been his clients.

The range was busy all day. You don't become a good player overnight, but every little helps. There was Faldo, all a-fiddle, twitch and tweak; and there was Els, shouldering his way into his stance like someone trying to squeeze into a tight coat. That familiar high loop – a man chopping logs – had to be Jim Furyk. Here came Nick Dougherty, acknowledging people with a phrase – 'OK-thanks-cheers' – he turned into a single word. If the links were a racecourse, then the range was the paddock. Players loitered between trucks from TaylorMade, Mizuno, Srixon, Wilson and Callaway. Coaches stood, arms folded, kicking balls out of divots and nodding.

It was one of those perfect Scottish days: the moment you stripped off a sweater, down came the rain, and just when you had climbed into those horrible damp waterproofs, out came the sun. There was almost too much to keep track of too. Crack: anyone see where that went? Thud: who the heck hit that thing? Look! There goes – oh, what's his name again?

On the course, engineers crouched over cables: 100 miles' worth. The company contracted to 'deliver' hi-tech communications – Envision Media, an 'integrated event marketing firm' – had inspected charts and planted 18 kilometres of fibre-optic wiring in the precious turf. It also created a halfway house where photographers could transmit images without having to trudge back to base.

The broadcasting presence was immense: a sizeable village of trucks, equipment and staff was installed on the site. The newspapers were full of bleary attacks on the BBC for sending too many staff to Turnberry, as if they were all here merely to take the waters and perhaps, oh, go on then, a small pink gin. Everyone knew that these attacks were motivated chiefly by corporate rivalry: most news organisations were desperate to charge fees for their online news, but could not for as long as the BBC did it for free. But the criticisms still stung, and it was routine to hear the Beeb spoken of as if it were a bloated fat cat. In truth, it was working flat out. It had raised towering scaffolds into key vantage points, so the course resembled nothing so much as a theatre. In golf, as on the stage, the play was the thing. The ingredients were natural – dunes, grass, gorse and sky – but the scenery was masking-taped into place.

The players have a phrase for it: the links are 'out there'. It is tough out there, they say, or cold out there. I did OK out there. Modern golfers are pampered, to say the least, so perhaps it is not surprising that they cling to this suggestion that their stage is a virile testing ground for warrior-heroes. They can't wait to get 'out there' – to tackle the beast, the monster that is Carnoustie, Troon, Muirfield, St Andrews, or in this case Turnberry.

The television production team understands this very well. It is not by chance that the TV audience is shown a brolly flying over a cliff, or a baby munching a bag of crisps, or a girl having a snooze in the long grass, or the elderly couple fondling each other's bottoms. These are part of the ritual iconography of the Open, a clear editorial choice. Those old-timers throwing sticks for their dogs on the beach, oblivious of the golf, the distant trawler and the hare darting over the green are major members of the cast – an enduring tribute to the power of the aerial view. The director wants the sky, the sea, the grass waving, and the massed ranks of spectators, moving like columns of ants around the course.

This is a predictably charming part of the annual broadcast, but it has a deeper purpose. It strives to suggest that the television audience is simply a privileged voyeur at a major social event, when in truth the presence of the television units on site are so intrusive that they form the foreground, not the background, of the scene. Find a nice view of a putting surface, and a buggy with a camera unit might well park smack in front of you.

Of course, the television studio does not mention this. 'Ah,' sigh the pundits, as the camera lingers on the view from the 17th tee – the Craig, the sun sparkling on the sea and the haughty hotel, 'it's not a bad old place.' Walk there yourself, however, and the view changes: there are three tall cranes, a forest of satellite dishes, an industrial estate, a pile of corporate cabins, huge grandstands, a burger shack, swirls of orange wire, endless roped walkways, a sea of waving canvas, crowds waiting for permission to cross a fairway, and clumps of wind turbines on distant hills. A lot of hard work goes into making the Open seem open.

It is hard work too, being one of those ants. The galleries for the most fancied players are too big and busy to permit a clear view, and there is nothing like an umbrella to wreck a good vantage point. Watching big-time golf is in some ways like going on safari or big-game hunting.

'Who's that?' someone in the gallery will whisper, squinting through the squall at a distant tee. 'I think it's Clarke! Or is it Els?'

'I'm sure I saw Casey a minute ago; but it might have been Leonard.'

It isn't easy, but it does make the Open a showcase for British manners. Large crowds are policed by elderly volunteers in uniforms (courtesy of Mizuno), who hold up delicate blue string and signs – 'Quiet Please' and 'Stand Still' – which, incredibly, are obeyed. Thousands of people hold their breath when a Tiger or a Monty set's a ball on a tee. It is a tense silence, one that would burst if held too long, but it really is quiet.

In this vacancy the ants come to realise that they are not truly spectators but extras, bit players in a TV spectacular. The camera wants them there: the shouts that echo across the links contribute immensely to the topsy-turvy suspense and time-honoured atmosphere. Queuing in the rain to cross a muddy path is a cherished tradition, as British as a wasp on a pork pie, and the laddish gags of modern pro-celebrity golf, where a clutch putt is a Dennis Wise ('a nasty little five-footer') and one that breaks late is a Booker prize-winner ('tough to read') – these have no place here.

The Open is very dispersed, and unusual in that the crowd – contrary to golf's image as a sedentary game – moves (football fans see their game as manly and energetic, though it breeds couch potatoes). It is not possible to see a golf championship whole, and hauling oneself around slippery dunes can be tiring, so the tented village is crucial: the market square for the event, a central trading floor for gossip, jokes and hey-I-didn't-know-you-were-here greetings. The rangy banks of marquee space form a familiar pattern: the Open Arms, with its generous swathe of tables and chairs, is there to quench the golfing thirst, while assorted caravans sell

Aberdeen Angus burgers, Chinese rolls, hog roast, chips, ice cream, flapjacks, cappuccino, the usual meaty-fatty works.

There's a Bollinger tent for the better-heeled, a cavernous VisitScotland zone full of promotional boosts for golf elsewhere (three free balls were on offer to those willing to book rooms at St Andrews in 2010). There was a cinema showing historic loops, corporate dining rooms (identifiable by the smart pot-plants outside), a junior golf arcade (bright plastic fun), a dark video-game booth, a camera stand, giant screens, leaderboards and a shopping precinct – all anyone could want for a grand day out.

Surprisingly, no enterprising soul seemed to have thought of setting up a newspaper stand, so readers had to make do (imagine!) with Rhod McEwan's superlative bookshop, in its usual corner of the merchandising tent, past the endless miles of sponsored golfwear. In the shower rooms, golf's literati can graze on nuggety old pearls with delightful titles such as *Out of the Rough*, *The Haunted Major* and *The Game's Afoot*. Legends of the game have always been happy (for a fee) to share their expertise: *How to Play Golf* by Harry Vardon rubs shoulders with lesser how-to lights such as *How to Break 90 Before You Reach it* by Steve Brody (humour) and Gay Brewer's *How to Score Better than You Swing*. Hackers could *Play Great Golf* with Arnold Palmer, *Golf My Way* with Jack Nicklaus, *Pure Golf* with Johnny Miller, *Natural Golf* with Sam Snead or *Power Golf* with Ian Woosnam. This was cheeky, since one could also play *Power Golf* with Ben Hogan – yours in a signed first edition for just £400. You could learn the *ABC's of Golf* from Tommy Armour, or the *Essentials of Golf* from Abe Mitchell. I looked at James Braid's *Advanced Golf* (with a chapter on 'Intentional Pulling and Slicing'), and wondered if it was wise to spend £250 on ball flights most achieve without professional help.

The whole history of golf is embraced in this small set of shelves. The first book by a professional (Willie Park) is here, alongside the first instructional book, which dates back to 1857.

The first great travel book on the game is the mighty *British Golf Links* by Horace Hutchinson, not cheap at £1200, but with priceless sepia images of stalwarts out on the links, and evocative images of 'the grip'. Andrew Bennett's *The Book of St Andrews Links* (1898, only slightly 'foxed', £4300) is one of the few source books on the early years of the Royal and Ancient. A 1913 guide to Scotland, meanwhile, included the train times from Charing Cross.

There were thrillers (*Death from the Ladies Tee*, 1925, or Agatha Christie's *The Murder on the Links*, 1960), biographies and even period cartoons. One pictured a 'tennis player from London' peering into the gorse and saying, 'I'm not sure I like this game – hitting it into a bush and huntin' after it.' Another caught the difference between the American golfer, who admiringly watched his lady friend practise her swing, and his British equivalent, grumpily telling the wife, struggling under the weight of his clubs, to please stand still, he was trying to concentrate.

Alex Salmond would have cheered to see *Golf for Women* by Genevieve Hecker, the first instruction book for ladies, only slightly ruckled by the way the dust jacket billed her as 'Mrs Charles Stout'. There were golf balls, matchboxes and a flicker-book golf lesson from Ben Hogan (£42). Pride of place went to a colossal art history book on Tom Morris (£395).

Talking of Alex Salmond, he was here, and wanted people to know it. As part of its 'Scottish Homecoming' celebration, Turnberry was staging a public 'putt against the pro' contest on a practice green. Sam Torrance and Bernard Gallacher were standing around missing eight-footers, laughing and sharing jokes. One of the early leaders was a six-year-old boy from Eastbourne who had already broken a hundred at his local course (off the men's tees) and looked, in his head-to-toe Nike golfwear, like a miniature pro. He was a walking photo opportunity, and within minutes Salmond was pushing in. Photographers lay on the ground behind the hole to record the delightful moment, and when one of Salmond's putts threatened to clatter into the Nikons behind the cup, a snapper kindly placed a ball on the front lip. Salmond stepped up to be pictured tapping it in, but was shooed back. 'Ah,' said the proud statesman, who had made such a high-minded fuss about golf's sexist ways, 'you want me to *pretend*.' Back he went; he punched the air in mimed triumph and held the pose. The next morning's papers showed him celebrating a successful putt, and invited Scottish voters to wonder at his mastery of so many essential life skills. For his bewildered companion (and a proud father), it was an important lesson: the camera does lie.

It is possible that no journalists are so well looked after as golf reporters. The media marquee is like the business centre of a top-flight hotel, and aside from all the usual comforts, writers do not have to move to speak to players. There is a well-equipped theatre for post-round interviews, and the R&A escorts a select but obliging band of players – the big names, or those who have done well – to come in and chat for 15 or 20 minutes to a roomful of reporters. There is no need even to take notes. Microphones capture every word, and within a few minutes printed transcripts are stacked outside, with word-perfect copies of what has just been said.

A couple of hundred yards away, by the 18th green, there is a smaller tent known, not elegantly, as the 'mixed zone', where reporters may request a brief word with any player they please. The players will almost always be happy to recall their round. If they ever decline (see under Montgomerie), the press poses as a wounded innocent. We only wanted to ask why he played such rubbish – where was the harm in that?

It is a privileged position, rendered logical by the simple fact that it is not possible to describe a golf tournament any other way. Reporters can't trail all over the course, though they may, every now and then, enjoy the luxury of following a single round. Golf is a strange sport in that some 60 players or so work their way round simultaneously; it is not possible to watch them all. Journalists face a stark choice. They can follow one group all the way round; they can stick on a single hole and assess each group as it passes through. Or they can stay in the tent, the information hub, watching television, listening to the players of note as they come in. In truth, reporters have no choice: they are obliged to stay close to base. But it does tilt what they write in favour of interview material, and it is also worth bearing in mind, when newspapers publish conversations with players, that the amiable-sounding chat was almost certainly conducted in a middle-size theatre, with a hundred or so reporters in attendance.

It is in these tense tents that trial-by-media happens. Here, where the smell of bacon sandwiches and coffee merges with the scent of spilled Coca-Cola and fiery electronics, is the fabled 'court of public opinion'. People talk about the press pack 'in full cry', but in fact it is quiet, polite, attentive and industrious. The hurtfulness is systematic and built-in. Journalists are pressed for time and want 'stories', so while they claim to be seeking 'news', more often they take refuge in the familiar, the already-known. Editors glimpse incidents on television and, forgetting that the TV coverage is itself a tightly edited collage of 'stories', want their own reports to reflect the live broadcast. And what everybody likes most is a spat. The ideal scenario requires one player to say something pungent about another. Any off-colour remark, recycled to the victim, can be used to draw an equally spiky response, and then, well, hold the back page.

So when Sergio Garcia met the tent the day before the Open, it was not long before someone asked how bad it felt, given that he had been a contender so many times, when 'someone like Lucas Glover' comes from nowhere to win the US Open, 'and everyone's like, who's he?'

What an extraordinary question. In effect: how sour are your grapes? Who's he? Who, one might better ask, was 'everyone'?

After all, if Glover was not widely known, there was a chance it was because he was not much written about in the newspapers. And whose fault was that?

Garcia had been round the block enough times to avoid a pit-fall like this. 'Lucas Glover's a very fine player,' he replied, killing the story flat.

This is a recurring syndrome, and since interviewees quickly learn how to play with dead bats, a counterproductive one. It is one reason why so many golfing pronouncements sound numb and lifeless: 'I was hitting the ball pretty good out there today,' they might say, 'but I couldn't buy a putt.' Or: 'I thought it was a six, but it turned out to be a seven.'

Yet here they came, one by one, polite and eager as lambs. There is a stock Ryder reflex these days (on television more than in newspapers), to present all golf events as Europe versus America, and at the Open there is also a brittle conceit to the effect that Americans hate it over here, the poor wee things. This is contradicted by the fact that they often win it – six of the 21st century's first nine Opens were won by US stars – but the stereo-type still grips. Most of them, asked how they feel about links golf (in the hope that they will fulfil the stereotype by express-ing nervous shock or awe), smile and say they love it, that this is what golf is all about; but still, they are always asked. If one unwary or bored soul admits that he finds it tough, he is hung out for public scorn like a scarecrow.

The two-time defending champion, Padraig Harrington, had been sought after all year, and still was. Maybe practice did make perfect: he seemed to have found a way of chatting freely and with surprising candour for a man who had missed six cuts in seven events. 'It's interesting,' he said. 'The last six months have been the worst in terms of performance that I've had since I turned pro, yet it may be the most productive time I've had off the course.' He had been working on his swing with his coach

Bob Torrance, who lived near Turnberry but who had flown to Paris and Dublin to help his star pupil. Back at Turnberry, like a racehorse sniffing familiar air, Harrington seemed to be finding his old snap. At one point, in practice, he tugged two drives into the hollows left of the fairway.

'What happened?' said Torrance.

'I just wanted to see what was over there,' replied Harrington. 'In case I happen to be there in the tournament.'

Harrington arrived on the Sunday clutching the Claret Jug in its black suitcase. For the third time in a row — why change a winning formula? — he had skipped the Scottish Open in order to play the Irish PGA, simply because it was played on a rain-swept links course. He won by seven shots, but did not delude himself. Afterwards he sat in the recorder's hut, with rain slamming down, and pronounced his ball-striking 'poor'.

He did not give much for his chances. He was approaching the Open, he said, with 'trepidation'. He was happy enough with his week, though. 'The weather really threw it at us,' he said. 'I'm as prepared for links golf as I could be.' He would not be working on his swing at Turnberry because, though he was zealously seeking 'some changes' to his position at impact, there was no point trying to re-engineer the machinery of his game while there was a championship to be won. 'I know the one way I can't win the tournament is if I am in the middle of a swing thought.'

Success, and the fame and fortune that it has brought, has not altered Harrington. 'I get one vote in the election,' he told a newspaper.

Rory McIlroy said that Tiger Woods was inspirational, but that he didn't fear him; Greg Norman thought that the new, lengthened Ailsa Course would not permit anyone to match his own course-record 63, set 23 years before. Ernie Els was hoping to put a difficult year behind him.

Paul Casey reckoned he would be able to handle the pressure,

thank you – he hadn't got to be the world number three by faint-
ing when the heat was on. He felt 'comfortable' and thought he
'knew how to win'.

There was extra 'pressure' on him this year thanks to some hot
recent form. In truth, he was golf's answer to Tim Henman or
Andy Murray – but there the comparison ended. Casey was no
tabloid personality; there was no sense that an Ailsa hillock would
be christened 'Paul's Peak'.

He had mixed memories of Turnberry, where he played in an
Amateur Championship as a teenager. 'I started off pretty good,'
he said, letting a mid-Atlantic (he went to college in Arizona)
idiom creep into his Surrey vowels. 'But then it went awry. I
needed par at the last. I went for it, buried it in the bunker on the
corner and made an eight. So that was that.'

There it was again: par at the last. Sounds easy, doesn't it?

Casey was sharp on the comparison with the grass-court game.
'Tennis is all about winning,' he said, deflecting the suggestion
that he try and spark up some Caseymania. 'Andy spends 90–plus
per cent of his life winning. Golfers don't do that – well, unless
you're Tiger Woods. That's why the hype isn't there in golf. And
I think that's a good thing.'

This was a significant observation. One of golf's unusual features is that it allows a player to perform at the top level for a
decade or more, travel the world, become a millionaire, and never
win. The American golfer Briny Baird, who would be teeing it
up at 9.53 the following morning, turned professional in 1995,
joined the PGA Tour in 1999, and in all that time had never won
a tournament. So far this year he had played 19 times, missed
seven cuts and finished in the top ten three times; but he had still
scooped up over a million dollars. And it was only July.

Argentina's Angel Cabrera thought his putting was *mucho mejor*
(much improved); Paul Lawrie still had 'loads of desire';
America's Boo Weekley admitted, 'I'm not very well, but I'm not
going to pull out'; and John Daly was discussing his slim new

look. 'I've lost 75 pounds,' he said. 'The doctors told me to go on a 1200 calories a day diet, so what I eat now in seven days is what I would eat in one day before.'

Rory McIlroy didn't feel he was 'any sort of superstar'; Ryo Ishikawa was invited to declare, in a bashful, princely way, that he loved Scotland ('I also tried haggis. So very nice. Very nice taste'); and Henrik Stenson was willing to be sensationally controversial about Woods – 'I've seen him play ping-pong, he's not super-human.'

Martin Kaymer was 'trying to sleep a lot, to get the energy back', and Lucas Glover was 'doing good' and thought that links golf was 'fun'.

What, someone asked, was he reading? 'The last one was Greg Iles, *The Devil's Punchbowl*,' he said. 'Good read, pick it up.' It turned out that Glover had once let slip that he liked books, and the media seemed inclined to see this as an astonishing and deeply eccentric diversion (since when did a book help a fellow hole a putt?) and grilled him on it.

There was also time for the media's favourite Tiger Woods question. If a player can be lured into an unguarded remark about the main man, even as a wisecrack, he can be guaranteed banner headlines ('"I Can Tame Tiger," Boasts Open Chump'). Quite a few have fallen for this one, and the question itself often seems innocuous, even flattering. Here it came.

Did Glover feel, as US Open champion, that he was a match for Tiger?

He might have been new as a major-winner, but he was too wily for this. 'I got paired with him at AT&T two weeks after,' he said. 'He beat my brains in for two days. I think he's still got me.'

Damn. A truthful answer, and the death of a good story.

Ernie Els was speaking freely, almost for the first time, about the grave difficulties in his own life. Woods might have a crocked knee, and Luke Donald's wrist might be jarring; but Els was adapting to the discovery that his small son, Ben, was autistic. This shocking news came hard on the heels of his own knee injury (a boating accident) and he had become, in the last three years, a pale shadow of his former magnificent self. He was still thought of as a leading player, on the grounds that class was permanent, but the figures suggested the opposite. He had won once in the last four years, had missed the cut in the Masters and the Open, and was sounding plaintive. 'I am searching, man, I am searching,' he said.

At precisely the point (he was 40) when he might have reaped the (huge) rewards of his enviable golfing style, he felt like a novice. 'It's almost like having to get myself in a frame of mind to start all over again.'

The most significant interviewee, of course, was Tiger Woods. After his practice round he went to the tent, as usual, and answered the world's questions with a polished assurance that seemed at once forthcoming and curt. What did he think it would be like to play with Ishikawa in the first two rounds? 'Very quiet.' If he had known how bad his knee was at the US Open, would he have still played to the end? 'Yeah, probably, knowing me.' Had Roger Federer been bragging about his 15th major? 'Our texts back and forth have always been jabby here and there, but also extremely supportive. That's what friends do.' Was a year without a major a failure? 'It's been tremendous. To sit here and say I was going to have three wins halfway through the year, I wouldn't have thought that.' What did he think of Scottish roads? 'Stevie drives. He's used to this side of the road. His racing mentality kicks in every now and again, loves these turns.'

Tiger was being modest: he once won a 'celebrity stock-car race' in New Zealand from the back of the grid. He could drive all right when he felt like it. But was this a clue that he would, after all, be using his driver?

He had not seen much of the year before's Open. 'My day consisted of trying to get from the bed to the couch and then back from there to the bed. That was my day. My leg was at that time – I was in pretty good pain. So watching this tournament, I really didn't do much of that.'

Everyone knew that Woods was not a diligent spectator. He does not require the escapist fix thought indispensable by so many executives, taxi-drivers or freelance writers. Nor had he been to Turnberry till now. He didn't, he had once said, 'do' golf vacations.

He didn't do vulnerable either. But at the end of his long discussion, he did let slip what by his standards was almost a sigh. As always, he had spent the past few days building a strategy. 'You have to make sure you know what you're doing out there. You have to be committed to either putting the ball short of the bunkers or skirting past them.' He was his usual self: serious, intent and in earnest. But for a moment he dropped his shoulders and his guard, as if weighed down by the thought of what lay ahead. 'But you know,' he added. 'It's not as simple as people think.'

Greg Norman had plenty to talk about, after his own performance in 2008, playing in the final group with Padraig Harrington and nearly making history, and Kenny Perry's excellent effort in the Masters earlier in 2009, when the 49-year-old was only one putt away from being the oldest ever winner of that celebrated green jacket. At Birkdale, Norman had been one half of a honeymoon couple, and Chris Evert was alongside him once again this year. On the Monday evening they went out to dinner with Watson and his wife: the two grand old Turnberry champions were planning to play a practice round together the next day.

At one point Evert asked Watson which would mean more, the Senior Open down at Sunningdale, or this one right here, in Scotland.

'You've got to be kidding,' said Watson. 'I would rather win, finish second, third or fourth at the British Open than win the Senior Open.'

'It's logical,' said Norman. 'It's the greatest championship on the planet in our mind. That's no slight on the Senior Open. It just shows the intensity and the magnitude of what the British Open means to us.'

He had other worries. In March he had made a quarter of the workforce at one of his divisions redundant, and he was bitter about the slowdown that made it essential. 'Some of them had worked for me for 20 years and I knew they would have no place to go. There's just nothing you can say. I just hope that one day I can swing that door open again and welcome them all back in.' As for the economy whose dip inspired this anguish, he said simply, 'It's dead, and it's a long time before it's coming back.'

Norman had a personal interest in this year's tournament. His daughter Morgan, who ran a wine division of his business empire ('She's proving a phenomenal businesswoman'), had been dating Sergio Garcia, but earlier in the year the pair had split up. Norman was a prime golfer and a busy wheeler and dealer; but he was also a dad. His own son (Gregory – an odd coincidence) would be carrying his bag this week.

When his turn came, Garcia himself didn't mind admitting that it had been hard. 'It's probably the first time I've been in love,' he said. And yes, he certainly was keen to break his major duck.

This was a noose that was now firmly stuck around his neck. For the time being he was in the unfortunate position of being the 'best player never to win a major', a title no one wants, for the simple reason that it peppers every press conference on the schedule. 'I'd love to get rid of it, yes,' he said. 'But I'd rather be the second loser than the 39th loser.'

For many years this had been Colin Montgomerie's cross to bear, and it had proved (some would argue) too heavy; but these days Garcia was the popular pick as the sweetest ball-striker out there. If he could putt, ran the received wisdom, there would be no holding him. He had come close to winning a major more than once, and his recent performances had been riveting. He was half an inch away from winning the 2007 edition at Carnoustie, and was no longer laughed at for squeezing himself into a sartorial hazard the previous year, when he went out with Tiger Woods in the final group wearing a canary-yellow outfit in which Poulter would have been ashamed to be seen dead. Not surprisingly (self-consciousness not being a recommended swing aid), Garcia played poorly that day; urban myth had it (on non-existent grounds) that Tiger Woods, after storming to victory, sent a text to a pal saying simply, 'I just crushed Tweetie Pie.'

Before leaving Loch Lomond, Colin Montgomerie was asked what he thought of his chances at Turnberry. 'I'm not expecting anything,' he said. 'And neither should you.' This was a sound assessment of his position in the golfing constellation these days. He was ranked 200th in the world, and was a 300–1 shot for the Open: no longer what the film business would call a 'player'. Anything was possible (that's links golf), but it was hard to imagine him ever recapturing his old accuracy and zest.

Montgomerie's poor Open record was a mystery. He had been raised in this landscape (his father was a golf club secretary) and this week he would be staying with his dad, less than half an hour from the Open fairways; he was one of the all-time great players in European history; and had gilded credentials as a top-flight links golfer with a 63 at St Andrews and 64s at both Muirfield and Carnoustie. But far too often he had played below himself; he had missed eight Open cuts and suffered a host of bruising lapses (just 24 hours after his 64 at Muirfield, a squall blew up and he shot 84). It was tempting, given his hair-trigger concentration, to ascribe this mediocre record to the scale of the bumbling Open crowd, but he had performed superbly in much more raucous conditions at successive Ryder Cups. It must be, the feeling went, just one of those things.

Montgomerie himself left Loch Lomond in a dark mood. He hadn't played well, and his only tactic for improving things was to stay away from Turnberry until the last minute. 'I will go very late,' he said sourly. 'Nothing else is working.' But he could not bring himself to renounce hope altogether. Montgomerie admitted that he hoped to sneak into the Open 'under the radar' and enjoy 'the best course in Britain'.

The radar might have been happy to ignore him, but his compatriot Sandy Lyle, alas, chose precisely this moment to ignite a bright and aggressive flare over his head. There had been whispers of ill-feeling between the two – the best Scottish players of recent times by a long street – ever since Montgomerie had pipped Lyle to the captaincy of Europe's 2010 Ryder Cup team. Montgomerie had actually been an eager and vocal supporter of Lyle's own credentials for the role – seemingly until he was asked to consider it himself. But now, several months later, and at the beginning of Open week, Lyle decided to make his distress public. He was in conversation with some journalists at Loch Lomond when one of them wondered, a little cheekily, if Lyle's conduct at the previous Open, when he walked off the course after playing horribly for a couple of hours, had been a factor in his not being given the captaincy.

It had certainly been widely felt, in sports pages across the golfing world, a poor show: ageing, past-their-best former champions are technically welcome, but it is not thought gracious if they occupy (and toss away) a berth for which an up-and-comer would have surrendered his eye teeth. In Lyle's case, his bail-out inspired yards of media scorn. Nor did it suggest brave leadership to golf's decision-makers. His excuse, cold hands ('They were virtually going numb'), did sound, even to his best friends, pretty feeble.

His reply to the question at Loch Lomond was astounding, however. 'You would have to ask the committee that,' he told the assembled recording devices. 'But you've got Monty with his situation where he was dropping the ball badly overseas. And that is far worse than someone pulling out because he has sore knuckles. It's a form of what could be called cheating.'

Ouch. A shock wave rippled along the golfing grapevine.

Lyle was referring to an incident in 2005, at the Indonesian Open, when play was interrupted by a storm. Montgomerie left his ball where it lay, in long grass above a bunker, but when he returned the next morning it had disappeared. He was permitted a replacement, and it certainly did seem (the television pictures were not really equivocal) that the new ball was in a kinder position. The previous evening he would have had to stand with one shoe in the bunker; now he had a clear footing in the grass. He went on to win £24,000, and a much-needed heap of precious ranking points.

It was a combustible incident to bring up, because on-course dishonesty is one of golf's most sacred cows. Ever since the great amateur Bobby Jones was congratulated for calling a foul on himself for an accidental transgression no one but he could possibly have seen (he replied, famously, that 'one might as well congratulate a man for not robbing a bank'), the game had been several hundred per cent (at least) addicted to the idea of itself as unimpeachably honest. It promoted itself as more or less the only sport that would not tolerate cheating in any form or shape. Some of its rules, indeed, bent so far in the opposite direction that they themselves seemed almost unfair. Ian Woosnam was disqualified from the 2001 Open when his caddie left a spare club in his bag, putting him over the 14-tool maximum; Mark Roe was banished from the 2003 Open because he failed to exchange scorecards with his playing partner, Jesper Parnevik. Both were riding high, with a chance to win the Claret Jug; neither was seeking an advantage. In cases like these, the punishment seemed to outweigh the crime by an unpleasant distance, and all so that golf could preserve its reputation for spotless chastity.

Turnberry quivered with horror. George O'Grady, chief executive of the European Tour, said, in one of those machine-milled statements that sound so unconvincing, that Montgomerie was 'absolutely the right man for the job' and that Lyle's comments were 'deeply inappropriate and ill-timed'. The television commentator Peter Alliss summed up both the general twitchiness and the Wodehousian silliness of it all when he said, 'It's a fact that if you're known as a cheat in golf, golfers ostracise you. You can be a womaniser, you don't pay your taxes, a whiff of BO – but he who cheats at golf, Oh Columbus, we don't want him in the club.'

He was right: golf can be sanctimonious, and Alliss himself was often pilloried for his own slightly old-fashioned assumptions (what other sort should he have: he wasn't a youngster any more), especially by people desperate, thanks to their own class nerves, to distance themselves from the old-school, clubbable persona he so cheerfully represented.

Lyle's allegation sent people racing to the archive. There had been a similar case in Arizona that spring, when television pictures suggested that Kenny Perry might, in the act of addressing the ball, have squashed the grass enough to improve his lie. There were still mutterings, 36 years on, about the time Tom Watson charged Gary Player with the same, um, accidental slip. Perry was exonerated on the grounds that there was no 'intent' – a confusing ruling that allowed elements of motivation into the black-and-white world of golfing fair play: a player hitting the wrong ball could not plead that it was an accident; a golfer who teed in front of the markers would never be let off on the grounds that it was unintentional.

There was much sporting politics engaged by matters such as these, because golf's pride in its spotless reputation is more than a sentimental pose; it is of burning commercial value. Corporate sponsors love golf's clean-living image. Those billboards in airports, those glossy spreads in magazines, love to hoist words like 'integrity' and 'values' over their own corporate logos. One of the reasons why golf continues to abide by the letter, rather than the spirit, of its plentiful laws is that its squeaky-clean image is a lucrative, maybe even a unique, selling point.

There are ironies here: the desire to punish players for innocent errors (such as Woosnam's or Roe's) reveals an interesting lack of faith in the reliability of the top pros. The assumption – a lingering legacy from the early days, when golf's gentlemen assumed that the 'professionals' could not be relied on – seems to be that they cannot be trusted. So it is at least possible that in Montgomerie's case the authorities were surprisingly forgiving. The former Tour player Gary Evans certainly thought so: he had been a busy critic of the European Tour at the time, and repeated his charge now that the top players 'get away with murder' while 'lesser lights tend to get picked on'.

Perhaps he was right. Maybe there was a hint of player-power here. Fact was, if the ruling bodies ever did start penalising Monty or Perry for such fiddly crimes, what on earth would they be obliged to do about Tiger Woods's club-throwing (if Roger Federer tried that he'd be hauled up for racquet abuse) or Ian Poulter's laugh-a-minute clothes.

Maybe it would have been better, in retrospect, if the authorities had accepted Montgomerie's apology . . . but penalised him anyway, on the firm-but-fair principle that accidental transgressions were as hazardous as deliberate ones. They would have been erring, as so often, on the side of golf's 'whiter than white' reputation, but they might have prevented it ever recurring, as it was now, as 'Montygate'. But it is easy, in seeking to be whiter than white, to seem merely holier than thou, and golf was also under perpetual pressure to sweep aside its finickity tones.

Sandy Lyle has rarely been known as a learned or a subtle thinker, but even he could not have been blind to the blaze that his allegations were certain to ignite . . . could he? It was a resonant way of dramatising why he had been passed over for the Ryder Cup captaincy. He wasn't just putting his foot in his mouth; he was kicking his own teeth out. These were not the sort of 'leadership skills' Europe's golf establishment was looking for.

The point, in any case, was that a decision had been reached, so this had expired as a controversy (or should have). Montgomerie, like Perry, had denied cheating. There was a brief procedure at which he apologised for any mistake he may have made, and he did donate his winnings to charity (though he did not relinquish the ranking points). Anyhow, his apology was accepted. To reopen the case now, in this most prestigious week, seemed self-indulgent in the extreme. The grapes in Lyle's mouth were not just bitter; they had fermented, and quite gone to his head.

But there it was, out in the Open: the ch-word. For the next two days it would be the top 'story' coming out of Turnberry. 'Hate and Lyle' sang the *Daily Mirror*. 'Lyle in Monty Cheat Blast' echoed Scotland's *Daily Record*, not trying to suppress its glee. In outline it was a perfect 'got-up-by-the-media' melodrama: a player bad-mouthing another, using a press conference as the means of communication. When Montgomerie arrived, the media were waiting to pounce. This included the TV cameras, of course. Television presenters are very fond of talking about 'the media' as if it were an embarrassing and misleading blot on their sport, but they rarely, if ever, hesitate to insinuate themselves into any squabble that comes to their notice.

Montgomerie announced (through his manager) that he was 'very surprised', but that he had no further comment, which seemed the only dignified way forward. After George O'Grady's terse statement denouncing Lyle as way out of line, Act One, Scene Two of the drama called for a Lyle apology. He came to the media theatre, sat at a raised desk with a jug of water, and looked over at the throng of newshounds seated expectantly beneath a bank of lights and cameras. 'Good afternoon,' he said, and launched into another of those pre-written formulaic 'statements'. 'Due to the extensive media coverage,' he said, he wanted to be clear that he regretted bringing up the 'incident in Jakarta'. He said that Monty was a 'good friend' and a 'great champion' whom he had 'always supported' as a Ryder Cup captain. He admitted that in his 'frustration' he had 'regretfully brought up an old incident' that had 'long since been resolved'. He ended, somewhat against the balance of probabilities, by saying that he felt 'especially bad if I have jeopardised his preparations for the Open Championship'.

As mea culpas go, it wasn't the worst (despite that wobbly use of the word 'regretfully'). If he had turned on his heel at that point, there wouldn't have been a great deal to add. But for some reason Lyle hung on to field further questions – which of course were merely the same question all over again. At first it seemed incomprehensible, but then, from the half-smile playing about his lips, a suspicion emerged: Lyle was enjoying this. When someone asked whether this 'fury and upset' had affected his own preparations, he was ready with a nice modest quip: 'Obviously my challenge is to get past the 9th hole and go from there.' The room laughed, and it was like the old days, when a scrum of journalists would hang on his every word. What he really needed was a friend to drag him away and save him from this greater folly, but it was too late. In as much time as it took to make a piece of toast, Lyle dug himself an even deeper hole. 'I'm only going from what other people have said,' he confided, letting slip that he had no first-hand knowledge of the event, 'but it was a pretty poor drop. It was his mistake, and it will probably live with him for the rest of his life.'

It was surreal. He had barely completed his clenched apology before repeating the allegation – seemingly with more relish than before, and with the sorrowful air of a disinterested elder statesman. If anything, he seemed wounded by the fuss, and tried to blame 'the media' for taking his words 'out of context'. But then he went on to chide his 'friend' Montgomerie for being 'a bit of a drama queen', as if it were Monty who was harping on this old sore, not himself. When he suggested that Monty needed to grow up and move on, no one knew where to look. He even gave expression to some comradely sympathy, as if the present furore were nothing to do with him. 'I've got no vendetta against Colin at all,' he said. 'I'm all for him. And the last thing he wants right now is for all this baloney going on right now before he tees off this week.'

These were the kind of noises he was supposed to be making, but when a journalist, suddenly apprehending that Lyle seemed ready to blurt it out all over again, asked him outright if he still felt that Montgomerie had cheated (an allegation he had just officially withdrawn), he launched right in. 'It was all there to be seen. I didn't prefabricate this thing. The drop wasn't close to where it should be. And of course on TV it doesn't lie.'

Prefabricate? The room shrugged. Good old Sandy.

It was a terrible performance, but it was possible to sympathise with Lyle. Of course he was old enough to know better, but by disparaging a rival he had stumbled into the cross-hairs of the media's favourite elephant gun.

A few hours later, Montgomerie was himself persuaded to say a few words. He said he was 'not very happy', agreed that yes, his preparations had been 'dented'. He was amused, he said, to hear of Lyle's hope that none of this would affect his chance of being vice-captain at Celtic Manor. 'I thought that was funny,' he said. 'I thought that was very, very funny.'

Not long after that, the two men passed one another by the clubhouse. Montgomerie glanced at Lyle, gave a brief nod, and said not a word.

In the media tent, for the next 24 hours, it was as if there were nothing else to talk about. Some were even heard to utter that the Open 'needed' a story like this, because otherwise there would be little to grab the attention of the back pages. The sad point here was that this might well have been true. 'Woods vs Harrington' was all very fine, but of interest only to golf fans, whereas 'Lyle Slams Monty' was one of those mass-market sensations that could inspire headlines across the board. In one way it would confirm the entrenched view of golf as a game for past-it fuddy-duddies, but in another dimension it made it seem hot and bitchy – a far richer commodity in our media-savvy, bully-boy, *X-factor* world.

The problem of media space was especially acute this week thanks to the casual way in which England's cricket authority had gate-crashed golf's historic calendar by slotting its Ashes Test at Lord's at precisely the same time as the Open. Even semi-intelligent sporting governance might have ensured that these two events – the twin peaks of the British sporting summer – did not coincide, but this year's Lord's Test had been knocked about by the Twenty20 World Cup back in May. 'For us, the mid-July date is fixed,' said Peter Dawson. 'The Open is when it always is.' It would have little impact on crowds, but the clash was certainly bad for commercial hospitality: the corporate demographic for cricket and golf is almost identical. A lot of companies that take boxes at Lord's also, in a normal year, rent a piece of the tented village; but this year the corporate chalets stood empty. Even the Royal Bank of Scotland, one of golf's most enthusiastic patrons, was obliged to scale back. It was not in the smart 'chalets' overlooking the 18th tee; it was offering a buffet rather than a sit-down gourmet festival, and it would not be serving champagne.

Quite right too, most people thought. The bank had accepted a torrent of taxpayer bail-out money; it was clearly not smart for its senior executives to be photographed throwing back bubbly at a golf tournament.

There remained the issue of media coverage. Sport's governing bodies are aware that they are locked in competition with each other for space in newspapers, and on television and radio.

However rude, intrusive and misleading the media can seem, their promotional power is priceless. And since the audience for big-time golf and cricket overlaps, the clash with the Ashes was painful. The Open would not struggle for airtime, and since it was broadcast on the BBC it was guaranteed a better audience (perhaps five times better) in Britain than the cricket could reach through Sky, but it might struggle to command back-page head-lines, especially in papers with a vested interest in the TV channel. Golf's heart sank when Andrew Flintoff chose the day before the Open to announce his retirement from Test matches. He was the folk hero of the national game: a silly spat between two once-great golfers could not match that. Lyle's attack on Montgomerie was intense, troubling, of no importance whatso-ever, yet potent enough to dominate the entire build-up to the Open.

Ironically, there was a possibility, despite the reputation for wild weather in these parts, that the Open might be saved by the rain. The forecast was predicting more water in St John's Wood than in Ayrshire.

At the annual Golf Writers' dinner, held on the Tuesday of Open week, some of the talk concerned this ghostly absence of corporate VIPs, but most revolved around Montgomerie (who had decided now not to come to the dinner after all) and Lyle. Els, Westwood and Clarke took a table together and chuckled about the whole affair; Harrington picked up his second golf writers' player-of-the-year award and made sure, in his earnest way, to thank the media for promoting the game so assiduously. And the after-dinner fun was provided by David Howell, a player down on his luck, but universally popular for his self-deprecating wit.

He began by saying he had always dreamed of giving the speech at the Open, but hoped it would be after the tournament, not before. But he knew he had much to be grateful for – indeed his wife was a particular inspiration. 'Only the other day we were in Harrods,' he said, 'and she picked up a piece of glassware and said, "Why don't we buy one of these and get it engraved, so we can pretend you won something."' There followed a delightful reprise of his brief career as a 'Ryder Cup legend', in particular the round he played in partnership with Henrik Stenson ('and there was water on the right'). There were quips about his lack of seniority in his own agent's pecking order ('I rang him up, but he was out walking Ernie Els's dogs') and unrepeatable gags about fellow players.

It was a fine performance. Everyone hoped he would win.

The last man in was Australia's John Senden. His speculative trip was rendered more than worthwhile when Jeev Milkha Singh did pull out, after struggling through practice with a 'nagging rib injury'. Suddenly, Thomas Levet was only the second happiest man on the links. 'It wouldn't have been nice to come all this way and not play,' said Senden. 'But it would have been far worse to sit at home thinking I could have been here.' After four top-ten finishes in America, he was not intending merely to make up the numbers. 'The course is great, and I'm feeling all right,' he said.

You had to feel for Milkha Singh. Back problems are a common golfing ailment, partly because the golf swing is a wrenching manoeuvre, and partly thanks to the ultra-frequent flying. But it was time to look forward, not back, because the pairings had been announced. If Montgomerie and Lyle had been in the same group, the media's happiness would have been complete. No such luck. The governing idea is that each group should contain one home player, one American and one international player, but other factors play a role. It is called a 'draw', yet the R&A admits to tampering in order to adjust for crowd control (it is best if the groups with the big followings are dispersed around the course) and the needs of the various television companies. It is not possible for television producers to track the whole field, so they like to have a few solid groups to focus on at any one time. America likes to have its own big shots (Tiger, of course) in full view during prime time, while the Japanese are keen that their domestic stars go out late in Scotland (cocktail hour in Tokyo).

The R&A had decided to put the two most boisterous galleries together. Tiger Woods and Ryo Ishikawa. Looked like bad luck on Lee Westwood, the third player in the group, but he accepted it with his usual breezy good humour. He was under no illusions what it would be like; he had played with Tiger in the past (notably in the final round of the 2008 US Open, when he finished just one shot out of a play-off) and had seen first-hand the excitement inspired by Japan's new teen sensation. 'I was at the World Match Play in Tucson. He wasn't even playing, but there were about a hundred photographers there.' It would be worse on Thursday, but what could you do? 'It'll give me a chance to practise my Japanese,' said Westwood, grinning. The next day he joined a junior golf clinic for some fun with the under-tens, and when one young boy asked him what he would find to talk about with Tiger Woods, he smiled again and said, 'Nottingham Forest. He's a mad keen Forest fan.'

Nottingham Forest? Is that the new golf spa in Robin Hood country?

Westwood could laugh, but it was possible that the chief victim of the draw might turn out to be Woods himself. Of course he was used to large galleries, and no one was better at screening out distractions, but he was emphatically not used to huge galleries that were focused on someone else. Over the years his rivals had grown accustomed to crowds moving when it was their turn to play, as people scrambled for a better view of Tiger's next shot; now he would have to see what that was like. The pool of photographers following Ryo Ishikawa would be record-breaking. When he played his first professional tournament, the

Japan Tour website crashed under the weight (two million hits) of public interest. And while no one was more likely to be polite and deferential than a Japanese golf observer overseas, photographers are notoriously thick-skinned about the mayhem they create in their quest for the perfect snap.

There were other strong draws, and some regular Open-watchers licked their lips at the thought of Woods–Ishikawa luring people away from the other groups. The man of the moment, Martin Kaymer, would go out with Ernie Els and Lucas Glover. Harrington would tee it up with the durable American Jim Furyk and the in-form Australian Geoff Ogilvy. It would be no surprise if the eventual winner came from the threesome including Rory McIlroy, Retief Goosen and Angel Cabrera. And everybody's favourite after-dinner speaker, David Howell, would play with the tall, steady Stewart Cink, as well as the most popular candidate in the first-Asian-winner stakes, Thailand's Thongchai Jaidee.

There was a flutter of press interest when Paul Lawrie and Davis Love III were paired together, because Love had allegedly mocked Lawrie when he won the Open in 1999, claiming that Carnoustie, a soaking obstacle course that week, got the 'winner it deserved'. This had all the makings of a good feud, but there was one problem: Davis Love denied ever saying such a thing, and Lawrie, dash it, seemed happy to believe him.

The most tempting group of all, however, included only one serious contender. Sergio Garcia, the bookmakers' second-favourite, was twinned with both the youngest man in the tournament, the 16-year-old Italian amateur, Matteo Manassero, and the oldest, Tom Watson. Manassero almost had the style and looks of a young Ballesteros. Having won the British Amateur Championship, he knew how to get the ball around a seaside course. He was one of several youngsters in the field – England's Oliver Fisher was 20, like Rory McIlroy; the German amateur Stephan Gross was just 21, and even the veteran Chris Wood was only 22 – so he would not be alone. But Manassero's presence was awkward for Garcia. In golfing terms he was the senior figure in the group, but beside Watson he felt like a stripling. Which was fine: boyish charm was his marketing edge. Yet in Manassero's company he could no longer think of himself as El Nino.

Watson had been enjoying himself. On Monday he practised with Daniel Gaunt, and on Tuesday with his old friend Greg Norman and Jeremy Kavanagh. He didn't seem to mind being gate-crashed by newcomers; on the contrary, he just smiled his grey, faraway smile, chatted amiably about his glory days, and played superbly on both occasions: all of his playing partners noticed how sharp and true his ball-striking was.

On the sixth hole something had happened that might – who knew – shape the entire week. He dropped a ball about 25 feet from the cup and rolled in a beguiling putt, the sort of putt a man would need to hole from time to time to compete at the week-end. He smiled, dropped a ball on the same blade of grass, and holed it again. It seemed like tempting fate to try one more (reality would surely bite), but he drew back the putter, eased it through, and there: three in a row. His smile, when he turned towards the 7th tee, was a tiny bit broader, and even more fixed, than ever. He looked like a man who had just found gold glinting in his old, mud-streaked pan.

The practice days were winding down. Bruce Vaughan, the reigning Senior Open champion, practised chipping for five minutes, then squinted at the setting sun. He was at the start of what one might call the North Atlantic swing; after the Open he would go to Sunningdale to defend his trophy. He had been able to play only one practice round, because his caddie had missed a flight and was gridlocked in London till the Tuesday.

He was somewhat alarmed by the way the youngsters played.

'I was saying to some guys on the Champions Tour,' Vaughan said. 'I go out to the range and see the ball disappearing. The way these kids hit the ball, I don't know . . .' A few yards away, Manassero was stroking putts and looking forward to the Open at an age when Vaughan himself had not even begun. 'I didn't know what golf was when I was sixteen,' he said.

It was a nice reminder that there were many different roads, some of them long and twisting, to the first tee at the Open. Vaughan had not been a serious pro golfer (he played one year on the American circuit in 1995, when his best finish was 22nd) until he turned 50, but then he joined the so-called 'Champions' Tour and won the 2008 Senior Open. He wasn't enjoying all the big-gun talk about the driver being a redundant club this week. 'I don't have that option,' he said. 'I hit it short.'

He was not staying in the hotel, and was half-regretting it. 'I thought I'd found a nice place, it's over that hill somewhere. They said it was 15 minutes away, but it's more like 15 miles.'

It is often said of golfers that if they can just break through to their first victory, more will follow. Few conversations about Sergio Garcia, for example, did not include this glint of folk wisdom. Victory allows players to graduate from believing they can win, or hoping that they don't mess it up this time, to the enviable plateau of certain knowledge. Harrington knew he could win, because he had done so twice before. So for him, preparation had the single aim of getting him into a position to challenge on Sunday afternoon – he was happy to take his chances from there.

As night fell, tongues loosened. Might 2009 be the year of the breakthrough, the year for a British winner, a youngster, an old hand, a legend, an outsider, a qualifier, perhaps even a journey-man? Those who had seen Markus Brier flay it around Kilmarnock Barassie a week before wondered if it might not be time for an Austrian winner; and wouldn't it be something if

John Senden, the last man in, was also the last man standing. What were the odds on a Lyle–Montgomerie pairing in round three?

People could say what they liked, as heatedly as they liked, because, in truth, anything was possible.

As the conversations went on late into Wednesday evening, I found myself dwelling on Harrington's conviction. 'I know if I can get into position,' he said, 'I can win. That's nice. Others can get there but they can't win. For me, getting into position is what's in doubt.'

Was it true that only a few players really could win? One of the most appealing things about the Open, it always seemed, was how open it truly was. The courses, the weather, the erratic nature of the game, the role of pure chance: there were so many variables – any player who had made it this far had some sort of chance to win. Wasn't that the whole idea?

I could not help noticing, however, flicking down the list of past winners, how many multiple champions there were. The Morrises had four apiece, Harry Vardon six, James Braid, J. H. Taylor, Peter Thomson and Tom Watson five each, Willie Park Sr, Walter Hagen and Bobby Locke four each, Jamie Anderson, Bob Ferguson, Henry Cotton, Jack Nicklaus, Seve Ballesteros and Tiger Woods three each . . . Getting on for nearly half the Claret Jugs ever won (64) have gone to just 16 golfers.

Maybe Harrington was right; maybe there truly were only a few players capable, in the decisive moments, of keeping their game together over the final stretch. Perhaps the advantage of having won before was greater than any other factor – perhaps knowledge really was stronger than faith.

In which case . . .

As the gossip swirled into the evening, Sweden's Alexander Norén was still waiting by the phone. He was a very fine player, a British Amateur champion, and now the next in line. If anyone dropped out, he would play the Open. Who knows, if that happened, he might hole a putt or two; his entire life might be about to change. Every time he turned on the news there was talk of Ross Fisher's baby. The call might come any time.

It never did. The Open, finally, was closed.

CHAPTER TEN

Day One

Few sporting galas begin with such a marked lack of fuss as the Open. At Turnberry, the first group went out at 6.30 a.m., so most fans, even those who had been looking forward to this moment all year, were asleep when the first shot was struck. The sky was blue; mist spilled off the hills; the sea was as still as a lake; the granite Craig floated like a mirage on the placid water; flags hung limp on the 18th green; and gulls squawked in the fresh morning light. Only a modest knot of early-risers nudged each other around the tee when the first players arrived. The sun was peeping above the red roof of the hotel, and the dew had been swept off the immaculate grass. George Brown had long since given his last pep talk, and his team had given the cool, misty fairways one last lick of loving attention.

Paul Broadhurst was playing in his 14th Open. He had won half a dozen times in Europe, had played in the Ryder Cup, and come here the hard way, through the qualifier at Sunningdale. He had seen a few ups and downs in his golfing life, but was unable to sleep, and rose at 3.45 a.m.

'This is something new for me,' he said. 'Playing first in the Open. I can sleep all I want tonight. I'll be out like a light.'

He was playing with a pair of major-winners in decline: Mark Calcavecchia, the 1989 Open champion, and Michael Campbell, winner of the 2005 US Open. Calcavecchia was supremely unconcerned about the time of day. 'I get up early anyway, it's not a problem for me,' he said. 'I just love coming over here, hanging out with the guys.'

He was not one of those who pretended that fierce competition was the lifeblood, the only motivating force in the world, and that he would not be here if he did not fancy his chance of victory. 'I'm the first to admit I'm not as good as I used to be,' he said. 'My thoughts of winning have pretty much gone out of the window. I'm not in good enough shape.'

The Met Office weather forecast was promising: 'Mostly dry and bright, with sunny spells' and only the 'chance' of a shower. The horses carried on grazing; sheep continued to lie on the damp grass. A generator hummed; a greenkeeper's chariot groaned to a halt on the other side of the gorse.

No detail had been overlooked. Euan Grant, the golf course manager, had set his alarm for 3.10 a.m. and hurried down to meet George Brown and the greenkeepers. Out they went, swarming over the Ailsa like Lilliputians, painting cups white, raking bunkers, fixing divots and grooming greens.

The yardage sheets measured distances to the pin in half-yards.

The first tee is a special place, because golf is a game of constant fresh starts. Hope springs eternal, and the game's delusions are chronic – it is forever erasing itself; every round holds the promise of a new beginning. This is another reason why golf demands a special kind of emptiness: subtle memories need to be left in the locker room. There is no greater enemy of ball-striking than a head swarming with contradictory thoughts. The game requires a determined lack of reflective inhibition.

This first hole, Ailsa Craig, was devised to tease the players. At 354 yards it was short enough to be reachable, but the ball would have to fly a dark expanse of wild rough, and there were four bunkers round the green. The 'safe' route involved an iron and a wedge, but two new bunkers on the left meant that accuracy was required even here. It looked easy on paper, but could fray anyone's nerves. What could be more annoying than playing for safety at the very first hole, and sloshing it into the sand?

While the caddies pulled on their white bibs, Broadhurst shook hands with his playing partners and with Brenda Calcavecchia ('Nice to see you again'), who was carrying her husband's bag. Then the famous starter, Ivor Robson (having denied himself any food or drink the night before to ensure he did not need a comfort break during play), cleared his throat.

The senior R&A officials were all there to see the start of play. Tournament director David Hill rose at five for an urgent appointment with a cup of coffee, before checking the state of play at the gates, the car parks and the catering tents.

'Good morning, ladies and gentlemen,' said Robson. 'May I welcome you to Turnberry for the first day's play in the 138th Open Championship. This is game number one. On the tee for England, Paul Broadhurst!'

Sunlight gleamed on Broadhurst's lilac sweater. He stood on the long shadows cast by the gallery, and struck the first blow of the tournament, a hybrid three-iron, at the bunkers on the corner. Calcavecchia and Campbell followed suit, and all three found the green with their second shots.

No one's putter was warm enough to produce a hot start, so the Open began with three pars. Calcavecchia had most to do; with his wife holding the pin, he tipped his ball in the side door to register a shaky version of a solid start. A heretical thought flickered across the damp grass: was that perhaps the putt that won the Open, or made the cut?

Twenty minutes later, Calcavecchia rolled in a putt at the second and became the first championship leader of the 2009 Open. He had a two-shot lead on Campbell, who had the lesser honour of being the first man (thought not the last) to become entangled in the heavy Turnberry rough.

The first ten players parred the 1st, and it began to seem that far from being a tense risk-reward, this was merely a gentle ramp. But then Mark O'Meara and Oliver Wilson holed putts for birdie, while Nick Watney missed a putt for par, and suddenly, when Calcavecchia gave his shot back at the 3rd, there was action on the leaderboard. Poor Watney: he tugged his approach on the 2nd into a gully left of the green, and while there was gleaming grass down there, it was also home to a mass of red, black and white electric cables. He duffed his chip and was two over par, three behind Calcavecchia. Watney was clad in pure white – he looked like an electrocuted cricketer, or a chic forecourt attendant. Now, on the 3rd tee, he shook his head.

The previous evening, on BBC radio, Bernard Gallacher, a one-time captain of Europe's Ryder Cup team, had been emphasising what a 'fine, fine' player he was, and how he was going to do 'very well' this week. Maybe he would: it was too soon to be categorical. But up in the group ahead, Rory Sabbatini had flopped out of a grass clump and holed a good putt for par, so one of the themes of this year's Open was already coming across loud and clear: missing greens was perilous. They were upturned saucers with slippery crowns, and the lies around the greens were rough and tangled: it was tough to chip up the bank and roll it close to the hole.

Another thing about the raised greens: the gallery could not see the hole. People only knew a putt was straight when it fell. As a result, that rising cheer as a ball neared the hole was nowhere to be heard, so the applause beginning to erupt across the links had a staccato, taken-aback quality.

Out they went, like hopeful onward soldiers marching off to war. Oliver Fisher and Greg Norman strode out together like father and son. Nick Dougherty looked spick and tanned as he secured par and then saw David Duval and Adam Scott miss putts

(Scott failing to be inspired by the lustrous support of his girlfriend, the tennis star Ana Ivanovic). Graeme Storm and Rafa Echenique watched Mark O'Meara's birdie at the first and glimpsed another big theme: the value of 'experience'. Storm could only sigh as his own birdie hung on the lip. Henrik Stenson, Steve Stricker and Liang Wen-Chong played the 1st like another joke-in-progress: have you heard the one about the Swede, the Yank and the Chinaman?

Across Britain (especially in England) sports fans climbed out of bed, switched or logged on, tuned in, wondered whether they could get away with not working, and settled in for the four best days in recent memory. The Open was under way, the Lord's Test would start in a few hours' time. Would anyone object if the phone fell off the hook till Monday?

Tiger Woods was on the range at this time, next to Westwood, belting balls 300 yards and tut-tutting on the rare occasions when they swayed off-line. Golf often seems a slow game, but the ball leaves Tiger's club at around 175 miles an hour, so it is a lot quicker than, say, horse-racing.

No one knew what would be a good score, but in these conditions it was certain to be under par, so after Campbell's dropped shot at the 2nd, and three more at the 3rd, he was ruling himself out rather early in the piece.

The second hole comes back towards the first tee, and ends near the main route out to the rest of the course. The big TV studio was up behind the green, and though at this stage the stands round the 18th were empty, the first tee was bustling. While Dougherty, Duval and Scott sized up their short putts for par, a greenkeeper's van beeped its way along the cart path, and a clamour burst out across the way. Matteo Manassero was stepping on to the 1st in a navy sweater adorned with a small Italian flag. An even heartier cheer greeted Tom Watson, wearing an old-hat, grey-diamond jumper and carrying a putter. But Sergio Garcia won the biggest welcome, a tribute in part to his brilliant play, in part to the fact that he had been seen smiling more than once, and in part because he had come so close to winning one of these things several times now.

It was sobering to think that Manassero's parents had not even met in the long, hot summer Watson beat Nicklaus on this same stretch of sandy soil: the Duel in the Sun was 16 years before young Matteo was born.

Garcia had the honour. Everyone commented on the fizzing sound his ball made, and it was true; it whirred off his club like a startled grouse.

Manassero pulled out a club, put his ball on the tee, took a quick look and cracked it away before anyone in the crowd was quite ready. This speed was universally called 'refreshing', but it was also, well, amateur. He was now in the oh-so-professional world of the five-hour round, and was going to get rather bored waiting for everyone else to inspect shots from every angle, then fall as still and silent as statues, inwardly reciting their positive swing thoughts before allowing their stroke to commence.

It was commonly said of the meticulous Bernhard Langer that though his pre-shot routine was 47 seconds, he could do it in 37 if the referee put him on a stopwatch, and he was not exceptional. Factor in a lost ball here or there, and this could be a time-consuming event.

The grateful cheer that Watson received reflected his standing in the game, rather than his actual game. It hardly seemed to matter that he plonked it down the middle, dropped a nine-iron just six feet from the pin, and rolled in the putt. Fifteen minutes after his first shot, he was one of several joint leaders (the others being Calcavecchia, Wilson and Stricker). It gave him a tangible surge of hope. 'I said, well, this is a continuation of the feeling I had in my practice round. With the wind down, let's take advantage of the old girl and get off to a running start.'

That is exactly what he did. At the second he hit a six-iron to 12 feet and missed, but followed up at the 3rd with a four-iron

to 20 feet and another smooth birdie. All across the course, and
on television screens around the world, a faint murmur of appreciative interest began to stir. It probably wouldn't last, but it was
good to see the old champ doing his thing.

By now the fans, or guests, were streaming over the bridge to the
course, and it didn't look like an Open crowd: the umbrellas were
rolled up, and some were wearing shorts. Cloud hung to the Ailsa
Craig like a signal.

The practice putting green was by the main route into the
course, so several hundred people gathered around to watch the
early starters warm up. The BBC had a studio truck at one end,
and the presenter Gary Lineker stepped out now and then to say
hello to his golfing chums.

A radio reporter grabbed a passing word with Rory McIlroy,
and asked him what was the first thing he did in the morning.

'Wake up,' said McIlroy, moving away fast.

This was no longer a relaxed practice day. Jaws were tight. This
was it.

For most of the fans this was their first glimpse of Ryo
Ishikawa. He certainly looked the part: it was as if Ian Poulter had
run away to the circus. Ishikawa sported turquoise tartan trousers,
a Day-Glo-blue shirt and sleek wraparound shades, while he hit
soft one-handed putts. Lee Westwood, in chunky white flannels
and azure shirt, grinned. Woods was yanking his neck about in
the far corner, where no one could talk to him.

He attracts some criticism for this kind of standoffishness, but
has a problem – insane popularity – which no one but Ishikawa
could imagine.

If anything, the odd thing for Woods today was that he might,
for once, not be the central attraction.

The players had been consulted about this coincidental 'draw'.

'I spoke to Tiger and Lee,' said Dawson, 'and they were both
happy.'

They weren't alone. Darren Clarke was settling his butterflies with a cigarette, Justin Leonard and Robert Allenby were checking their strokes, and Luke Donald was tapping putts. One missed to the left; one slid past the right edge; the third went dead centre. That would have to do.

Donald and Clarke disappeared, with Japan's Azuma Yano, to receive a rapturous home-nations welcome before ploughing off down the first.

It was 9 a.m., but it felt like lunchtime. The first groups were already coming to the lighthouse. But the main event was arriving on the first tee: Woods and Ishikawa were in the alley behind the tall empty grandstand and marching, like actors entering a stage, on to the golf course.

It was not a wise time to ask for autographs, but that didn't stop people. Woods, hands in pockets, strode between thickets of outstretched arms, eyes down. Even if he had wanted to sign, the officials would have tried to prevent him. It would have taken him hours to march 100 yards.

The crowd awaiting them might have been the biggest gallery ever to watch a first-round grouping – and the media presence was remarkable. The R&A had limited the number of Japanese photographers to 15, but there were 35 from the rest of the world, and another 70 or so reporters, analysts, summarisers, technicians, marshals, policemen, rules officials and other attendants jostling for a view inside the ropes. The Masters, in Augusta, does not permit this, but the Open gives the media unbeatable access, even at the risk of upsetting the paying spectators whose view they block. Long lenses poked from the grass like the snouts of beasts.

Woods was well used to media scrums, of course – but this was new, even for him. The cameras were here to snap images of . . . someone else.

Gloomy clouds were gathering overhead. The delicious clear light of the early morning was turning into a mild, damp, grey Ayrshire day.

This was the point at which the BBC's coverage began. Hazel Irvine invited viewers to settle in for 'every shot' of the Open – an unsettling remark, since the cameras had already missed at least a thousand in the two and a half hours so far. The coverage may be magnificent, but it does not include 'every shot'. At any one time it can track no more than half a dozen players (one of whom, inevitably, is Woods).

'On the tee from USA,' sang Robson's high burr, 'Tiger Woods!'

'Play well, guys,' said the main man, stepping up to his ball.

A charged silence fell upon the scene. There came a rustle of polite applause from behind the starter's hut – someone tapping in at the 2nd, by the sound of it – but otherwise there was a tremendous, clotted stillness in the air. Then Woods cracked his ball away, and a chorus of camera clicks streamed after it, like bats swarming from a cave.

In the distance, Clarke and Donald were walking onto the 1st green and missing birdie putts. From this distance it looked like snooker, on a vast, landscaped cloth. Donald, dapper and tidy, had hit his ball high and soft to the flag, but his putt refused to fall. Was that, one wondered (just for the cruel fun of it), the putt that would end up costing him the Claret Jug?

Woods and Westwood fired their irons down the centre, clean into a shallow gathering area already pockmarked by divots. Ishakawa took a greedier line up the right, and stayed in the light rough.

Woods hit to ten feet, Westwood to six.

Ishikawa lagged up and holed for par.

Woods allowed too much break; Westwood eased it in.

Minus-one: a good start.

On the 2nd, Woods wafted his ball to seven feet and holed. Swish. But then, on the 3rd, he pulled a rash tee shot into a TV tower on the left. A gang of photographers rushed to take pictures of his ugly lie, but he was in luck: he was allowed a drop, away from the temporary obstruction. He shoved a tee in the ground, tossed the ball to caddie Steve Williams for cleaning, and let it fall into deep grass two driver-lengths away.

'Come on,' he muttered.

Not surprisingly, the ball scurried on through the back of the green, and for once he failed to get up and down from the fringe. His chip was a duff, and he ended up having to hole a beady-eyed five-footer for bogey.

Back to square one.

It didn't seem to matter: he hadn't become the world's best player by being a metronome. He often started poorly, like this; one of his strengths was his ability to locate his game mid-round. Time after time he had come back from lapses that would have sapped the will of lesser players.

Half a dozen holes ahead, Tom Watson was stuttering too. So far it had been one of those days where nothing goes awry, but at the twisting par-five 7th he made a tiny mistake and pushed his second into a greenside bunker. It looked as though his brief honeymoon was about to end. Thanks to those early birdies he was still two under par, but this was tricky, and might well signal the beginning of his slide back into the pack.

He didn't waste any time. He shuffled his feet into the sand, slid his wedge firmly beneath the ball, clipped it up almost vertically, and raised the club in meek acknowledgement when the ball landed smack over the hole. And in the sustained burst of applause, something stirred, some hungry communal recognition that rose above (or dug beneath) mere sentiment. Up till now Watson had been lapping up a warmth inspired by old glories. But this one had nothing to do with age, experience, medical intervention or folksy charm – it was skill, pure and simple, and the crowd saw it at once. He missed the putt for birdie, but even so, this was the moment when his Open began in earnest. It was only a par, at a hole where the top contenders hoped for more, but it announced that something was afoot out here, something none of us had seen before.

At the 9th he got up and down from a bunker again, and at the spectacular 10th, with its tee at the foot of the lighthouse, he carried the rocky shore safely and fired a six-iron to 12 feet. When that went in too, he was three under par, and the crowd, like a kicked beehive, was awake and buzzing.

Long forgotten shouts began to tumble from the stands.

'Come on, Tom.'

'Go for it, Tommy.'

'You've still got it, Tom.'

While all eyes and lenses were on Woods and Ishikawa, Westwood was helping himself to three birdies on the first three holes. He hadn't been lying when he said he didn't mind a bit of 'atmosphere'. He looked rock-still over the ball, and the writhing tension around him seemed to sharpen his calm. Thanks to Watson's miss on the seventh, he was the pacesetter on his own.

The 4th was a trim par-three, right on the beach, called 'Woe-Be-Tide', a clumsy tribute to the water on the left-hand side. It was a notable beauty spot, and Westwood kept his eye off the tall bank on the right, encrusted with photographers, and laid an emphatic iron four feet from the hole. He missed, and grimaced – could one afford to blow chances like that?

Ishikawa holed from a greater distance to register his first Open birdie. He was dashing, colourful, adventurous . . . and also, it seemed, skilful.

Tiger Woods is rarely last in a three-man group. He didn't look happy.

Every eleven minutes, three new players stepped into the arena, and suddenly things were beginning to tumble and accelerate. Westwood backed away from his tee shot at the 6th, disturbed by an apologetic cameraman who murmured something about it being an 'accident'. As he walked down the steep slope, he could hear applause from the 17th green just inland to his right, where Calcavecchia was collecting a tap-in birdie to join him on minus-three. A minute later, a more sustained burst up by the lighthouse announced that someone – perhaps Watson, to judge by the happy laugh that lay in the heart of the cheer – had done something good.

It was Watson's birdie at the 10th, and the crowd was hoisting him on its figurative shoulders. Spectators began to change their plans, and head for the back nine. How many more opportunities would there be to see Watson in full flight? This might be his last hurrah. And the turmoil round Woods was so obstructive you could hardly see anything, anyway.

Now there were three co-leaders. Others were advancing and retreating like the tide. Michael Campbell, nursing an injury, was a shadow of his former self, and needed par at the last for an embarrassing 78. Duval dropped two shots on the first three holes. Norman was double-bogeying the 5th to fall a brutal six shots behind the leaders.

The much-fancied Henrik Stenson was stumbling at two over par, but Graeme McDowell, a Northern Irishman well used to this kind of golf, had stolen two early birdies to put his name high on the boards.

Of course it was too early to read much into these beginnings, but good starts help – they both indicate and breed confidence. Nothing succeeds like success. It was also clear that even in these conditions the Ailsa had teeth. A missed fairway spelled various depths of trouble.

Garcia, not to be outdone by Watson's sand shot, had stabbed in an eagle on the 7th, and Stricker, still flushed from victory a few days earlier, helped himself to birdies on the 2nd and 8th.

Both slipped up at the 9th, however. Garcia had six feet for par, but – story of his life – missed. He wasn't alone. The 9th, like the 10th, was a special place, built above the ruins of the castle;

but the fairway was not visible from the tee (Jack Nicklaus once called it only a 'rumour'), and was a hog's back designed to throw balls off on both sides.

Another of the strong, underrated Americans, Stewart Cink, had birdied both the par-threes, no easy feat. The 6th, in particular, was a beast, requiring a big shot (231 yards) across a valley to a raised green protected by three bunkers set in steep, unforgiving banks.

Several of the players were fooling with their mobiles this week, posting messages to e-groups. Watson was not interested ('I don't tweet'), but Poulter and Cink had already attracted a large fan base to their one-liners.

Reading them, it looked as though Woody Allen was safe.

'Morning Open viewers,' wrote Poulter. 'Watching the golf this morning on TV. It's flat, calm and no rain there – I'm staying five miles away and it's pouring.'

Poulter seemed on the brink of a big win, but this didn't bode well. He had sent out press releases announcing what he was going to wear, and knew that the papers would print these advertisements as if they were scoops. But rain was spitting from a heavy sky, and Scottish wind was no respecter of colour-coordinated stormwear.

On the 7th, when Woods found the rough again, Westwood followed him in. Then a wheel came off. It did not help Woods's darkening mood that a television buggy had been abandoned in his line, so he waited, glowering, for its red-faced owner to weave away. But then he forced the ball close to the green, rolled it close with his putter, and holed for birdie. It was almost as though he needed adversity. Somehow, despite his unrivalled success – perhaps the first billionaire sportsman in history – he was striving to cultivate an embattled, world's-against-me quality.

Westwood, less fortunate with his lie, floundered his way through the long grass and made bogey – or double bogey really;

this generous 538-yard hole could be reached in two (provided the tee shot avoided the rough on the left and the sand on the right). So this was a rich moment. Westwood had played superbly and was two under par; Woods had been a walking horror show, yet by seizing this chance was only a stroke behind. Of all the reasons for his dominion over the game, this was the most telling: he could carve it around like a cab-driver, and still haul in a score.

As Westwood sank back, Australia's John Senden found a third consecutive birdie at the 15th to scoot past him into the joint lead.

That's how it is, on the first day of an Open: the Championship has no shape. On the second day, the leaders would be looking to consolidate their position, and there would also be the race to make the cut. On the third day (so-called 'moving day'), the contenders know that they need to stay in touch with the lead to have a realistic chance of victory, so the golf resembles the pre-race time trials in Formula One. The final day produces the winner, and greets the players emphatically with triumph or disaster. But the first day is a free-for-all. Anything can happen, at any time. It is the hardest to follow, but in some ways the best: each birdie might be the start of a run; missed putts can be decisive. It is no day for a long lunch.

Some of these early tremors would turn out to be significant in the larger scheme of things; others would dissolve into the general story. But the Claret Jug was not the only prize. For some, just being here was a giddy triumph in itself. 'As a player,' said Daniel Gaunt, 'words can't really describe it. Back when I was playing practice rounds with my brother, it was always, this putt's for the Open. It's always been the tournament, and actually to be here, playing in it, well, as I say, words can't describe . . .'

At Final Qualifying he had spoken about giving himself just three weeks to make enough money to continue – he was nearly at the end of his tether – but now he was trying to forget or move beyond such remarks.

'I was angry with my swing. But the fact is, I've worked my butt off trying to do this. I don't know how many people are working in a shop 12 hours a day to earn entry fees, but it's something I do. And it's hard. But if I got to be 40 and didn't do anything, I know I'd look back and think, Why didn't I take the gamble? So I am taking the gamble. This is it.'

When John Senden swiped another birdie on the 17th hole he lit a bright beacon for Daniel Gaunt and everyone else like him in the field. The last man into the Open was in first place. Truly, anything could happen.

Senden, fired by the euphoria of gaining a foothold, parred the first dozen holes – the best run of pars, it would turn out, in the entire day. He would have been happy to par his way home from there, but fate had a better idea. At the 13th he hit a seven-iron to 30 feet and holed for birdie; at the 14th he hit a six-iron to 20 feet and rolled that in too; at the 15th he hit a tee shot to six feet for three in a row. After parring the 16th, he hit his long approach to the 17th into the left hand-bunker, splashed out and holed another unfeasibly long putt to top the leaderboard with 66.

By this stage he was getting greedy. When he missed a make-able birdie on the 18th he tilted his head, as if cross with himself. But he knew as well as anyone that though the birdies were the gilt on the gingerbread, it was the run of pars (not all of them solid) that built the foundations of his day. 'I hit the ball well,' he said. 'Especially early on. I had a couple of good saves. That kept the momentum up.'

When Senden left the 18th he walked through the gap in the grandstands, put his lucky coin back in its lucky pouch and stood for interviews like a patient horse. Outside, Ernie Els was trying to find his old putting stroke on the practice green – he was due on the 1st tee in a few minutes' time.

Senden wasn't laughing at the irony of the thing. 'Any man can come here and win,' he said. 'I have a chance. Everyone has a chance.' He had not been to these parts since 1994, when he tried to qualify. 'That's right, I was outside the ropes, watching. I remember seeing Nicklaus, Norman, Watson and Price have a practice round. That was pretty special.'

He had just matched Nicklaus's Duel in the Sun score. That was pretty special too.

The turn at Turnberry is among the prettiest places in the golfing world: the rocks, the lighthouse, the sea, the islands, the sky, the curve of beach, the clumps of harebell and heather – it is heroic golfing scenery. Woods could barely see it for red mist. At the 9th his approach scuttled along the ground, and he swished his club in fury. At the 10th he was so disgusted by his tee shot that he hurled his club away with a curse.

He had been attracting behind-the-hand remarks about this sort of thing for a while; many believed (in truth there was not much doubt about it) that a lesser player would not be permitted such histrionics. But while golf's spotless restraint was important publicity, so was Tiger's glamorous intensity. If he seemed to be flaring up too often, well, who were we to complain?

It was a reminder, either way, that golf, even at this high pitch, is maddening. And its frustrations are unavoidable because the better a player becomes, the higher soar his expectations. A fat three-iron that might inspire a novice to throw his hat into the air (anyone care for a drink?) would leave a Woods looking thunderous, ready to punch someone. The world's best player – an enviable thing to be – looked frantically unhappy. Golfers are like swans: their steady gait and imperturbable manner is a pose achieved by willpower – we cannot see the frantic paddling beneath the water. There seems to be no calm plateau on which they can relax.

The unvarnished fact is that, by definition, you only hit your best shot once. But golfers are greedy: even duffers want to hit their best one every time. And most are deluded enough to believe these to be their true self, exemplary chips off their golfing soul rather than rare aberrations bound, by the law of averages, to happen every now and then. One of the ugliest disciplines in golf is that you are only as good as your worst stroke.

To digress: I once heard a cheerful coach in Florida ask a group of golfers whether they were, by any chance, looking for more consistency. Every single hand went up – not surprisingly, since 'consistency' is the game's Holy Grail. The coach startled them (were they paying to be insulted?) by saying that they should give themselves a pat on the back. 'I've been watching you,' he confided. 'And you're all consistent, each and every one of you. You do the same damn wrong thing every time.'

It was a nice reminder that golf, as Padraig Harrington's 'mind coach' Bob Rotella would put it, was 'not a game of perfect', but a quest. As Woods once observed, if it were perfectible it would lose its grip: with a bit of practice we could all knock it round in 18 strokes, and need a new game.

This, oddly, is what computer-golf resembles. Absent-minded teenagers can biff a few bright pixels round digitised versions of St Andrews in 51, sending texts with their spare hand.

When Calcavecchia rapped in for par on the last he became the clubhouse leader on minus-three. This was no great feat: he had only beaten his two playing partners, one of whom (Campbell) was ready to quit. But it was a good score, and he was a fetching story: a 49-year-old former champion still able to bash it around the links. He would do – until Watson, who had just hit a soft seven-iron at the 12th flag to go to minus-four, finished – as a stick with which to beat the pampered modern game, with its tranquil greens, toothless rough, imported sand and computer-generated water hazards.

He was even happy with his caddie. 'We get along great,' he

said of Mrs Calcavecchia. 'If anything goes wrong it's my fault. It's just something I enjoy. She gave me a couple of good reads and a lot of cute smiles. But she knows what she's doing out there. When it started raining on 16, she said, "Don't worry about me, I don't care if I get soaked." The bag weighed a ton today, and she's got to be exhausted. But she's doing great.'

Behind him, the field was trembling. It was only the middle of the day, but the early starters were marching in fast now. The tide was out, and the sea still looked like a pond. A big Hugo Boss yacht posed out by the lighthouse, but all it could do was drift about in this sudden micro-doldrum.

At the 10th Woods three-putted for bogey, a rare sight; but at the 11th Manassero found the cup to join the maestro on level par, an impressive move. Matthew Goggin, like Senden a late reserve, rolled one in to go to three-under, and David Howell provoked an appreciative rumble in the media tent by birdying the 9th to complete the outward half in 31 (four under par). As always, Woods willed it close on the 11th and forced himself below par again. But he gave the shot back at the 15th. It just wasn't his day.

Garcia looked like he was getting sick of the applause for Watson and Manassero. Of the three, he was the one with the best game, the best chance. And finally, at the 15th, his ball ran true into the hole. A miracle! He was two-under. If he had let his caddie putt for him he might well have been in the lead, but he was close, as golfers say, to where he wanted to be.

The 16th was the most altered hole on the course; it was a left-to-right dog-leg, making the burn running across the front right of the green a far more dangerous hazard, since players had to come towards it, not merely over. And it looked as though the R&A wanted to show off their new toy, because the pin was in a brutal position, on the sharp slope at the front. Balls that pitched by the flag would ricochet down into the stream. No wonder there was a grandstand here.

On the tee Garcia, with an iron in his hand, cried, 'Fore left!' –
not so much a warning as a plea to the ball-spotters on the outer
limb of the dog-leg. It worked: they spotted the ball. But his
approach plummeted down behind the green, leaving a nasty
downhill chip that would be hard to stop. If it got past the hole,
it would accelerate.

He coaxed it on to the green with enviable delicacy, but the
ball dribbled on and on and on, like a drip of rain on a wind-
screen, paused at the hole, then wandered on, gathered pace and
sped down into the water.

He took a drop, played a fine chip, but could not hole the putt.
Just like that, the two shots he had spent the day gaining were
snatched away.

The received wisdom is that you cannot win the Open on the
first day but you can lose it. This is consoling, yet means only that
you have time to make up lost ground, a luxury not available at
the end. And there was no hiding from the fact that Garcia's
Open boat had just taken an ugly dent, and was shipping water.
He was the kind of player who thrived with wind in his sails.
Two under par was a platform from which he could launch an
assault. Level par was a flat tyre.

Watson knew this hole well; it was not one to take liberties
with. He found the middle of the fairway, plonked his ball safely
over the flag, and cosied it to the hole for par. When he birdied
the par-five 17th (the old-fashioned way, by chipping on and
holing an eight-footer) the five-time winner was in front again.
Par at the last would see him home as the leader.

His drive carried to the light fringe on the far side of the fairway, just over 200 yards from the pin. He took a seven-iron, the
same club he had used to stab Nicklaus in the heart, more or less
from this spot, 32 years earlier.

'The most important thing is the right weight,' he said. 'And
that shot came out the way I wanted. I hit it flush.'

The first putt ran five feet past, but if this day had a theme, it was that Old Tom Watson had given way to his younger self, to the man who did not miss chances like this.

'This to take the lead,' whispered Peter Alliss, to the television audience.

The ball rolled at the hole and dropped. Watson beamed, took his black cap off, and turned to congratulate Manassero on his own fine round.

'Well done, Tom,' said Alliss, in the avuncular, told-you-so tone that grates on some viewers.

The kitchens in the tented village were starting to serve lunch, and the Aberdeen Angus burger hutch was sending a plume of smoke across the grass. Watson was ushered off the green to a microphone.

'I enjoyed it out there,' he said, 'though I suspect 65 will not be leading come the end of the day.'

What did it feel like to be 'rolling back the years'?

'I don't live in the past,' he said. 'But obviously what happened in 1977 is at the forefront of a lot of conversations. Some of the kids playing today weren't even born then.'

It was left to Sergio Garcia to give his achievement the proper weight.

'I think if Watson plays the way he played today,' he said, 'he can beat Tiger Woods and everyone else. He flushed it. The only thing he could ask from Tiger was length, but he hit quality shots, as well as anyone.'

Yeah, yeah. Who wanted to hear that Watson was good at golf? He had a chance because he was old, because he was experienced, because he was channelling the spirit world, and because he loved Scotland. The idea that he was simply very good at hitting a ball with a stick – please.

It was unlikely that there would be a finer story for the newspapers than 'Watson Born Again', so he was escorted to the media tent to amplify on what he had just done. He was an old hand, and saved everyone the effort of bringing up the subject by declaring, as soon as he sat down, that he had detected 'something spiritual' about his day. He had received a message, he confided ('a modern text'), from Barbara Nicklaus to say that she and her husband were watching and thinking of him, and wishing him luck.

'I texted her back and said, "We really miss you over here." And I really meant it. It's not the same without Jack.'

He could not have said anything more disarming, given the media's appetite for sentimental drama. Pressed for further memories, he recalled the time, in 1994, when he missed putt after putt with 'these hammer mitts', and ended up losing the Open to Nick Price. 'That was about the most disappointing tournament I ever had. I really, really felt I could win, but the putter totally let me down.' After a consoling dinner ('and a couple of bottles of wine'), he and Nicklaus had sneaked down to the hotel's pitch-and-putt for a friendly game. 'It was about eleven o'clock at night. And here comes the security man. And I said, "Jack, you go talk to him." And the guy, he starts walking up sternly, he's going to run us off the course, and then it was, "Oh, Mr Nicklaus. Carry on, please."'

For Watson, there was more than easy sentiment to these tales. He was trying to explain that he knew and liked it here. The memories weren't just sugar frosting: they were of tangible pragmatic value.

'I've played this course, what, in six championships now. And I have to admit I do play off the memories of '77. That helps you. I can stand up there on the 15th hole and say, I cut this four-iron in there against a crosswind. I know that helps me. That's experience. Experience wins.'

Was Watson seriously saying he hoped to prevail this week? It seemed a presumptuous thought. But he had been to hundreds of these conferences, and knew what the room wanted. Nothing goes down so well in golfing circles as a wry reference to advancing years, so when Watson admitted that 'when you

get to my age', it was as if Woody Allen had blown in. The
media like to seem cynical, 'hard-bitten', but in fact give the
top priority to weepy drama. For one instant Watson's mask
slipped ('I hit a lot of quality shots,' he admitted), but no one
wanted to hear about them. He had played well because he was
old, because he was a legend, because he had a false hip,
because Turnberry had a special 'aura', because, dammit, he
was nice.

It was noticeable, however, that an awful lot of people out on
the course, queuing politely for tea and sandwiches, waiting at
crossways for stewards to let them through, lending each other
binoculars and swapping spine-relief tips, were the same age as
Watson, and none of them could play like him. He was the
exception, not the rule. He wasn't even proving that old men
could play golf – just that one old man could.

Shaking himself back to the present day, he cut to the chase.

'How am I going to do? That's what you all want to know.
How am I going to do in the next three rounds? Well, I don't
know. I wish I could tell you. I wish I could tell you that I'm
going to break the Open record . . . We'll just have to see where
it comes to.'

This was true and helpful, but the cat was out of the bag, gam-
bolling in the spotlight. In mentioning a 'spiritual' feeling – 'the
serenity of it was pretty neat' – Watson had given a grand day an
even greater resonance.

It was, as it happened, his best-ever first round in an Open.

All the dials were spinning now. The leaderboards were flicker-
ing like the departures screens at airports. Greg Norman was
finishing with a distressing 77, but Steve Stricker snared one last
birdie for a racy 66.

It was a fine effort, but he was a bit dazed. He still had an
'emotional hangover' from the previous week, when he won the
John Deere Classic on Sunday and jumped on a red-eye flight. 'I

kissed my wife and kids goodbye and I was on the plane and I was here. It is almost like last week didn't happen.'

Stewart Cink had a putt on the 15th to go five-under, but just – thank goodness – missed. No one wanted Watson to be caught. He might not win, but it would be nice if he could be permitted one last day in the sun.

The slender Colombian, Camilo Villegas, was producing a storming late run, birdying the last three to jump into the limelight with Senden on 66. He was no newcomer, but there was still confusion about his name (Vee-yay-gas). Thanks to his time in Barcelona, the BBC's Gary Lineker had enough Spanish to pronounce the double-l as a 'j' – Vee-jay-gas – and enough authority to make this the standard version. But South American Spanish had its own rules, which seemed to have been mislaid here.

Woods was still playing as if in a gale. On 13 he railed at his ball – 'Don't do that! Don't do that! Goddammit!' – as it flew the green, and then, fuming, he tanked a tee shot into the heavy rough that lined the 14th. It was unexpectedly moving to see him playing so badly. Like a bruised prizefighter driven repeatedly to his knees, he refused to surrender, and kept dragging himself up again to face the next blow. Somehow he clawed his ball back into play, got it somewhere close to the hole, and made what Peter Alliss, on television, called a 'rather scruffy four'. The putt circled the rim like a spinning coin before falling, a piece of fortune he acknowledged with an ironic bow.

Ishikawa still had his sunglasses on, though the sky was gloomy again. And while Westwood and Woods tried to plot routes short of or between bunkers, the bashful prince continued to blast it at distant targets. Along with his other attributes, he had nerve, and he was holding things together very well. When he blazed it at the short 15th and slid home a birdie, he went below par. He was, beneath all the razzmatazz, only 17.

Woods bogeyed that hole, but worse was to come. At the dangerous 16th, Westwood, who had put barely a foot wrong, leaked his approach right and into the burn. Woods, amazingly, followed him in. ('It was 20 yards right of where I was aiming. It was not a good shot.')

At the 17th Tiger didn't dare take his driver, even though an eagle would have put him right back on track; but his three-wood wasn't a friend either – he pummelled it 275 yards into the gallery out by the 6th green. The lie wasn't bad, but the recovery shot was: it stayed in the rough. Once again he saved par, but on this hole that was a dropped shot.

'Goddammit, Tiger,' he snarled, one last time, before finishing with par for a not-dreadful 71 – a better score than at times seemed likely.

'I certainly made a few mistakes out there,' he agreed, for once declining to relive his round in detail. Instead he headed for the range with his puncture repair kit.

It might not have helped that Ishikawa had flicked home a birdie at the 17th to complete a fine two-under-par 68, a more than impressive first effort.

Westwood's 68, meanwhile, was 'as bad as it could have been', he felt. All he could see were dropped shots. 'I didn't birdie the par-five, the 7th. I made a double at the 16th, and then didn't birdie the 17th . . .'

Normally a sanguine man, he was trembling at the thought of what might have been. 'I could have gone out in 29 quite easily,' he said.

This was one of those bad news–good news remarks. It was a shame he had failed to make the most of it. On the other hand, he was in very good form indeed.

Little had been heard or seen of Luke Donald. He did not feature in the television coverage, and was therefore ignored by the radio team, and was therefore unable to make an impression on anyone not walking with his group. But he holed a long putt on 18 to recover from a so-so start and finished with one over par, the same as Woods. This score would prove the most popular tally of the day: 28 players would settle on 71.

David Howell was three shots better off. He hit a reef at the 15th, where he missed the green and fluffed a chip; and though he salvaged a bogey he went right on and dropped a shot at the 16th too. Annoyed, he leaked another at the 17th (a birdie opportunity if ever there was one), and suddenly he had tossed away three of the shots he had gained on the front nine. It might make a funny speech one day, but he wasn't smiling at the time. Fortunately, or bravely, he holed a putt at the last to go back to minus-two, a score he would have settled for at the start of the day.

It was a fair return to form for a man who had been able to play only four tournaments so far this year, after dislodging his back helping a friend lug a washing machine downstairs. 'My crazy decision to move into the removals industry,' he said, 'wrecked the first half of my season.'

At two o'clock Ian Poulter attempted to turn the Open into a catwalk for his own-brand designer sportswear, and it didn't take long for people to query his priorities. He was wearing a Union Jack waistcoat with mock-tartan trousers, and looked, some said, like a Spice Girl in royal bunting.

His playing partner, Miguel Angel Jiménez, was too bluff a fellow (nickname: 'the Mechanic') to be flustered. He was wearing different shades of biscuit-beige: good camouflage wear for bunker play.

Yet while he laid up in front of the bunkers, Poulter went straight in.

It was no surprise. Poulter is likeably cocksure, but look-at-me clothes require booming play to avoid looking preening or idiotic. Senden wore blue, Watson grey. Quiet uniform clearly worked. Poulter shovelled his ball out, chipped past the flag and missed. Then he bogeyed the 4th and 5th. 'I couldn't have done worse with a set of spades,' he said.

Jiménez, in contrast, made a case for the wet-sand look by

nailing three birdie putts to reach the turn at minus-four, seven strokes clear of the limp British flag.

A little while later, Paul Casey birdied the 1st, the 3rd and the 5th and eagled the 7th to reach the turn in 31 strokes as well. It felt almost tidal; while some players came home, others were still setting out. The course shivered with the sound of golf, which has many distinctive notes. Here on this treeless shore there would be no ball-on-wood clatter, or ball-into-windscreen chime. But there were, drowning out the birds, planes and rising wind, the noises of the crowd. There is a language to the whoops and sighs that echo in the hummocks of an Open: there's the missed putt hmmmm, the so-close aaahhhh, the how-did-that-miss gasp, the sympathetic oooh, the knowing, nodding yeeeeees, the astonished woof, the encouraging growl, the buoyant roar and half a dozen other distinctive trills.

That deep, rolling, sustained cheer, for instance, could only mean that Jiménez had holed another putt to join Watson on minus-five.

In truth, for on-course spectators the state of play can only be followed by radio, so the R&A sells small tuners on neck ribbons with headphones that broadcast their own temporary station, Radio Open Golf.

They are great, though it soon becomes apparent that the commentators are in a booth somewhere, watching television. You could sit in a stand at the 18th green, watch David Howell chip up to the hole, tap in, wave, wander off and disappear – and a few minutes later the commentary would cut, as if live, to 'Here comes Howell, chipping at 18.' A wind that looked to the imprisoned pundits like a 'gentle zephyr' might well be ripping caps off out by the lighthouse, where seagulls flapped impotently into the gale. Either that, or time really does stand still at the Open.

A new and unfamiliar name suddenly appeared on the leaderboards. Jeremy Kavanagh had learned a lot from his practice days with Watson, Norman, Stricker and Glover, and was scorching through the front nine to reach the turn in three under par. He was playing with Daniel Gaunt, who was having a less happy introduction to Open golf, double-bogeying the awkward 6th and then dropping strokes at 8 and 9 as well.

It is not a pleasant feeling to look across at your playing partner, at this early stage, and realise that you are seven shots adrift.

That was nothing, however, compared with the misfortunes of the young American, Anthony Kim. Suffering from a ricked neck, he came to the second hole, drove the ball into the rough and then snaggled it into a fairway bunker. His third shot stayed in the sand; so did his fourth; so did his fifth.

Welcome to Scotland.

While all this was happening, Padraig Harrington was grinning on the 1st tee for all the world like a man who had won this thing the last two times, and expected to do so again. His quick, crisp swing swatted the ball away and he was off, quick and jaunty, teeth bared, splay-footed – with the rolling gait that Alliss liked to call 'a touch of the drunken sailor'.

At the 2nd his approach ran off the green, but he chipped up the bank to five feet, and holed. On the third he drove into the rough, blasted it up near the green with a rescue club and again chipped close; at the 6th he banged in a birdie, and he missed a chance on the 7th, before somehow saving par on the 8th from an awful tangle of grass beside the green. It was in many ways a typical, combative Harrington opening: by scrapping for every shot, and seeming to relish the trickiest ones, he was one under par, right in contention, when he might easily have been several over.

Rory McIlroy had the opposite experience. He was fancied to repeat the fine form he had showed in his first Open, as an amateur at Carnoustie in 2007; and he nearly took this one by storm. From the word go he swished the ball with the whiplash swing that was now the envy of almost every golf observer; he picked up birdies at the 3rd and 7th, and nearly holed two more. But at the 8th he took a slightly greedy line, dragged the ball into long grass, and, striving to get it up the fairway, clomped it only 20 yards into even longer rough. Fortunately it flopped close to the feet of his coach, Michael Bannon, who promptly embarked on a determined search. As the minutes passed, it looked bad, but then the ball appeared right beneath Bannon's feet. It was, McIlroy knew, 'a bit ugly'. Sometimes, he said to himself, double bogey was a good score.

It might, he knew, have been worse. But he was back where he started.

He blazed up the 9th and holed a putt for birdie, then flew his drive into the rough once more. This time, more cautious, he took a drop, and played a wonderful mid-iron approach to limit the damage to one stroke.

'You have to take your medicine,' he said.

This was true, but it had a bitter taste. Barring a couple of loose shots, he could have been half a dozen under par. It was a hard lesson: one slip and you could lose everything.

John Daly came to the first tee determined not to let Poulter steal the show. He was wearing a pair of brilliant-green-and-yellow clown's trousers, and he too dropped a shot at the supposedly easy opener. Was it possible that hand-eye timing mattered more than disco colour schemes. Who would have thought it?

Daly was one of many players with a bad back, and watching him spin his weight around his spine, it was small wonder. 'If they rub it any more I'm going to feel like a piece of gingerbread,' he said.

But he was quite good at rising above such nuisances. He had realised in practice that he would not be needing his driver on these narrow fairways, so he took a hybrid four-iron and bent the loft down to 12 degrees to keep it lower. That wasn't all. 'I cut the shaft about an inch to get it a bit stiffer . . . hit about 200 balls on the range and fell in love with it.'

On the 7th he horseshoed around the cup with his second shot, which nearly dropped for an albatross. Who knows, if he had been wearing black and white like everyone else, it might have dived in.

Far ahead of the fashion parade, Stewart Cink was standing tall, holding his high swirly follow-through, and bombing his second up the 17th. A few moments later, he bagged his sixth birdie of the round to join Tom Watson at the top of the leaderboard, on five under par. He was one of those excellent American players – along with Furyk, Leonard, Stricker and many others – who did not much feature on the European television radar, which noticed little besides Woods and Mickelson. As a result he tended to be dismissed as 'steady' or 'reliable' or 'solid' – faintly disparaging terms for a condition to which all golfers aspire. It is hardly more glamorous to be unsteady, unreliable and airy.

On the 18th Cink made his first mistake of the day, and found the bunker left of the fairway. He hacked it out, played to the green and missed the par putt. Perhaps it was for the best. It was early in the afternoon of the first day, and the media were already happy to have their story: the return of Old Tom Watson. The next best headline was the awful form of Woods. No one was much interested in other challengers.

There was still a bit of mileage in Lyle, however. He came off after a 75 – not too terrible – and spoke to reporters. Obviously he would not be so foolish as to say anything further on the subject, but, hello, here we went again. 'Monty,' he said, was 'milking it a little bit' – an odd description of someone who had resolutely said nothing. 'We do sometimes call him a bit of a drama queen,' he said, trying to act the wronged party.

As he spoke, Monty was dropping shots on the back nine. But he won a handsome cheer at the last, when he popped in a putt for birdie and a first-round 71 (four better than Lyle, thank you very much).

Padraig Harrington just carried on scrambling. At the 15th he clutched his head when a putt for minus-two stalled at the hole, and then he made a mistake at the 16th. But though he scuffed his second at the par-five, it scuttled like a hare past the bunker and on to the green. He had an eagle putt. Hole it, and he would be, somehow, within spitting distance of the lead.

In the past few years he had proved himself to be very good at clutch moments such as this. This time, success eluded him, and he failed to exploit another chance on the 18th too.

He had played, he felt, with a 'slight amount of trepidation'. He hadn't attacked the pins with his irons, or holed many putts. 'But you know,' he added, with his earnest grin, 'one shot ain't going to make a difference when it comes to Sunday.'

This was good therapy, but was it true? It was all very well to say that missed putts in round one were, in the context of the Championship as a whole, just tiddlers that got away – of no importance in the final result – but shots gained here could reap big psychological dividends.

There was something else. The monthly golf magazines were all swollen by Open pull-outs, and one included an interview with Harrington in which he explained that his own lack of experience around Turnberry meant nothing, since it was shared by all the leading contenders.

'I don't think there's anybody who's played this golf course competitively,' he said firmly, 'that's going to be in contention.'

Did he perhaps shiver when he said those words? Did the ghost of Tom Watson not drift into his peripheral vision? Evidently not.

Paul Casey was living up to his warm billing as the new best player in the world rankings after Woods and Mickelson, collecting no fewer than five threes in the first seven holes to reach the turn on minus-four. Jim Furyk, meanwhile, was completing a fine score (67) that left him only half-pleased. 'Everybody is going to come off the course saying they could have done better,' he said. 'I putted well during the practice rounds, but didn't do a good job today.'

Perhaps the flat feeling came in part from the emptiness of the stands around this final green. The classic amphitheatre was in place, and had been for weeks; but the crowd (more than 20,000 paying spectators) were out there, not in here. The famous eighteenth green thrust between the stands like the prow of a ship, the traditional yellow pennant fluttering bravely on the tip.

People talk in hushed tones about the spine-tingling atmosphere on this sporting stage, but in the early rounds it feels provisional. The one-way system, with one staircase allowing people in and another letting them out, means a constant process of change; some leave, others arrive, and there is a rapid turnover. When Harrington putted out, people abandoned the scene like water being sucked out of a plug. By the time Stuart Appleby walked up, acknowledging the non-existent cheers with a raised club, for form's sake, the only noise was the sound of feet shuffling on temporary flooring and metal stairs.

When Davis Love hit his second to four feet, the bored, indifferent footsteps barely paused to notice. Was it for this that he had burned his way around 36 holes in Texas, to qualify? He walked past the bunker and holed the putt for an aw-shucks round of 69, which was a more heroic effort than it seemed: after three bogeys on the outward half he had sprinted back under par by completing the back nine in just 32 blows.

You wouldn't know it to look at him. He shook hands with a detached, businesslike air and walked off to the scorers' tent . . . and as the few remaining spectators looked at the abandoned green, a voice in their ear said, 'Quickly to 18 to see Davis Love. This for birdie. Come on, Davis.'

A few minutes later, an Australian man and his girlfriend tried to get into this deserted grandstand, only to find their way barred. The whole gaping maw was reserved for 'composite' ticket holders – people (mainly corporations) who had bought a seat for the entire four-day contest – and the rule was: no admittance.

'We only want to be here for a few minutes,' said the visitor, gazing at the empty acreage of wet plastic. 'That's my brother coming on to the green.'

The steward took pity on him, and Christ Gaunt, having missed out on qualifying himself (by one stroke), was able to perch in an empty stand, and watch his brother Daniel competing in the world's great golf championship. His score was disappointing – five over par – but it was better than Nick Faldo, by no means a bad player, even if he was a bit of a laughing stock this week for having his knighthood emblazoned on his bag. He was no longer Nick; he was Sir Nick, and don't you forget it.

The smart alecs decided to call him 'Snick' and have done with it.

'This is just great for Daniel,' said Chris. 'And no one deserves it more.'

His brother was playing with Jeremy Kavanagh, whose superb front nine (32) had crumbled into dust in the last 40 minutes. On the 16th tee he was on cloud eight, at least, on two under par. But the treacherous 16th undid him: his ball sizzled out of a grassy lie clean over the green, and his chip, like Garcia's, cantered past the hole and into the burn. He was unable to get up and down and ended up with six. Suddenly he had tossed away all his heady winnings. More was to come. Another double bogey on the 17th was followed by one more lost shot at the end, a miss that completed what would usually be called his 'misery'. But Kavanagh had no interest in misery.

'You won't hear any disappointment coming from me,' he said, elated despite his sad ending. 'No way in hell I'm going to let those dropped shots at the end spoil it. You've got to love it. It's such a beautiful place. I even loved that bogey at the last. It's been just an amazing day.'

Elsewhere, blood was being shed. As a fighter jet screamed overhead, and the promo-yacht did slow-motion stunts beyond the rocks, Graeme McDowell came a cropper at the 16th to spoil another round that had started so well. As he dropped his ball in the rough on the edge of the fairway, some of the spectators grinned: they weren't given such favourable drops when they sliced at their home clubs. The old idea of playing the ball as it lies does not quite apply in major championships.

Elliot Saltman played well for 70 ('I made a lot of pars from the middle of the green'), even if he could not reproduce the sizzling form of the previous week, but his brother Lloyd fared worse (75). Denmark's Søren Kjeldsen seemed to have the kind of drilling ball flight that suited this terrain, and his putter was hot: he birdied the 10th, 11th and 13th to go to four under par.

There was a new joint leader, Ben Curtis. The surprise winner of the 2003 Open was posting 65 to join Watson and underlining the extent to which there were horses, in the Open, for courses. Some players just liked this kind of golf, and could make a success of it. A good start helps; Curtis made a steely eleven-footer for par on the first, and after that he rarely missed. 'To be honest I was just hoping to find a fairway,' he said, a nice nod to the idea that links courses respond better to humility than to swagger.

Where Kavanagh had finished 6–7–5, Curtis finished 3–4–4 to complete one of those whooping yet invisible turnarounds with which first-day golf is studded. With three holes to play there were only two shots between them. Now Curtis was joint leader and Kavanagh was nine shots back.

As Curtis finished, there were still players whose Open had not yet begun, swishing clubs on the 1st tee and preparing, at last, to let fly. The final threesome did not go out until half past four. They were chased by a platoon of greenkeepers who spread out with mowers, rakes and divot repair sets. For them, tomorrow started right here.

Josh Geary, winner of the qualifying in Melbourne, spent the morning watching Tiger Woods on television (what else was on?)

and began nervously: 'I was shaking for the first few holes.' But when he rolled in a birdie on the par–three 4th he relaxed, and two late blows at the 16th and 17th took him to even par, level with Elliot Saltman.

At 6.40 p.m., a time at which the day seemed as though it ought to be drawing to a close, it flared into life again. Tom Lehman . . . John Daly . . . players were bringing home scores to be proud of. Rory McIlroy rattled in two birdies on the back nine to finish below par – not quite the score his play seemed to warrant. He had eight threes on his card, but was only one under – the same as Woods, who played like the driver of a runaway train. There is a gap between playing well and scoring well, and while McIlroy's brilliance was obvious, his carefree manner was costly.

His playing partner Retief Goosen played one of the shots of the day, an amazing up-and-down out of a bunker at the 17th. He had one foot in the sand, one foot out and was half-kneeling on the bank, but he splashed out to prevent a fine opening round (67) from being derailed.

Walking to the last tee, McIlroy congratulated him on his contortions.

'All that gym work has paid off, I guess.'

Goosen gave his ghostly, faraway smile. 'I've had 20 more years to stretch than you.'

Boo Weekley, the popular Floridian whose shit-kicking, country-bumpkin persona always went down well with the media, notched the same score. Could he continue? 'I think I know I can.'

Camilo Villegas had gone one better, thanks to his amazing finish: four birdies in the last five holes. He had played in the United States long enough to have learned a more anodyne American English – he aimed to 'hang in there' and 'play smart' – but was able to rely on the words of his caddie, the Irish sports columnist and author Colin Byrne.

Byrne caddied for Goosen for years and wrote a book about it; this year he worked on and off for the injury-hit Alexander Norén, until a new call came. 'For some unknown reason Villegas decided I would be worth a few weeks on his bag,' he told the readers of his *Irish Times* column.

Villegas was a hard worker and an early riser: he liked to get going at 6.15 a.m. 'There is a sense of the early bird catching the worm . . .' He was also superstitious: his lucky ball-marker, an Australian 50-cent piece, had been in his bag since he turned professional, and Byrne knew he must not mislay it – 'I guarded that with more care than I did the clubs.'

How Villegas knew the coin was lucky is a deep question. Who knows: if Byrne had lost it, maybe his man would have smashed the Ailsa record. Maybe that coin was the only thing between him and endless victory.

In other respects Villegas did not rely on luck; he had a finicky attention to detail, especially when it came to yardages. 'It wasn't as simple as 150 yards and ten to the pin,' wrote Byrne. 'It was plus two for the hill, three for the temperature and four for the wind.'

Branden Grace, the South African qualifier from Sunningdale, played smartly in his first Open and said it was 'mind-blowing, all the people'. He played well without holing putts, but a birdie at 15 and a sudden eagle on 17 swept him to four-under. Chris Wood finished on 70 and called Turnberry 'the best course I've ever played'. And Søren Hansen came within an inch or two of taking the outright lead.

This was by no means popular. 'Don't go in!' voices cried in the media tent, as a putt filtered towards the hole.

The picture was still fuzzy enough for some papers to read into it what they pleased ('Harrington Showing Positive Signs,' said the *Irish Times*), but for almost everyone the story of the day – the Return of Tom Watson – had already been written, and no one wanted a twist at this late stage.

Watson's heroics inspired opinion-formers as well as reporters, and there were rival points of view. On the one hand he was a sporting legend – all very lovely. But he was also proof, for the game's detractors, that golf was a game for duffers – not a sport at all. Some senior sportswriters subscribed to this bland view, arguing that you wouldn't catch a 59-year-old competing with a 20-year-old in a sprint or a boxing ring. This was no great perception; but to say that a sport was not a sport because it did not resemble other sports seemed inane; couldn't a sport have its own unique characteristics? One might as well see sprinting and boxing as non-sports because one is a momentary drug-fest, while the other induces brain damage – or horse-racing as a non-sport because the players sit down, or rule out gymnastics because it involves only bullied teenagers.

All such thoughts were interrupted by a heavy roar from the 17th green, where Miguel Angel Jiménez nudged in a birdie putt to go to five under par. Normally a sedate mover (there is something of the river barge about the way he chugs, prow high, from green to tee), Jiménez twitched like a man who had been stung by a wasp when the ball fell in.

His playing partner, Ian Poulter, cut a more dejected sight. The union flag on his chest was not tattered, but this was a bulldog with his tail between his legs. He chewed a tee between his teeth, bounced the ball on his driver, and could only sigh as Jiménez went on to hole a long putt (50 feet) at the 18th to knock Watson back into second place. The Spaniard's grin was wide and friendly. Next stop: a glass of Rioja and a big cigar.

He had hardly missed a fairway. 'And also I had a nice day with the putter, what you need to make a score, no?'

The whole day had gone well. 'Since I woke up this morning, you can see through the window and you look at the sea, it looked like a pond, so nice, so calm. No windy, no nothing, and it took care of me.'

Like all overseas golfers he was invited to say how much he loved Scotland. He was happy to oblige. 'I like very much the Scottish public, the British people,' he said. 'They very well understanding this sport.'

Some reporters were fascinated by the fact that he smoked – a wild eccentricity. He must, they suggested, be in a hurry to light up right now.

Jiménez smiled. 'Never get in a hurry to make good things in life.'

He couldn't leave without being nudged to say something about Watson. Was he aware what he had just done? Had he ruined the great man's day?

'No, no, he's going to be legend for ever,' said Jiménez. 'Tom Watson is one of the guys you still have to look for, guys like him. He's a legend here with us, and we have to feel very proud to play with him.'

Everyone was being asked this. And since there is no sport like golf for insisting on generosity between competitors, there was unanimous warmth in the replies. Everyone had something nice to say.

'Tom Watson is one of the best ball-strikers of all time,' said Stewart Cink. 'I am not surprised to see him up there.'

John Daly thought he was 'just awesome' – 'I watched every shot of his round this morning and it was amazing, a great day.'

Ben Curtis agreed. 'He can still hit it. I think for him it's a matter of how well he putts. On a day like today he's probably licking chops.'

Tiger Woods had spotted a trend. 'Mark is up there,' he said. 'Both Marks, Calc and O'Meara, and obviously Tom, so three Open winners. They obviously understand how to play this kind of golf.'

O'Meara echoed his pal. 'Experience counts for a lot. Calcavecchia is on the board, and Watson at nearly 60. These guys can really play.'

Rory McIlroy could not imagine being so old, but was equally fulsome: 'It's incredible. I think he's 39 years older than me. If I can go round Turnberry in 39 years' time in 65, I'll be very happy.'

No one had enjoyed quite as good a view, of course, as Watson's playing partners. For Matteo Manassero it turned an already precious day into a historic one. 'Tom was unbelievable,' he said, in fine school English. 'He really helped me feel good, just asking social things and questions about where I won my Amateur title, but he played fantastic too.'

There is a reason why the first round of an Open feels like the longest day: Scotland's northerly latitude generates enough mid-summer daylight to allow the first group to tee up before breakfast, and the last to wander in after dinner. The Open crowd files on to the course soon after first light, and is free to stay for 14 or 15 hours. But they can deny themselves a whisky for only so long, so the closing groups play in a strange, empty theatre. Seagulls reclaim their hunting rights on the fairway; groundstaff fan out with brooms and mowers; electric buggies nose along pathways collecting rubbish sacks and flags; marshals wander off to the car park, the day done. They do not dignify the final players with so much as a backward glance – they've seen enough golf for one day. The corporate marquees have lowered their blinds; you can almost smell the steaks and hear the tinkle of conversation glimmering from the fabulous public rooms of the hotel up on its hill. It feels like the end of a party, with a host who would be very much obliged if you hurried up and left.

Some players thrived in the tranquillity. Japan's Kenichi Kuboya was not much known in Europe, so it took a conscious effort to remember that so far as he was concerned, he was the central character in this event. He had learned golf at his father's driving range in Kanagawa, well enough to win four times on the Japanese Tour. He was ranked 125th in the world, 74 spots ahead of Colin Montgomerie. He was no novice, in other words, and in the seaside hush he found his best rhythm. On the 15th he was on level par, not at all a bad effort, but on the last four holes he went 2–3–3–3: birdie-birdie-eagle-birdie. While almost everyone connected with Open was having dinner, he was joining Tom Watson on five under par.

There wasn't time to rewrite the news, nor room to mention that he had taken only 26 putts – the lowest number of the day. Only one other player took so few: Stewart Cink. But who cared about him?

Even that wasn't quite the end. In the very last group, the qualifier who shot a course-record 66 at Glasgow Gailes to win this eerily quiet evening slot was also bringing home a score. Steve Surry made up for a lapse at the 13th by slotting a birdie putt on the easy 17th; four at the last gave him a 69.

Four birdies in a round in your first Open is not bad. Surry had shot the same as Harrington, McIlroy and Els; he was one ahead of Garcia, and two ahead of Woods – a fabulous day in the life of a wannabe golfer who had been a professional for nearly five years now, mustering career earnings of around £40,000. In the winter months he took jobs in supermarkets or fixed drinks in the bar at his home club near Bath.

He was coming off a EuroPro tour win, however, and was in good form. Earlier in the week, eager to live the dream, he had signed for practice with Harrington and Paul McGinley, but then got cold feet, or a hard head, or both.

'I decided that I'd be watching them rather than concentrating on my own game. So I backed out and played on my own.'

He jumped at the chance, though, to play with his fellow Wiltshire golfer David Howell – a friend of a friend. At one point a boy approached the pair of them and asked for signatures, and Surry modestly said he was sure the lad didn't want his: he wasn't famous.

'That's not the right attitude,' said the youngster. 'If you are playing in the Open, I want your autograph.'

'It was a bit weird being told off by a 12-year-old,' admitted Surry.

Almost everything about the Open was eye-opening. As an unknown, Surry was a prime target for equipment companies keen to get their clubs on live television (no point bothering Woods). 'I could probably fill my garage with what I've been offered by the various club manufacturers this week,' he said. It was quite a contrast to his usual beans-on-toast, will-the-car-start life. And he did pick up some gleaming new Callaway irons.

At the start of the week he said that (like the golf fans here at Turnberry) he was 'determined' to get Woods's autograph, but when he saw the man practising, just yards away, on the range, he didn't like to interrupt.

'I couldn't help noticing how calm and composed he was.'

He wouldn't have minded celebrating his great day with something or other, but everything was closed, even the Players' Lounge.

'We had some rank fish and chips, and went to bed,' he said.

About 20 minutes after he finished, a fat orange printout appeared in the media centre, full of names and numbers: a statistical summary of the day's play. Not everyone had found life easy – the Durban qualifier Jaco Ahlers shot 83 – but the average score was sharp enough to give credence to the idea that Turnberry was a soft touch: 51 players (a third of the field) achieved par or better. But the weather forecast suggested a more arduous challenge, and there was no sense reaching a verdict too soon.

The hardest hole to score well on was the long par-three 6th, where only nine players managed a birdie. The most obliging was the with-the-wind par-five 7th, where there were 82 birdies and nine eagles. But the 17th, predicted by Watson to be tough, was

benign: 78 birdies and six eagles. The easiest green to hit, not surprisingly, was the 1st. Yet nearly a quarter of the field failed to hit
the target: not bad for an easy-peasy, 354-yard par-four.

The putting statistics told an obvious story too. Dustin
Johnson was the third-longest driver, with an average distance of
317 yards. But he took 34 putts to be 78, fully eight over par.
Jiménez, meanwhile, fired it 'only' 294 yards, but found 12
fairways against Johnson's seven, and needed only 27 putts. It is
a game, in the end, of accuracy, not distance, and no one exem-
plified this tedious truth more clearly than Manassero, who came
fifth in greens-in-regulation, but lagged in putting, with 35
shots.

Putting statistics are unreliable, favouring players who miss
greens and chip close, but they are at least a rough guide, and
Manassero's numbers did not bear out Tom Watson's generous
assessment.

'I wish I had his putting stroke,' he said. 'Bang, in the middle
of the hole. I remember that, vaguely. I just vaguely remember
how to do that.'

The room laughed when Watson said this – what a charming,
not to say hilarious, reference to his own advancing years.
Everyone knew that youngsters putted with 'no fear': it was a
rock-solid golfing cliché.

A squint at the numbers told a different story. Watson had
taken only 28 putts, half a dozen fewer than his youthful partner.
And since he was too old and wise not to have been aware of this
decisive discrepancy, it meant that the old champ might be soft-
soaping us all, hamming it up.

Of course it might have been that Watson's eyes did water with
envy at the way Manassero rapped in three-footers without a care
in the world. But it was also possible that he was lying doggo.
There are conventions governing media encounters, and it would
not have been the done thing for Watson to broadcast any serious
self-confidence. Much better to mock his faltering faculties and

promote the idea that he was back here in his old haunt, hitting a few balls for old time's sake.

He had a strange, pale glint in his eye, though.

Nor was it true that Turnberry was 'defenceless'. The new 16th hole, a once-easy downhill par-four, was now a treacherous dog-leg that on this first day had ruined many promising rounds. Fredrik Jacobson approached it on four-under, took a three-over-par seven and sank into the pack. The list of double bogeys was an Open who's who: Graeme McDowell, Lee Westwood, Sergio Garcia, Søren Kjeldsen, Søren Hansen, Adam Scott, Ken Perry, Johan Edfors, Paul Lawrie, Francesco Molinari, Chad Campbell, Anthony Kim, Rod Pampling, Martin Laird, K. J. Choi, Greg Norman and Michael Campbell . . . all of them dropped two shots here.

The average score on the hole was 4.32, well over par, and barely lower than the average score on the par-five 7th (4.45).

One last thing. Every pundit agreed it had been a grand day for the old guys, but if you looked at the back end of the list (the loserboard?), it had also been a bad one. After his 77, Greg Norman said he had never driven the ball worse. Nick Faldo shot 78, as did Bruce Vaughan. If we forgot about Watson and Calcavecchia for a moment, it was clear that golf was a young man's game, and that experience counted for nothing at all.

CHAPTER ELEVEN

Day Two

Everything would depend on the weather. The forecast on Friday was predicting showers and a breeze, so anyone who dodged the downpours and kept the ball low might be able to grab a score and sit back while others suffered. In contrast to the accepted view that tournaments could be lost (but not won) on the first day, it looked as though the opening round might prove decisive – the best way to win this Open might be to swipe a low number on Thursday, and then fight like a mongoose to protect it. One glance at the pin placements was enough to show that the R&A had cut holes close to the edges of greens and hidden them behind bunkers. Tough pins plus weather made it unlikely that anyone one would match the birdie blizzards achieved the day before by Watson, Jiménez and Kuboya.

The authorities were frowning at the prospect of rain. 'It's the umbrellas,' said David Hill. 'Spectators hate them. And in wet weather people get depressed. There isn't enough shelter – but that's links golf.'

There had been few such problems on the first day. A modest threat of lightning never materialised, and at the end of play a camera rostrum on the 3rd hole had to be moved, because it had become a temporary bail-out area from which errant players could drop to safety.

By the time play began the putting green was full, while caddies stood to one side smoking, keeping up golf's class division between faddish millionaire players and their puffing spear-carriers. In spite of Angel Cabrera's famous remark that 'other players have psychologists – I just smoke', there were few smokers on tour. Jiménez had his cherished post-round cigar; Darren Clarke liked the odd puff; and Daly often had a cigarette clamped between his teeth. But for the most part golf was non-smoking.

Speaking of Daly, his trousers were again catching the eye. Some were calling today's pair – a psychedelic fountain of colour – 'an explosion in a pizza factory', while America's most famous golf journalist, Dan Jenkins, was tweeting, more abrasively, that 'the trailer park wants its shower curtains back'.

Traffic from the north was backing up halfway to Ayr, loitering past sleeping shops, pubs and tea-rooms and giving drivers time to smile at the ironic-sounding village signs – 'Haste Ye Back' – on the road.

In a polite British way, security was tight: spectators were funnelled down a steep path and through a strictly policed entrance. Had anyone wanted to, there were miles of barely guarded boundary – the beach, the fields, the road – across which anyone could have stepped. But the law-abiding masses were subjected to fierce electronic scrutiny.

'Oh no,' wailed one man, patting his pockets. 'I had it a minute ago.'

'Is this anyone's?'

Somewhere behind him, a woman held up the missing card.

What would he have done if it hadn't been found?

'Blown £55 on a new one, I suppose,' he said. 'I'm here now.'

In the second round the playing order is reversed, and late finishers get first crack. The way the sky looked, this could be providential – though late starters would be able to watch the morning on television, see how the course was set up and make mental notes about the breaks on greens.

As a result, the qualifiers Jeremy Kavanagh and Daniel Gaunt headed into the drizzle as the second group of the day. They were playing with David Higgins, who, like Gaunt, had qualified only the week before. For all three this was a heaven-sent chance to take a step towards the golfing firmament. On day one Higgins had shot a three-over-par 73, one better than Kavanagh and three better than Gaunt, who now bogeyed the 1st.

His shoulders didn't sag, however – on the contrary, he relaxed. He was timing the ball well and felt calmer than on the nerve-racking first day. The quiet, early-morning scenery offered the kind of tranquil, hushed golfing atmosphere he was used to, and he rolled up his mental sleeves, went to work, and started pounding pars. On the 5th he missed the green but shut out memories of double bogey the previous day, pitched cleanly over the flag, and drained a tricky one down the hill. He was playing all right.

One or two newspapers had picked up on Gaunt's situation – he was a neat emblem of the wealth gap that yawned below the top tier of pro golf. He had won on the EuroPro tour, earning himself £10,000 – very nice work. But entering such contests took a fee of £350, plus the best part of a thousand pounds in expenses, and you couldn't win them all. He was a good player (he wouldn't have made it here otherwise), but he had taken money out of his house to sponsor himself.

At the 6th both Kavanagh and Gaunt took three-woods and made three – no easy task into a vigorous breeze off the water – but while Kavanagh then made three fives to slide back, Gaunt sprang into life. He birdied both the 8th and the 9th and went to the turn on one under par. Then he cracked it long off the downwind tees on the back nine, birdied the 14th and the 17th,

That sinking feeling. Tiger with Japan's Ryo Ishikawa.

'It was just problem after problem.'

'No one saw it?' Woods searches for his lost ball in the rough beside the 10th.

Excuse me. Only accredited photographers need apply. Getty Images

The final day. Ross Fisher and friends inspect the lie in the rough at the 4th.
Mike Egerton/Empics Sport

To the 7th green. Was this a course on which Watson could do well? 'Yes.'
Jon Super/Press Association Images

The 9th tee. 'I said yesterday that the spirits are with me.' Jon Super/Press Association Images

The lighthouse: 'How am I going to do? I don't know.' Peter Morrison/Press Association Images

'Be the right club!' Watson, with a one-shot lead, fires the fateful eight-iron at the final green. Stephen Pond/Empics Sport

'I didn't think Tom would drop a shot at the last.' Lee Westwood three-putts the 18th to miss the play-off. Anthony Devlin/Press Association Images

This for the Open. Tom Watson watches his final putt, and his winning hopes, fade.
Peter Morrison/Press Association Images

The beginning of the end. Cink and Watson set off on the four-hole play-off.

Getty Images

'I think it's me, Tom.' Cink plays from sand on the first play-off hole.

Alastair Grant/Press Association Images

'Links golf and I really like each other.' Cink plays his final approach.

'I was never really in it, but I was never really out of it.' A victorious Cink salutes the crowd.

'It's a survival test out there.' Cink is driven to the media tent.
Jon Super/Press Association Images

St Andrews, home of the Open in its 150th year. The Claret Jug on the Swilken bridge, looking up the 18th hole. Rebecca Naden/Press Association Images

and did not drop a shot. Maybe the course wasn't playing tough, after all.

The field streamed after them, each group lugging its own little army on the march. Rhys Davies, the only Welshman in the field, birdied the first, but gave it back at the 2nd and slipped to 38 (three over) on the front nine. He was playing with the promising Gaganjeet Bhullar, who had made an impressive debut the previous afternoon to be only one over par.

This was no Indian summer, though, and after a double bogey at the 5th, Bhullar was chopping it out of rough on the 7th to drop a further stroke. With this left-to-right breeze the pot bunkers on the right were catching a lot of drives; a few minutes later, Ben Curtis was chipping out sideways as he tried (and failed) to hang on to his first-day gains. He was in a bad run – five bogeys in six holes – that would end his chances. Experience seemed to be of little help. He had birdied the first too.

He was playing with Ross Fisher and Mike Weir, whose combined score of minus-eleven had made this the best-performing group of the first day. Fisher, one of the form players, was clocking the ball long and straight, and when he pushed in a birdie at the 4th he was one of very few going in the right direction. Mclroy and Goosen, playing together, also made a move, but Sandy Lyle was adding self-inflicted injury to the insults he had been hurling around: he dropped three shots on the first five holes.

With the wind helping, somebody had to have a crack at the 1st green, and to no one's surprise it was Alvaro Quiros, the Spanish big hitter who was proving, if proof were necessary, that length was not everything. He cleared the green, found a claggy lie in a clump, and made bogey. Word soon spread: most of his successors took five-irons; Garcia took a six.

By the time the leader, Miguel Angel Jiménez, set out he had almost lost his advantage, because the American alternate, Steve Marino, was repeating his first-day form. Cameras, curious, began to swing in his direction, and were surprised to find a man who, in his red woollen hat and shapeless rainsuit, looked like the bloke delivering Christmas trees rather than a silky skilled international sportsman. His father had fetched his passport, but had clearly forgotten his son's razor.

Now, he seemed to be saying, where the hell was that wrench?

Jiménez, a strolling advert for Andalucia, stepped out of his way with three bogeys on the first four holes. At the 6th he found the bunker on the left and couldn't get out. Second time around he still left himself a 20-foot putt, and though he holed it (bravely), he was no longer leading the Open.

On the other hand, he was still two under par, and well placed. It was a shame to have tossed away the shots he had banked, but they had given him a cushion against precisely this. Only a handful were under par, and the wind was freshening. The radio's 'gentle zephyr' was snapping hard at flags and trouser legs.

Padraig Harrington also started badly, but hung on by his chirpy, defiant fingertips. When the wind dumped his ball left of the 2nd green, he chipped dead and saved par. He had plenty of support, which came in handy at the 7th, when he lost his ball. A team of well-wishers tramped through the grass, and found it – before noticing that his playing partner, Geoff Ogilvy, was also searching for a lost ball, alone and unhelped.

Suddenly, the course felt full. There were various vantage points where spectators could feel surrounded by comings and goings: the mound between the 6th and 17th; the grandstand behind the 4th, with its view down the 5th; the seating at the 9th, which opened up the 10th and 13th too. Watching golf is often a matter of glimpses, flashes of familiar swings and faces. There was Faldo, short of the 7th green, taking three, four, five, six, seven practice swings before risking a chip. That sudden burst of applause meant that someone – Brian Gay, maybe – had hit the flag. That tiny figure down on the beach below the lighthouse was Tomohiro Kondo, who had pulled it left at the 10th, and was lucky the tide was out.

At the 6th tee there was a pleasantly scented sausage and coffee van, and, in case you were hit by a Srixon while enjoying a fluffy bacon roll, a medical centre. It was polite of Azuka Yano to choose the 5th hole to soar over the green and hit a lady spectator on the head, because medical help was only yards away. In the event she was fine, though another young spectator, watching her being tended, promptly passed out.

Thus the rich variety inherent in golf-watching. How was your Open? Great. I watched a Japanese player bounce a ball off a woman's head, and then I fainted. The weather was awful. Can't wait till next year.

Modern health and safety meant that fairway marshals were obliged to wear blue plastic hats, like Lego characters, damaging the dignity of the scene while doing no good whatsoever.

It certainly put Paul Casey off. He three-putted the 4th and then, at the 5th, missed an 18-inch tap-in ('It just popped left off the club'). At the 8th he lost his tee shot into the wind and chided his driver by snapping it.

'It's been in my bag for four years,' he said. 'It's had a good run.'

Fisher stood on the 15th tee at level par. His manager was under orders to alert him if the childbirth hotline rang, but so far there was no sign. But the tension was helping, because although the two birdies on the front nine had been cancelled out by two bogeys, he was not surrendering.

'I'm trying to put it to the back of my mind,' he said.

His tee shot to the 15th green was unremarkable, but golf, though a slow game, is susceptible to sudden detonations, and when he holed a 50-foot putt it was as emphatic as a bull's eye, and changed the whole shape of his round. With the wind helping, the par-five 17th was practically a gimme; if he held his nerve, this could turn out well.

The role of confidence in golf has never been overlooked, and Fisher, feeling dandy, tapped in a birdie at the 16th for good measure. When he pocketed another at the 17th he was on minus-three, and riding high alongside players – Watson, Senden, Villegas, Cink – who might well slide back.

He finished on minus-three, two behind Marino and very much part of the story. He was still unequivocal about his birthing plans, however.

'My wife comes first,' he said. 'If she were to go into labour tonight or tomorrow, I've got no choice. I want to be there.'

His sponsor had a jet standing by at Prestwick. If necessary it would zoom Fisher to Farnborough, a short race down the M3 from Kingston.

This was an unusual modern stance for the highest-placed British golfer, and it led some commentators – who might not themselves have quit such a nice assignment for a mere birth – to depict him as a drip. It was a sign – welcome in the bubble that had fallen on Turnberry – that golf was, despite appearances to the contrary, junior to life. With neither song nor dance, Fisher was striking a blow against the locker-room tyranny that saw family life as a menacing encroachment on a chap's game.

Nor did it affect his level-headed assessment of his own play.

'I was with two major-winners,' he said, 'and the way they struggled showed just how easy it was to get blown off course out there.'

Daniel Gaunt, meanwhile, had completed a dizzy round of 67, with only 23 putts, a dozen fewer than the day before. 'It suited me to have tough conditions,' he said. 'I had nothing to lose.' Unlike Fisher, he was not looking for his name high on the leaderboard, but this brilliant day put him on three over par for the first two rounds and made it possible, indeed likely, that he would make the cut. If the guillotine had fallen on the first day it would have sawn off anyone worse than minus-one; but today's weather was going to drive the cut line higher. Plus-three would probably be right on the mark. Once again, he was in for a long wait.

Some of the other early starters were looking bedraggled. Ben Curtis was heaving himself off greens like a man wondering if he had left the gas on (he should have asked Marino to pop round and fix it), and Ian Poulter was deflating like a burst balloon. At the Open, the build-up is louder than usual, which makes poor performances seem doubly abrupt.

Jeremy Kavanagh, playing with Gaunt, had finished less strongly but was the opposite of downcast. There are different forms of triumph and disaster in golf, and winning is not everything – Kavanagh was refusing to let a few missed putts spoil his day, or his life. At the 17th he had pushed his drive into the right-hand rough in front of the spectators, who had to shuffle back. It is a mystery how players manage to concentrate at such times, but Kavanagh was all business. A thought flashed into his mind: a keen golf historian, he recalled the piercing one-iron Ben Hogan struck to secure the US Open at Merion in 1950. It was the 36th hole of the day, and Hogan, aching from the car crash that had broken his legs, had lost a three-stroke lead. He needed par on the last to join a play-off, and faced a 200-yard uphill approach to a small green, with sand on the right. There is a famous image of the shot, a stinging iron that sent the ball whistling up a narrow alley through the crowd to the heart of the green.

Kavanagh pulled off something similar. The ball took off low and carved up the left side before falling to the right to set up a birdie that would make no difference to anything: his triple bogey at the 10th had long since put the cut out of range.

Still, a burst of cheering flared up on the ridge above the fairway – his family fan club shouting its approval. Kavanagh took off his cap and whirled it above his head with eager, unabashed, Jimmy Stewart glee.

Each group at the Open is accompanied by a walking scoreboard carried by a volunteer. This one showed that Kavanagh was on plus-eight.

'Christ,' murmured a spectator. 'Eight over, and playing shots like that. How good do these guys have to be?'

Tom Watson wasn't watching any of this. He knew without looking that the weather was going to change things. He break-fasted at his usual perch high above the course, and surveyed the scene with a near-nautical eye.

Looked like the wind was getting up. Oh well.

He answered 'about a hundred emails' and read up on climate change (possibly to keep up with his caddie, Neil Oxman, who when not toting Watson's bag was a political consultant and film critic).

Then he headed for the range.

At that moment, Steve Marino was coming in with a miracle score that included even fewer putts (just 22) than Gaunt's round. So much for experience. He had not been to Britain before, and was finding everything quaint ('What is it, shepherd's pie? Not bad'). He was breaking all the rules of links golf too: he was way-ward off the tee ('I drove into the rough a bunch') and missed greens. At the par-three 4th he misfired a windy tee shot into a bunker ('I hit it terrible'), but it cost him only a bogey because his putter was on fire. He rolled in a series of long bombs, includ-ing one for eagle on the 17th, and was now, improbably, joint leader of the Open.

'There were points where I felt I was one-putting every hole,' he said. 'I don't think I could have shot one stroke less, to be honest with you.'

He was genial enough to pose as a happy-go-lucky innocent abroad – 'I'm having a blast. Mum's probably about to have a heart attack when she hears I am leading' – but this was a dis-guise. He was no novice. He had lost a play-off to Steve Stricker a few weeks earlier, and was big news in Arizona, where he once shot 59 in a tournament.

When the questioning became too folksy, he took a deep breath.

'I'm not in a daze,' he confessed. 'I know what's going on.'

Jiménez was finishing too, not quite so happily. But he made up for his awful start (out in 39) by picking up a shot on the way back, and if, a week ago, you had offered him three-under at halfway, he would have lit your cigar.

The applause on the first tee for Watson was sustained and warm, but almost melancholy: no one seriously thought he could do it again. Yesterday had been a delightful cameo; sadly, it was time normal service was resumed.

He found the fairway all right, but his wedge did not threaten the flag. So the roar when he sank a sliding 30-footer was fuelled by shock as well as pleasure. Here we went again. The papers were full of Watsonian references to 'something spiritual out there', and this was indeed uncanny: it did feel as though a larger force were smiling on his game.

Only for a moment. An hour later, the feeling had melted in the grey air. Watson bogeyed the 2nd, the 4th (three putts, the old failing), the 5th and the 6th to surrender his lead, and when he failed to save par at the 7th there seemed nothing to stop him from sinking into anonymity.

Enough good things had happened the previous day, however, for him to feel sanguine about a poor front half. He was four shots worse off than he had been at breakfast, but everyone was stumbling, and he was still in the top group. 'Wait for the turn,' he told himself. 'It will turn around.'

Later, he amplified on this insight. 'I said, you're probably going to struggle going out. But I knew the incoming nine was going to play, you know, a little easier.'

A friendly word of encouragement from Garcia might have helped. As the threesome made their way down the 8th fairway, Garcia gave his ageing playing partner a playful pat and said: 'Come on, old man.'

'Well, I feel like an old man,' Watson replied. But he was smiling.

He then hit a pure shot with his two-hybrid into that 8th green, missed the putt, but followed it with two more on the 9th.

'It wasn't necessarily right at the hole, but I was pin high,' he said.

One of the hallmarks of champions, even elderly ones, is their ability to snatch opportunities when they present themselves. Watson now holed a putt that saved him more than one shot: it signalled to himself and to everyone on the links that afternoon (the roar from the lighthouse was heard on the 18th green) that he had not given up.

'Now we're playing downwind,' he told himself.

The Open day is too long to allow for anything but a rolling meal-time. Technically, Tiger Woods was due on the 1st tee after lunch, at 2.20 p.m., but since this was eight hours after the start of play, it felt much later. He had spent post-round time at the range, and now he warmed to his task like a champion, working the ball through the wind as though he loved this sort of golf. His all-black outfit made him look especially serious, but the gallery was subdued. There was something odd about his poor start yesterday . . . No one knew what it was, but something had changed: the man seemed less godlike, less . . . himself. There would be no smiles today.

Out on the course, Kenichi Kuboya was still going bewilderingly well – had no one told him this was a day for folding himself out the way so some bigger celebrities could march on to the advertising hoarding that was modern television? Golf is unusual in that it does not cheer on the underdog for long, but Kuboya did not seem to know the limelight was temporary. Birdie at the 1st gave him the outright lead; another, at the 4th, put clear sky between himself and his pursuers. One of the ways golf is a winner-takes-all game is this built-in fact that when you play well, it doesn't matter how hard the course is: the rough and bunkers play no role. The hazards punish those who err, those

who are already playing badly. This encourages a moral interpretation: only those who keep it on the straight and narrow
(what golf calls 'the short stuff') are rewarded.

And then, as so often, Turnberry pounced. Kuboya dropped
a couple of shots and then, at the 13th (straight into the teeth of
the gale), he lost his drive and the ball could not be found. He
had to take a buggy back to the tee, and did well to get away with
double bogey – he had to chip and putt from behind the green.
But the slip-up rattled him. Another bogey came on the 15th,
and though he snatched one back at the 17th to be only two
strokes behind Marino, the momentum had turned against him.

Elsewhere, scores rose and fell like gulls on the ocean breeze.
Stricker and Villegas dropped back, while Calcavecchia holed
twice for birdie. Manassero knocked in a long one at the 9th, but
Cink was in trouble at the 4th. McIlroy and Anthony Kim were
having a fit of the giggles at the 8th – Kim's shoulders shook as
he stood over a putt.

Their partner, Retief Goosen, was his usual impassive self. 'I
made my putt for par,' he said, failing to recall anything funny.

Todd Hamilton was playing well, by his recent standards, but
still missed the cut and struggled to suppress the idea that he
might never recapture the form that brought him the Claret Jug
in 2004. 'Sometimes,' he sighed, 'I wish there were something
else I could do for a living.'

Another man struggling to rekindle former glories was
Europe's Colin Montgomerie. Lyle's remarks may not have
helped, but Monty's own form offered few grounds for optimism
(his best result of the year was 13th at the French Open – a quiet
performance by a one-time great).

At Turnberry his favoured pose was whipped and hounded.
He hunched over practice putts with an air of grave, injured dignity, accepting the consoling words of passers-by – Butch
Harmon one moment, Gary Lineker the next – with the hurt
gratitude of an exiled monarch.

'Let's go and do. This. Thing,' he said, leaving the green with the air of a man compelled to clamber down into the Glasgow sewers. On the way to the 1st tee he brushed past autograph-hunters and then stood on the tee, swishing his club, wondering where the others were (they were signing).

It was a classic worst-of-both-worlds scenario. He had offended his fans, and now he had to hang about waiting for the others.

It was a bad start to a round that went from moan to grumble.

'Unbelievable,' he said, when his ball tipped into a bunker.

'Unbelievable,' he said again, looking at the sky at the end of his round, when it looked as though the weather might be easing.

The world, he seemed sure, had it in for him – even those students with their rag-week Monty wigs. By the end he was glaring at marshals for holding up those distracting 'Quiet please' signs.

These marshals are not paid – their one reward is a privileged view of the golfers. But when one tried to help, he was slapped down.

'It's behind that big bush, Colin,' said the man on the 7th.

'I know where it is, thank you.'

His father was following him round, and might have been given an idea for his son's Christmas stocking: Teach Yourself Public Relations. Montgomerie strode the course as if in a funeral cortege. It was true that the Open had never been a happy hunting ground: this was his 20th go, and his best effort was four years ago, when he came second to Tiger Woods. But the mind gurus back at the range could have told him for nothing that lugging your own private cloud of misgivings was no way to set about a challenge like this. As he passed, the crowd lowered its eyes.

One fan was off-message, and risked a cheer.

'Well played, Monty!'

'Well played?' Montgomerie muttered. 'I've just shot double bogey!'

Everywhere he looked he saw sarcasm. But many golf fans admired him despite his filthy moods, and he treated them to a tense finish. At the 18th his ball ran off the green, and his chip wasn't close enough, and the putt crept past to leave him on five over par, at least a shot the wrong side.

He had achieved four birdies – the sign of a good player – but every single one was followed by a bogey: the sign of an irresolute one.

'You can't do that,' he fumed, stating the obvious.

In a way the first two days of an Open are the final final-qualifying stage: the halfway cut produces the 70-strong field from which the winner will come. It was looking ever more certain that plus-three would be in: not enough players were doing better than that. So when Rory McIlroy also missed a putt at the last he looked (on plus-three, the same as Gaunt) to be safe.

Harrington, however, came to the 17th on four-over. He had let shots go early on and fought a losing battle ever since. A couple of putts trembled on the lip, and decided to stay above ground – revenge perhaps, for the ones that had fallen in years past. At the 17th he turned to the club that had settled the Open the previous year, when he speared a five-wood past the bunkers on the penultimate hole, and it did the trick again. This time he took two five-woods to reach the green, and though he missed the eagle putt, he did pick up an all-important birdie to take up the final fairway.

The applause was warm and sustained, and uncharacteristically he let himself float a little. He made the edge of the green with his second and walked towards the enclosed arena where jugs were won and lost. 'I was thinking, I'm eight shots behind. And somebody was being cheered on to the 1st tee – I think it was Lee Westwood. And I was thinking about that and I was thinking about this . . .' He ran the ball close and walked up with a light head. 'By the time I got over it, I was happy it was only two

feet. I struck it in the left half. It wasn't my most glorious putting stroke there.'

Plenty of people were finding it hard. John Senden finished on
80, 14 shots worse than the previous day, and nowhere near the
cut line. Paul Casey was missing putts and was five-over – he
would probably be going home too. Nick Dougherty shot par on
the first day, played twice as well on day two . . . and shot par
again. His decisive moment came on the long 6th hole, where
Adam Scott hit a rescue club and came up well short of the green.
Dougherty took a three-wood, biffed it to two feet and smiled.

Harrington was upbeat about his day. He was happy with his
ball-striking; he just hadn't been able to knock it into the cup.

'I think the longest putt I holed was two feet out there,' he
said. 'I certainly can't remember holing anything.' But at the 6th
he, like Dougherty, nailed a birdie that was especially welcome
after double bogey at the 5th. 'It spurred me on,' he said. 'Any
time you are hitting three-wood on a par-three you know it's
tough. Most of my golf was superb.'

He had pretty much abandoned any serious chance of winning, though.

'I am hoping to get out nice and early tomorrow morning, in
beautiful sunshine, shoot a good score and then the weather to
come in. We can always dream, can't we?'

John Daly was hanging in there too. 'This course,' he said.
'Whether it's calm or blowing, you are five inches from disaster.
I am happy to be here for the weekend.'

So was Calcavecchia. 'I'm actually kind of using my head,' he
said, 'which is unusual.'

Until Watson returned, the media were keen to cast
Calcavecchia as the elder statesman, and suggested that he must
feel sort of like a captain to the younger players.

Calcavecchia declined the role.

'I would never think I'm the kind of guy anybody could learn
anything from, to tell you the truth.'

Tiger Woods, meanwhile, was ready to go. As usual he was tucked in a private corner of the putting green, and even Australia's Geoff Ogilvy, a multiple winner around the world, was shooed away by security guards when he strayed too close.

Heading away from the lighthouse with a birdie in his pocket, Tom Watson negotiated the 10th, hit a seven-iron to 15 feet at the 11th and rolled it in to go back to three under par. A rousing chorus of cheers rolled along the shore like a thunderous wave. He was not finished yet!

'My thinking, going out, was that if I could shoot around even par with that wind I'd be right there,' he said.

Nothing much happened in the next three holes, and he was pleased when, from an awkward lie short of a bunker he had been lucky to avoid, he cleared the water at the 16th, even though he faced a long downhiller to the pin. Everyone knew that this hole had been the ruin of many Open hopes on day one – it was a hole you wanted to get out of in one piece.

Watson's fans were pleased too, because the 17th, with wind helping, was a clear birdie chance. Their man really was right in this.

First things first. Watson felt a surge of clarity as he stood over his ball. It was 60 feet down to the hole, with a right-to-left swing; several players, the previous day, had popped it into the burn from here.

Watson didn't plan to join them.

'I really felt,' he said. 'I had a feeling I was going to make that putt.'

Golfers quite often have these feelings, and they are often wrong, but in this case the ball tracked into a perfect line and drifted to the hole.

Watson started walking after it a yard or so before it fell. He picked it out of the cup with remarkable agility for a man with a new hip, kissed it and held it high. It was a miracle – and a throwback: Watson had holed a few like this in 1977. What was going on?

One minute later, with spooky precision, Manassero sent a putt down the same line: it was as if Watson had left a scorch mark on the grass.

Lightning did strike twice.

'It didn't surprise me,' said Watson. 'He's a beautiful putter.'

Garcia had the shortest putt of the three. This had been the story of his Open so far: he was peerless from tee to green, but his two playing partners – the oldest man here, and the youngest – were sinking putts.

This time he followed them in, and at one under par wasn't out of it either.

At the 18th, however, Garcia lost his ball left, and thumped a provisional with extra fury, racing past the bunker at 335 yards and bringing to mind one of golf's most frequently asked questions: why didn't he do that first time around?

Watson and Manassero did not totter, however, and as they walked up the final fairway, the multiple winner gave the teenager a word of advice: 'Don't change anything. You'll be there some day.'

Manassero's courteous response was to stand back and join the applause as Watson advanced, with that pecking little stride, into the colossal arms of the waiting public. The young Italian had two years of school ahead of him, but this hadn't been a bad summer holiday so far.

Watson's approach to the 18th came to rest on the right edge of the green, in three-putt country. It was not far from the spot where Nicklaus had put his second in the final reel of the Duel in the Sun.

The crowd held its breath.

Surely not.

If I can make it at 16, thought Watson, why can't I make it here?

It never looked like missing. He kicked his knee high and swivelled, squeezing his replacement hip into what he called 'my Scottish jig'.

He was immediately whisked aside to tell the world how he felt.

'I said yesterday that the spirits are with me,' he said. 'They kind of keep me focused.'

This was exactly the right thing to say. It allowed him to be modest and as self-effacing as he pleased, as if this were nothing to do with him. It was . . . destined: he was a mere pawn in some supernatural game.

He could even thrill the media tent by referring to himself as an 'old fart'.

Perfect. If Ishikawa could be a bashful prince, why couldn't Watson be a bashful king? He made only one slight false step, when, continuing his poetical musing of the previous evening, he said chivalrously: 'Lady Turnberry took off her gloves today and showed some teeth.'

Not all golf courses hide their teeth beneath gloves, but no one minded.

The bigger question was: could he win?

'I don't think that way,' said Watson. 'I never have thought that way. You stay in one shot at a time, the old cliché.'

That would have to do. It wasn't true, however. His speech was littered with glints of another idea. 'I still am competitive,' he said. 'I still play competition. And I enjoy it . . . I can still kind of get the job done . . . physically, I'm in good shape . . . mentally, I'm in a good place . . . It's been 34 years I've played links golf, it's a fabric of my life, I'll tell you.'

Few heeded this note in his conversation. They preferred to enjoy the reference to his elderly little knee kick on the 18th and nod sagely over his praise for Manassero's 'no fear' putting stroke (this time with more justice: Manassero took 29 putts to Watson's 31).

There was still talk about how the wind was getting up, to favour players who teed off early. The efforts of Marino and Watson seemed to bear this out, but Kuboya was showing few signs of relinquishing his high position; indeed he was punching his way back towards the lead. The previous evening he had eagle-birdied his way home with only mowers, greenkeepers and refuse trucks for company. After his stumble, he picked himself up, making it hard to assess the relative merits of innocence and experience. If the latter had helped Watson, then what were we to say of the co-leader, Steve Marino, who had never been here before?

Watson himself acknowledged that experience was not everything. 'I never played links golf before Carnoustie in 1975, and it turned out pretty well for me there.'

A few moments later he ran into the producer from ABC Television, for whom he had agreed to commentate over the weekend.

'You just fired yourself,' said the producer with a grin.

Out at the 7th, Tiger Woods, having parred the first six, holed a putt to go to level. Only four men were under par today (Marino, Gaunt, Fisher and Japan's Ryuji Imada) and Woods would soon turn inland. With the breeze at his back, he was odds-on to pick up a shot or two, and if he began the weekend only three or four off the lead, he would, as usual, be the hot favourite.

He soon slipped up, however, dropping shots at the next two holes before stepping on to the intimidating 10th tee.

This was a bleak spot for a man who had been missing fairways. The wind was rippling off a boisterous sea that foamed on sharp tongues of cold rock, and ahead lay a broad, wild cove. The contrast between the rocky waters to the left and the meek strip of mown grass in the distance, studded with deep bunkers, was exhilarating, but the lighthouse was an eloquent reminder that this was a place of dashed hopes, wrecked dreams.

It was tough from the golf point of view too. On the first day players could thump it over the bunkers and fire wedges at the green, but in this wind it would take a driver and a three-iron. Woods's tee shot flared right and vanished into long grass at the foot of the war memorial, way out beyond the bunkers. The names of fallen servicemen – Bateson, Calder, Fairweather, Jenkins, Squires – formed a poignant roll-call on the cross, thrust into the hill like a stone sword, on top of the mound. It was a sober tribute to the imperial nature of the war effort: Australians, Canadians and Americans were remembered alongside Scottish and English airmen.

It was not a playable part of the course, however, and as the crowd streamed towards the spot it was clear the ball would take a bit of finding.

Woods strode into the mêlée with a grim expression.

'No one saw it?' he asked, with outlandish rudeness, as if it were the job of these tubby dullards to find his mishits.

His severe black costume, which at the outset had seemed dashing – a touch of Zorro in the countryside – suddenly seemed merely gloomy.

It was not clear that the crowd was helping; a good number seemed more concerned with being on TV than with finding a missing Nike.

A ball was found – a Callaway, which Tiger tossed away with a sneer . . . and a minute later someone yelped and found the same ball again.

His own much-publicised brand seemed to have vanished.

As the minutes passed, a shock wave of alarm spread out from this grassy knoll, through the tents of Turnberry and out, through the television signals, to the watching world.

Woods was in trouble!

He rode a buggy back to the tee, popped a safe provisional into the middle of the fairway, and returned to the throng. No sign. He had to trek back to his second ball and hammer it towards (and short of) the green.

His fifth shot stuttered close, and he had to hole a testing one for a double-bogey six that put him on, perhaps even the wrong side of, the cut line.

As if Watson's triumphant finish wasn't a great story, here was another; Woods looked to be on the way out of the Open.

None of this was fun for his playing partners. Ryo Ishikawa's second shot on this hole plummeted into the most unusual bunker on the course – a big lake of sand with an island of tall sea grass in the middle – and was also lost. It was bad luck on the slender Ishikawa, who was looking more and more like a wind-buffeted Pokémon character. Again, scores of assistants trampled in search of the missing ball, but in vain. He too had to play again, leaving a hefty job for the poor steward who had to rake the sand.

While all this was happening, Lee Westwood hit his second shot to the front of the green and nudged it close for par. What was the problem?

Inevitably, the camera dwelled on Woods throughout this episode, and while some berated the BBC for its endless pre-occupation with the world number one, it was dramatic footage. This was a moment of golf history, not least because it looked more serious than a mishap. Woods wasn't playing like himself or even looking like himself. Something was wrong, and the meta-morphosis was alarming, because Woods wasn't just fallible – he was abysmal. The mask of easy dominance was slipping; he resembled nothing so much as a gunnery-school biplane flopping to earth.

In this evocative spot, the fighter ace was in a tailspin.

It had often been rumoured that Woods enjoyed the odd cig-arette from time to time (it might even have been true: it was in a newspaper) and it made sense for such scuttlebutt to be sup-pressed, because nothing could be allowed to contradict the presentation of Woods as an immaculate perfectionist – com-posed, assured, clear-thinking and devoid of self-pity. A lot of high-powered image-control made it hard for most fans to imagine this super-driven golf machine doing anything so loose and irrational as light up. The commentators were calling him 'human after all', and while few people had ever thought of him as anything else, we knew what they meant. Only later, when winter fell, would we discover that he had deeper reasons for seeming so tightly wound, but even at this moment of golfing dissolution he seemed ferociously, and destructively, unhappy.

In a way it was understandable. Even Tiger's unearthly self-control had its work cut out to endure the tyranny of athletic excellence imposed on top sportsmen these days: the body fascism that controlled their diet and musculature, the infinite practice drills and workouts that sought to refine and eliminate error, the impossible media pressure, the insatiable public thirst for heroism, the bitter psychological struggle against self-doubt.

It was impossible, as Woods scowled off the 10th green, not to feel that something momentous had happened. He had often seemed too good to be true, but now it seemed possible that he had built up a persona of such unerring calibre that it might not survive even the smallest fracture. His odd, Mozartian upbringing had merged fluently with an American college system that turned out smooth golfers the way other factories turn out streamlined cars, and he was a top-of-the-range model; he made it look easy. But the sour and self-lacerating bad temper on display here suggested something that most of his life so far contradicted: the possibility that his victories were hard won, and came at a price, that the pressure cooker of so many final-round dramas had left him steaming.

Something else was in the mix; Woods was so handsomely marketed – a walking billboard for Swiss watches, Irish financial engineering and a smoother shave – that it was common to see him as a Californian dude who just happened to be coolly half-black. Suddenly, as he stalked these Scottish clumps in search of his lost ball, the singularity of his colour leaped to the fore. For

years, top-flight golf had included this strange and historically
unusual spectacle: thousands of white people dancing attendance
on one black man. Woods had chosen to make nothing of this,
so it had faded as a theme; but at tense moments like this it
rushed in.

Look again at the footage of those moments. Of the hundreds
of fans swirling around the base of the war memorial, not one
had a black face. Not one. The only non-Caucasian in the frame
was the star, the favourite, the special one. The extent to which
Woods contradicted the demographic of golf – portly old white
fellows – had not been so striking since his first, mesmerising win
at the Masters back in 1995. He had jokingly drawn attention to
this disparity, years earlier, when he said that golf was a game in
which 'white guys dressed as black pimps'. Since then he had tip-
toed away from such controversies, but as he stormed to the 11th
tee the depth of the chasm over which he hung seemed greater
than ever.

It was like watching a man fall from a tightrope, and suddenly
it became possible to imagine something new: Tiger looked like
a man who hated the game, a man who could walk away and
never look back.

He had been in jams before, and recovered, but now things
went from bad to worse. He bogeyed the 12th and fell short of
the green at the 13th, where his chip foundered on the front edge
and tumbled back to his feet.

Spectators and viewers shook their heads in disbelief; Tiger
himself could only bow his neck, like a man awaiting execution.

No one could have anticipated what happened next: it had
never been seen before. Woods walked to his ball and, without
the least attempt at rehearsal or planning, shunted it roughly up
the green.

It was the shot of a man who was no longer trying, of a man
admitting defeat. Hardly anyone could believe it. Years of watching him stalk such shots, and, against the odds, holing them, had

encouraged us to see him as bulletproof, invulnerable to the doubts that afflicted lesser souls. Now he looked like a bolshy teenager: if he couldn't win, he wouldn't play.

He was seven over par. This truly was over.

It was no consolation to know that there was a bigger picture here, that at the start of the day there were 50 players under par, and now there were only 20. Turnberry had bitten back in style.

Woods would normally have been happy with those odds. Not today.

For a few moments, when he secured a majestic birdie at the 16th and a more routine one at the 17th, it was as if the familiar Tiger were asserting himself and would now birdie the last to dive below the bar into the weekend. There were only 75 players on plus-four or better, so it looked now as though this would be the cut line. Birdie at the last might do.

According to the radio he was still being quoted – at 100–1 – to win.

'Gawt tae be wurth a poond,' said one spectator, peeling away.

It wasn't. This was almost a new experience for Woods – he had missed the cut in a major only once before – but the pressure of making cuts is in some ways more severe than the pressure of trying to win. Indeed, this is one of the appealing things about the Open: there are prizes all the way down the leaderboard. Television presents it as a race to the trophy in which everyone but the winner is a loser, but at Turnberry it didn't look that way. There were players busting a gut to make the top ten, or evade the cut, or make a few extra pounds. Adam Scott was striving to impress his watching girlfriend; everyone was striving for something. Thongchai Jaidee was hoping to finish high enough to get him into the world top five – which would bring automatic qualification to the other majors. Half a dozen players were praying not to finish last. There was lots to play for.

Even in the Duel in the Sun there were other things at stake. In the final round the English player Tommy Horton was paired with

Ben Crenshaw ('Ben and I both knew that we were playing for third place from the start') and finished 9th, a long way from the Claret Jug. But he was the highest-placed Briton in the Championship – a source of colossal pride – and back at the hotel he found a crate of champagne in his room, a gift from a grateful gambler who had bet on him to achieve this notable distinction.

It was strange, the different forms the game took. In Scotland it was a dour spiritual examination laced with salty aphorisms; in America a fierce competitive arena and a forum for businessmen. In England, it took a more leisurely, clubbable form: harmless if maddening fun, a bit weak on esprit de corps, but handy if there weren't a cricket match on. P. G. Wodehouse caught (and perhaps invented) this tone perfectly by scoffing at the witless enslavement of golf's disciples and rendering everything in life – wives, careers, literature, all – as junior to the daily round. 'A golfer needs a loving wife,' he wrote, 'to whom he can describe the day's play through the long evenings.' In his world, bunkers poked fun not just at wayward shots but at conceit, pride, malice and romantic folly.

But when Woods approached the final green, with a long putt that would, if holed, keep him here for the weekend, his nationality did not matter. He was one of golf's supreme creations, and he was in trouble. The ovation as he stepped into the embrace of the final grandstands was immense. All past champions get a big hand, but this was a full-throated roar not just of appreciation, but of encouragement and something more – sympathetic fellow-feeling. Pretty much everyone there had played golf a bit; everyone knew the game could be a killer.

In his increasingly curt way, Woods rarely failed to salute fans, but at this moment, with one of the grandest galleries of the year on its feet, whistling and yelling him on, he did not even take his hands out of his pockets. He was losing friends faster than he was losing shots, and he looked as out of place as a shark in an aquarium.

Ishikawa was out of the running by now, though it was interesting to note that despite dropping seven shots on the back nine
he was only two outside the cut, while Westwood fired his
approach close to the pin and was on two under par, only three
shots behind Marino and Watson. He missed the putt – was that
the one that would cost him the Open? – but he was certainly
going to be part of the final two days.

These moments were rich ones in the politics of celebrity –
celebritics – because when Ishikawa's approach fell short, it meant
that neither of the two golfers who had dominated media coverage around the world for the last two days had made the cut.
In the media zone, Gonzalo Fernández-Castaño and Johan
Edfors were giving interviews, switching between Spanish,
Swedish and English, about how glad they were to be here for
the weekend, but both had to raise their voices to be heard over
the barrage of camera clicking – Ishikawa had been spotted
through a flap in the tent.

'The wind completely did me in,' he was saying.

A hundred yards away, Kenichi Kuboya was holing out to be
two shots off the lead, but even the Japanese media were not
interested.

Thus *X-factor* golf: popularity is a stronger currency than good
play. It reminded some of the story about Arnold Palmer, whose
clothing line at one time was popular with teenage Japanese girls.
Palmer, marvelling at the sales figures, kept offering to go over
there and boost the brand, but his wise agent, Mark McCormack,
told him to stay in North Carolina. The last thing the Japanese
market needed was to see that this super-cool new American
clothing line bore the name of a leathery old golfer.

'It was just problem after problem,' said Woods, impatient to
get away.

The BBC commentators, pressed for a snap verdict, were
cautious.

'He's just had a bad week,' said Alliss. 'It's like Don Bradman coming into his final innings and he's out for nought. It's only about the fifth bad week he's had in 13 years.'

Ken Brown agreed: 'I don't think his swing is quite as good as it was in 1999 and 2000. But you kind of feel like you're criticising God.'

Mark James was happy to risk a word of advice: 'He will be thinking all the way back home about his swing and what he needs to do next.'

And Wayne Grady felt the same: 'There's definitely something in there he needs to work on. The ball is not taking off on the right line.' He felt sure it was temporary, though. 'He'll come back with a vengeance.'

Lee Westwood had been closest to the centre of the drama, and was too genial a man to mimic the unearthly concentration of Ben Hogan, who once, so the story went, was so wrapped up in his own game that he failed even to notice when his playing partner shot a hole in one. But while he did not want to pry ('I was in my own little world'), he could hardly help noticing that Woods was struggling.

'You don't often see him play shots like that,' he said. 'But everyone's entitled to a bad day. It happens to all of us.'

It hadn't happened to Westwood. Two closing birdies cancelled out an annoying late bogey, and turned a fighting round into a competitive one. Indeed, to have had to watch two days of mayhem and still get his own ball round in such good style boded well for his own chances.

'I'm calm and happy,' he said. 'I had a fair idea the golf course was going to play like that. Two under par is a good position.'

At the end of the year, the news of Woods's extra-marital indulgences would put his poor display (and foul mood) here in a new light. At the time, few guessed that Woods might have done anything so likely to endanger the smooth functioning of his swing. The instruction manuals rarely mention it, but a guilty conscience is not a useful swing thought.

'I made my share of mistakes out there today,' said Woods, offering no excuses. 'I just didn't play certain holes well. I figured if I shot two under par today, I would be right there in the Championship. But you have to play clean to win a major championship, and I just didn't do that.'

He could say that again. A couple of bleak statistics summed up his Open. In two days he had hit only 15 fairways out of 28. In one sense it was a heroic effort: he was misfiring badly, ditched his driver, lost seven shots in six holes and still only missed by one. If there were such a thing as a classy missed cut, this was it. But after years of seeking to 'Tiger-proof' courses with length, the R&A had found a different solution: by promoting accuracy over distance, the Ailsa was punishing those who had grown used to pounding the ball miles and snatching birdies with their short game.

Woods had achieved three birdies, ten pars, three bogeys . . . and a pair of double bogeys. That, for him, was the engine flaming: on a normal day those double bogeys might have been eagles, and he could have been eight shots better, two off the lead and ideally placed to 'make a move'.

No one even asked him about his chronic temper.

This only seemed like the only game in town. Elsewhere, golfers' hopes were rising and crashing like the salt water on Bruce's castle. Stewart Cink was sliding; Leonard and Villegas were signing for level and minus-one: both were in the hunt, the shake-up, the frame, or whatever they called it. Howell was dropping back to two-over. Johan Edfors had seemed to have fallen out of the contest with bogeys at 15 and 16, but had limbo-danced back under the line with a birdie at the 17th.

Elliot Saltman was coming in like a plane with only one wing. 'I played absolutely horrendous,' he said. 'I've never putted so bad in my life.'

It didn't help that he had beaten his brother, Lloyd. 'I missed four putts of around a foot. It makes me feel I want to throw the clubs away.'

Another qualifier, Steve Surry, was missing the cut by half a dozen – disappointing after a promising first day. Three shots vanished in the first five holes, and he then double-bogeyed the 8th to go out in 40.

'Six of the front nine are straight into the wind,' he said, sadly. 'And I missed every fairway. I got found out. The conditions were a lot different. I drove terribly and spent a lot of the time chopping out of the rough. Once a round starts to get away from you it is difficult to turn it around.'

He then said something it was hard to imagine a big-name player saying. 'I had a great week and I won £3000 in total, so I cannot complain.'

Could not complain? He had a lot to learn.

When Luke Donald came down the closing holes on plus-three, he found himself unsure of the rules, and asked his playing partner and Ryder Cup teammate Darren Clarke whether the ten-shot rule was in operation – the agreement that anyone within ten shots of the lead makes the cut. It wasn't. The top 70 and ties would make it through, and it was looking as though plus-three would make it. One dazzling round, and who knew?

'It's now or never,' he said. 'I've got it in me to shoot low.'

A while later, Thomas Levet finished one shot worse and broke into song in the media zone – 'Renne-drerp kip foalin' on ma 'ead' – in an attempt to encourage the weather to raise the cut line (it worked).

Chris Wood managed to pluck a decent score from an up-and-down round and was relieved. 'I played absolutely awful,' he declared, 'but it was a great mental day. It is the worst I've felt and played on a course for ages. I've got a splitting headache and indigestion. I think it's down to the wind. It can dehydrate without you realising it.'

There was even time for some laughter. When the three-ball of

Stenson, Stricker and Liang Wen-Chong came up the 18th, some evidently amusing mishap in the fairway halted their progress. It turned out that Liang Wen-Chong had lost his first drive to the left, hit a provisional down the middle and was exploring the long grass in search of his first attempt. Stenson, meanwhile, marched to his own ball, and Stricker strode to his. When Liang Wen-Chong found his wayward first ball, Stenson picked up the provisional and tossed it back towards him. Only then did Stricker peer down and realise that the ball at his feet was not his own: he had not, after all, outdriven Wen-Chong's provisional. And now Stenson had gone and tossed his ball into the rough.

For once the Rules Gods were kind. The attendant rules official deemed him not to have identified his ball, and he was given a free drop. He was so relieved he nailed it close and holed out for birdie. Stenson, on the other hand, could not stop giggling, and only just made par.

By the time the last groups turned for home, the course was running fast and dry, gulls were jabbing the fairways, and men in buggies were waiting to collect flags. The South African Branden Grace stood on the 13th tee, narrowed his eyes, took aim at the green some 413 yards away, and, like Elliot Saltman a while earlier, hit his ball clean through it.

Golf's senior executives were just emerging from their long wrangle about the grooves on wedges: the large 'box' grooves on modern clubs were deemed to suck away too much grass at impact, giving players serious spin and control even from the rough. One answer lay in Turnberry's trophy cabinets, where you could marvel at the smooth, polished surfaces of 'plain-faced' cleeks and niblicks from bygone times. Sights like this, however, suggested that distance remained the big problem. The 18th hole at the Ailsa was 461 yards, and Sergio Garcia could reach it with a drive and a wedge. How long before he and his big-firing colleagues decided to carry the grandstand on the left and still stop the ball by the pin?

Out in the deep, wind-ruffled sound, a Navy submarine lifted its tall, dark conning tower a mile offshore. It looked like the dorsal fin of a nuclear-powered killer whale, and as the sun dipped towards Arran, sober and warlike thoughts stole across the links. It was cold. The front pages were full of pictures of military coffins processing through wet Wiltshire towns, and even the littered course looked like an abandoned battlefield.

One late onlooker broke the mood with a quip.

'Oh look,' he said, pointing out to sea. 'Tiger's cab's arrived.'

The daily factsheet once again contained many useful truths. The old lady, as Watson liked to call Turnberry, had bared her fangs: there were only seven players below par. In all, eleven players missed the cut by one, including three champions: Curtis, Hamilton and Woods, one Masters winner (Weir), and the eight-time holder of Europe's Order of Merit (Montgomerie). It was no disgrace to finish beside players of this stature.

A few players whinged about the pin positions. Rose found them 'inaccessible', Casey called them 'ridiculous', and Daly thought them 'brutal'.

No one sympathised. The Open was not easy; and fans did not mind, given the mountainous sums on offer, seeing great golfers in trouble.

One man still not complaining was Jeremy Kavanagh. He had not survived the cut, but if you had told him at the start of the week that he was about to shoot more birdies than Tiger Woods, he would have bought drinks for everyone in Ayrshire. He had also beaten Ian Poulter: no mean feat, even if Poulter's 14 over par was not at all what the swing doctor ordered.

'That was horrible for two days,' Poulter said. 'Horrible. I hit my last good shot on the third – yesterday. It could have been the easiest municipal down the road and I would have missed the cut. You can only laugh.'

The only thing that may have ruffled him was a stray remark

about that 'Union Jack waistcoat' by the observant author Lynne Truss, who called it an 'unforced error'. It was, he insisted, huffily, 'a cashmere cardigan'.

Yet again, much was being made of the value of experience, and the performances of Watson and Calcavecchia seemed to confirm it. But Mark O'Meara seemed to think innocence could be an equally effective swing device. After his ugly triple bogey at the 18th, he said, 'I fatted it and chillied it and chillied it again like an amateur.'

As for the obituaries being prepared about Woods, facts had to be faced: his Open record was still second to none. Watson was a links specialist, but in 31 Opens he was 70 over par (an average of worse than two over par per Open). Faldo could claim a slightly better average – plus-48 after 32 Opens. Sergio Garcia had suffered a traumatic start to his Open career, at Carnoustie in 1999, where he shot a first-round 89 and burst into tears, but since then he had five top-ten finishes, one of them a lost play-off. The result was a cumulative total of plus-40 in 12 Opens. Retief Goosen was plus-26 in 12; Cink was plus-68 in 11, and Westood was plus-79 in 14.

Padraig Harrington, a linksman par excellence, had played in 12 Opens, won twice, and still had an aggregate score of 20 over par.

Tiger Woods, for all his problems today, occupied another dimension altogether. Up till this year he had played 13 Opens (roughly the same as Westwood and Harrington), but was a whopping 41 strokes *under* par.

Only one other player in the field could compare notes with this achievement and not blush. After 18 Opens, Ernie Els was 33-under.

In all the hoopla surrounding Woods, few noticed that the low round of the day was Daniel Gaunt's 67. But the man himself was very chuffed.

'On the first day I over-focused,' he said. 'Tried to block out all the stuff and didn't really let myself enjoy it. But the second round I let more in, and it was fantastic. And that bogey at the first, funnily enough that relaxed me a bit too. I played well in practice, probably shot four or five under, so I knew I could play these holes, I knew there were birdies out there. I just had to be patient. And it just started to come . . .'

How did he explain the nine-stroke difference between his two rounds?

Most players, asked this question, toe the usual line: that's links golf. Gaunt had a more personal explanation. 'I've had no money, I can't play week in week out like a lot of the other players. I was working on the Saturday before coming up to Turnberry. It's a struggle to be consistent.'

His brother Chris could only applaud. 'From now on, July 17th is going to be a special day in our family,' he said. 'Whatever happens now, on July 17th 2009 Daniel was the best player in the world.'

CHAPTER TWELVE

Day Three

The finale of the Open is a two-day race to the line with a staggered start. The first man out was the first man to have finished on the cut mark – Johan Edfors – and because there was an uneven field of players he set off on his own in what the forecasters were calling 'strong winds'. The coastal waters once more looked wonderful; this was the best sort of sea – it had land in it. The shadowy outlines of islands floated in a drab, grey drizzle as an early ferry shoved through the waves out of Troon.

It had been a strange year for Edfors. When he won three times in 2006, he looked ready to step into the highest rank of international golf, but although he finished in the top ten five times in 2008, and matched it in 2009 with a third and a second, he seemed to have mislaid the winning knack. He qualified in fine form for the US Open, and played well in the tournament itself despite being heckled for his rakish, piratical looks.

'Captain Caveman!' came the cry. 'Looks like Tarzan, putts like Jane!'

Edfors didn't mind – 'It was a great atmosphere, and enjoyable,' he said – but he preferred it up here. 'It's a lot more civilised in Scotland.'

He had failed to qualify at Sunningdale (where he also ended up playing alone), but here he was, setting a pace few could match by racing round in three hours (the R&A-recommended time was 4 hours 25 minutes). 'I was offered a marker [Turnberry's director of golf],' he said, 'but I chose to play on my own. I enjoyed it too.' The crowd was sympathetic. 'My coaches told me not to rush, and I tried not to. I had a nice walk with my caddie, took my time on the greens, and we enjoyed the day. The wind died down on the back nine, but I didn't really take advantage.'

The fairways were empty apart from clusters of wagtails and the occasional marshal in a hard-hat, so he strode away from his pursuers. By the time he turned at the lighthouse, he was two holes clear of the group behind (Allenby and O'Meara). It helped that he played all right. 'I hit the ball well,' he said, after a level-par round. As he fizzed the ball down the last two holes, big crowds were streaming the other way in pursuit of Harrington and Garcia, who were just beginning. Most amateurs can be put off by the cough of a squirrel, but Edfors had the professional gift: focus. 'I didn't even notice them,' he said.

He did, however, notice the surroundings. 'I always try to take in the scenery, but in a place like this you can't not breathe it all in.'

Luke Donald still hoped for something special, and seemed to think that a spiffy little tartan twin-set might help him find it. He began with a smart birdie (unlike Thomas Levet, whose hopes exploded when he took an improbable six) and remained below par (in the golfing sense) until the 9th, when he skewered his drive into long grass. At first it couldn't be found, but then a young boy trod on it ('You felt it under your feet?') He took a drop, put his third into the hollow left of the green and took double bogey, but this was his only lapse. He parred his way to the 17th, collected a shot and finished the day where he started, on three over par.

'I played very well,' he said. 'It's hard to give yourself birdie chances.'

That was true. In one way this was a classic links test – the ball had to be kept away from the rough and the bunkers – but because it was hard to get the ball close to the teasing pin positions (an aspect of the game not easy to judge on television), players were aiming at the middle of greens. The result, not for the first time, would turn on the holing of long putts.

Donald didn't manage any, but his playing partner did. The American Bryce Molder, shrugging off an unusual disorder which made his left hand smaller than his right (maybe it helped), woke up and, after 'fighting my swing' in the early rounds, urged himself to relax. 'I said a little prayer, just help me enjoy the day' – and it came true. Three long putts helped him to a 67, which put him on even par for the Open, three ahead of Donald and certain to start late tomorrow: he was the day's biggest mover, up from 53rd to 8th. 'Sleeping and eating might be a problem ahead of the final round,' he said, smiling. 'But I'm loving every minute of it.'

Padraig Harrington knew it wasn't going to be his day when he made a mess of the 7th – a par-five where he needed to gain a stroke. He was playing with Ryuji Imada (nickname 'Spanish' – ho, ho) and when he drove in a birdie at the 1st it still seemed possible that he could mount a charge. He of all people knew that any score under par would be competitive, and though he let one slip at the 3rd, he was in good shape when he walked off the 6th with a par. But he hacked his way up the 7th and, faced with a 77-yard wedge for his third (a shot he would normally hope to get close), he smudged it into the rough short of the green.

'That was the shot that deflated me,' he said. 'On another day . . . but I just couldn't convince myself to hit it. After that it was tough-going. But these things happen. I only got three putts up to the hole, and I three-putted all of them. It wasn't my day.'

When Watson went for a hat-trick of wins, in 1984, he came second (behind Ballesteros). Harrington wasn't going to be able to match that. But he had seen signs of an improvement in his

game and was not downhearted. It was, 'you know, professional
golf'.

Daniel Gaunt was still floating on air . 'It's a big thing for me,' he
said. 'I always believed I could play at this level. Now I know I
can.' It earned him a prestige pairing with Rory McIlroy, who
was soon struggling. He showed Harrington how to play the 7th,
powering a drive up the left and firing a high three-wood to four
feet to set up an eagle, but that was the only flash of his glittering pedigree (he turned professional with a handicap of plus-five;
he hoped to be five under par most times he teed up). It said a
lot for the difficulty of Open set-ups that he was five-over on the
front nine alone. Gaunt was steadier, though a costly double at
the treacherous 5th knocked him back. On the 16th tee he was
still ahead, but then he spun a wedge back off the green into the
burn, and that was that.

'It's the most relaxed I've been the whole week,' he said.
'Maybe I was too relaxed. I just hope I didn't kill anyone off the
tee. But I'll go for the flag tomorrow, and try to pick up enough
money to keep going.'

Rory McIlroy appeared to give up long before he tossed his
ball to the little girl with the 'Go Rory' sign on the 17th. But he
wasn't grumbling about anything. 'The crowds were fantastic,' he
said. 'Even though some of the people out there probably
thought they could play those first five holes better than me.' He
didn't believe it had been a burden, being second-favourite ('The
favourite missed the cut, so I've done better than him'), but he
did feel that some of the hopes had been unrealistic. 'I still feel
it's too early for me to win a major. I've still got a lot of improving to do.'

If Gaunt and McIlroy had looked over the crowd on the 18th
fairway – in the gorse hedge on the outside of the dog-leg – they
would have seen Sergio Garcia hitting two perfect shots to five
feet on the 3rd, and failing to touch the hole from there. The

mysteries of putting continued to vex him, and this week it looked as though reading greens might be his weakness: he was forever rolling the ball beautifully just wide of the hole.

He wasn't alone. For Justin Rose the day was 'bittersweet' – quite a fancy word for a round of golf. He played 'really, really well', but just couldn't find the cup. 'I can't strike the ball any better,' he said. 'I was just the skin of my teeth away from something like a 65.'

As a former winner and the leading Scot in the field, Paul Lawrie was in a special situation, and it wasn't a comfortable one. 'I played awful on Friday, and today was even worse,' he said after a 76. 'On Friday I made 73 but it was more like an 83, if I'm honest. My short game is brilliant at the moment. Now I just want to do something positive on the final day.'

In all there had been nine Scots in the Open, but only one other had made the cut: David Drysdale, who had once played here as a marker, was enjoying a fine year and had qualified in style at Sunningdale. But things weren't going his way. At the 16th he had to call a foul on himself when his ball moved. 'Whether I moved it with my practice swing or it was just an unstable lie, I don't know. But it was a one-stroke penalty.'

There were hard-luck stories everywhere, and little to be done but grin and bear them. Montgomerie had been happy to imply that he might have done better if Lyle hadn't put wasps in his hot milk, but Casey, after a clumsy day that dropped him to eight over par, could only shrug: 'It's good fun. I love the golf course and just wish I was playing better.'

Graeme Storm eagled the 17th, but by then it was too late. A damaging pair of double bogeys – at the 5th and 14th – sealed his fate, though it was the location of the pin at the 15th that left him fuming.

'The flag position was a disgrace,' he said. 'The worst I've ever seen. The wind is directly right to left, and the pin is four yards from the right side of the green. And it's on a slope. Until someone gets the sack or gets punished for it, nothing will happen.'

There are always remarks like this at the Open, and they always leave golf fans bemused. They betray a sense among the top players that par-threes ought by rights to be clear birdie opportunities. The public, on the other hand, knows that golfers as good as Storm, the runaway winner of the Sunningdale qualifier, could hit a six-iron 200 yards to a green, even in a crosswind. They do not especially want to watch a succession of birdie putts, some of which fall. They are, however, interested to see if the world's best golfers, forced to target the safe side, can two-putt for par.

This time, Watson did keep an eye on the television. 'You can see a lot of golf, see what people are doing,' he said. 'They should make it illegal.'

After hoovering up a lot of energetic goodwill at the practice range – still the best place to watch the players stretch into their wings – his round began with two ovations. The first came when he walked on to the tee, but then he walked up the fairway to escape the shelter of the grandstands and feel the breeze, and when he returned there was a second roar. While television loves the crowd – the columns of ants – it diminishes the impact it has on the play. Those present could sense the force of the gallery's will.

Not for the first time, he started unevenly, but did not lose his balance. At the 3rd he drove into the fairway bunker, splashed out, hit a seven-iron to nine feet and holed the putt; at the 5th his second shot flew in the crosswind and fell into the right-hand bunker ('I did a dumb thing, because I remember that shot, how much it goes right. You just can't feel the wind'); but he swept it out and rolled in a crowd-pleasing 20-foot putt for another save. These were crucial moments; the longer Watson stayed up with the pace, the more emphatically his shadow would fall across his pursuers, and the more potent would become the support of the crowd.

'I missed three out of the first six greens,' he said, 'and I was one over par. A little bit different to yesterday.'

Nor had he used up the heat in his putter. On the 14th he holed another 20-footer for par, and then his special 'feeling' at the 16th allowed him to roll in another, to a wicked pin position close to the burn which, a while earlier, had been the undoing of Zach Johnson. The 2007 Masters champion saw his approach fall in the water, dropped out, chipped long and, afraid of putting back into the ditch, lagged short and walked off with a seven.

Johnson was one of many invisible players today. This often happens on day three; the structure of the tournament and the editorial imperatives of television set an agenda that excludes those not in contention. A number of high-flyers – Vijay Singh, Ernie Els, Angel Cabrera – played to small galleries and were barely noticed by the electronic media. The leaders – Watson, Marino, Fisher, Westwood – sucked up all the attention.

But there was melodrama all over the place. It was soon obvious that the shifting wind had made Turnberry a different proposition all over again. The 10th, the hole that had ripped off Tiger's tail, was unrecognisable: players were flying the fairway bunkers (290 yards away) with ease.

The third round is often called 'moving day' because it is the last chance for players to shoot their way into contention, and when Henrik Stenson came to the 18th on level par, it looked as though he might be doing just that. But his drive went right, hit a spectator ('I caught a guy straight on the head') and crashed back to the 17th green.

'I was trying to come in on the wind,' he said. 'I blocked it a bit.'

It cost him a double bogey.

'Well, I'll see tomorrow if those shots would've come in handy. It would've felt much nicer to be two shots closer to the lead tonight.'

There was not even much interest in Jim Furyk, who in the last three Opens had come 4th, 12th and 5th, and was a live challenger. He was 'real pleased' with his round of 70, but Dougherty was disappointed with his three-over ('I didn't feel like I got what I deserved') and Daly also felt short-changed: 'I gave myself a ton of opportunities.' He wasn't the first player anyone expected to be canny, but he had been cautious: 'I am proud of my patience. I've hit three drivers in 54 holes. If I can get my putter going, you never know. But Tom, it's great to see.'

Bryce Molder's was still the best round of the day, but now Thongchai Jaidee came in unnoticed with a 69. 'I very happy,' he said. The most surprising round of all came from Tasmania's Matthew Goggin, whose 69, achieved in a shocking pink shirt, made him clubhouse leader on three under par. He was a player who had not, in 15 years, won a tournament, and his best effort this season was fourth place. But he had kept his ball out of trouble and holed putts – a sure recipe for success. He was within inches of coming unstuck at the 16th (like Johnson) when he hit an eight-iron to the slope at the front-right of the green, broke into a run, and didn't dare stop until he had crossed the bridge on to the putting surface, and marked his ball.

'I'd be going a lot quicker than that,' said Mark James in the commentary studio, watching Goggin trot up to the green.

'You think you would,' replied his old friend Ken Brown.

There was a generous cheer when Goggin marked his ball.

It is an odd sort of game, to be sure, when a sportsman can excite the crowd by pressing a coin into the grass.

'When it landed where it did, I was a bit shocked,' he said. 'My heart was racing. It probably wasn't a very good idea. I was kind of messing around, too.'

Like Marino, Goggin was here as a last-minute call-up. It seemed to say something about the unpredictability of golf, the strength-in-depth of the modern game, or the meekness of so-called 'top' players, that so many unfancied golfers were emerging at the head of affairs.

Goggin himself didn't see it as a surprise. 'I've worked a lot on my short game and putting,' he explained. 'And that's the pointy end of the stick, really. I've always hit the ball well enough to be around about.'

Lee Westwood wasn't messing around – not on purpose, at any rate. He slipped up once on the front nine, missing a putt at the 3rd, but thereafter he was solid. He made up for missing birdie at the 7th by nailing one at the 12th, and when he picked up another at the 17th, he was three-under, level with Goggin. All he needed to complete a near-perfect day was par at the last – never as easy it sounds. He found the fairway, had just over 200 yards to go, and picked a 'hard eight'. But his tee shot was up the left-hand side, so the pin was hidden behind some grassy mounds.

Billy Foster, the caddie who had walked here through the bogs of Irvine, advised him to keep it right, not risk the straight line in, but Westwood was feeling confident. He took dead aim . . . and dropped it in the clump.

The lie was awful: his first attempt flopped the ball forward less than a yard; it took a fine recovery to cosy it close and hole out for a five.

It was only the third round, and convention stated that it would make no difference in the final analysis, but this looked like being a tight Open – one shot could make all the difference, no matter where it came or went.

'It was my error,' admitted Westwood. 'If it lands five yards right of the flag it probably hops up and I've got a 25-footer for birdie. If I hit it where Billy tells me to, then it would be one shot better.'

This was an unusual remark. Golfers do not always resist the temptation to blame their caddies for errors. Caddies return the favour by invoking team spirit only when it suits them. 'We played well,' they will say after a good round, whereas, in less happy circumstances, 'He blew it.'

It was a sign that Westwood's head was level. 'Just a small error,' he concluded. 'Better today than tomorrow, I guess.'

Westwood was playing with Stewart Cink, who was hanging in there, without exciting the kind of cheers raised by the others. When he dropped a shot at the 5th, and another at the 7th when he missed a tap-in, one or two sighs of relief ran round the media village: he was one of the players who could ruin Watson's fairy tale without providing one of his own in return. He was a powerful, seasoned golfer who aroused no great passion in anyone.

But he didn't sulk. 'Links golf and I really like each other,' he said.

You couldn't say that Cink was being overlooked by Britain's media through any anti-American bias, because Watson was by no means neglected, while a young Chris Wood was barely noticed as he stole around in 72 to be two over par. Perhaps it was his haircut, which still resembled the Turnberry rough; perhaps it was the low-slung trousers; perhaps it was his youth. It couldn't have been his tall, angular swing, which kept launching the ball miles. For whatever reason, he did not catch the eye of the judges.

Cink, meanwhile, birdied the short 11th and pulled out something better on the 17th, when he chipped close from the rough for another timely birdie. At the 18th, when Westwood stuffed himself in the mound, Cink played to the front-right edge and let the ball bound on to the putting surface.

'That's the way to play it,' said Peter Alliss, watching on television.

Was anyone listening?

Cink made no mistake at the last and signed for a total of minus-one, in some ways the ideal score: near enough to the lead to win; not close enough to be rendered giddy by any booster headlines.

'The weather dictates what your score is,' he concluded. 'I feel like I've played the same every day.'

He wasn't even too gloomy about the tap-out at the 7th. 'It's a shock when it happens but you just have to gather yourself and kinda roll on. I got myself one shot deeper in the hole, but I'm still in it. It wasn't a day where I got everything out of the round, but I think there's still hope.'

Cink wasn't the only man tripped up by the 7th. Harrington had been rebuffed there, and so was Goosen.

'I played stupid golf,' Goosen said. 'I was too greedy there with my third.'

He holed a big one at the 14th, though, which 'really made me feel good', especially since it followed a pushed four-iron that headed towards the crowd. 'Slow down,' murmured Goosen – by his standards a hissy fit. Two fine shots down the 17th gave him a chance at an eagle that would bring him right on to the shoulders of the leaders. He gave the putt a nudge and while it was not in his nature to sensationalise things – 'I hit a nice drive off the tee and a nice five-iron in there' – there was enough in his body language, in the way he began to walk backwards, club raised, as the ball veered towards the hole, that looked in deadly earnest.

In his understated way, he was ecstatic: 'I'm feeling pretty good going into tomorrow.'

It was easy enough to poke fun at Goosen's equable temperament; people did sometimes wonder how he would play if he ever woke up. But there was a mild defiance in his soporific reluctance to talk about game plans or mental strategies. Somewhere in South Africa, where giraffe nibbled on acacia thorns and leopards dozed in trees, he had uncovered golf's original magic formula: 'Try on every shot and see what happens.'

His playing partner, Jiménez, went the other way. Like Goosen, he was level par on the 15th tee, but he dropped a shot there, and then two more at the 16th. He failed to birdie the 17th and par at the last left him at three-over for the tournament. It spoke volumes for the value of first-round scores that he was six-over for the day, yet still in with half a shout of the title.

The alligator-hunting Boo Weekley was another player to resist the lure of modern methods. 'I'll prepare for the final day as I always do,' he said, after slapping the ball around in a second consecutive 72, to be one over par, within an eagle or two of the lead. 'Go up to the hotel, have a couple of cocktails, a few beers, eat some food, go to bed and and get up Sunday morning and do the same thing.'

Two years earlier, at Carnoustie, someone had forced haggis on him, so this time, he said, he was only eating food he could spell.

Luckily he knew all the letters in chicken wings – his nightly treat.

The atmosphere was strangely subdued. When Martin Kaymer, winner of the last two tournaments and not far off the lead, strode off the 18th tee, just one person leaned on the 100-metre-long outdoor balcony of the corporate chalets. The crowd swelled when Lee Westwood marched past, as you would expect – he was a British player leading the (British) Open. But there could not have been more than eight people cheering him on. Far below what was now an exhilarating golf contest, the subterranean groan of a lapsed economy could be heard in the empty canvas rooms.

Ross Fisher reckoned that he could be at his wife's side in 90 minutes, if necessary, so he could afford to set family life to one side and concentrate on golf for a few hours. In truth, setting things to one side looked well within his compass; his quiet temperament made him Berkshire's answer to Goosen: an affront to those who find politeness a personality defect. He walked with a fusspot waddle, as if someone had put broken glass in his shoes, and the closest he came to a cavalier gesture was the twitch that accompanied a holed putt; he jumped as if stung, and gave a dainty little curtsey when he picked the ball from the hole, like a shoplifter.

Everyone knew he was long off the tee, but in his younger days it was equally well known, in Surrey golfing circles, that his ball took a bit of finding. But his confidence, after nearly winning the US Open, was high, and life was good. He lanced it down the middle every time.

Playing with a major champion (Calcavecchia) for the third day in a row, he gave that distinctive twitch on the 3rd, for birdie, and again on the 6th, where his tee shot found a bunker and he feathered it out to four feet for one of those par saves that is said to 'feel like a birdie'. It made up for the one he had missed on the previous hole, the 5th. He hit a two-iron into the gale off the tee, and then a three-iron over the bunkers to the back of the green. He faced a big putt: 40-odd feet with about 15 feet of break.

'I actually watched Harrington hit that putt earlier on, so I knew how much it broke,' he said.

He curled it down to four feet, but missed.

That was a theme too. Putt after putt ran close, but not in.

Those pundits who said that Turnberry was easy had clearly not tried to reach these into-the-wind greens. There was more to golf than yardages.

On the 7th Fisher drove into the rough, hacked out and hit a sumptuous approach to give him a shot at birdie (which he also missed). So when he dropped a couple after the turn (one of them a lip-out), it looked as if he might be wondering what colour to paint the cot. He promptly bashed in putts at the 16th and 17th to go back to where he started: three under par, and only one shot off the lead. He was, he said, 'very, very delighted'.

What, he was asked, did he make of Watson's performance? Even as he spoke, Watson was looking at a possible birdie at the 17th to go to four under par.

'He's just a legend,' said Fisher.

This compliment was diminished only a bit by the sense that it might also apply to the bloke at the club drunk enough to park his golf buggy on a Wentworth helipad. Fisher added that it was 'a real Cinderella story'.

This was confusing too. Did he mean that Watson would have

to hand back the magic slipper? And who were the ugly sisters? Not, surely, Fisher and Westwood, the British hopes (though, this being surly Scotland, there was a fair amount of anyone-but-Westwood going on).

But it didn't matter. The big question was: what to do if his wife rang?

Again he was unequivocal. 'If Jo does go into labour,' he said, 'I won't be here. I'll be with her. It's something that I definitely don't want to miss.'

Their private dilemma was fast becoming the talk of a nation – Britain loved nothing better than opining forcefully on what other people should do. Around Turnberry it was hard to imagine anything more pressing than the destination of the silver jug, but, elsewhere, talk was centring on the evident 'uselessness' of men in birth situations. It didn't seem to make any difference that Fisher was not hoping to be there 'for her' – it was what *he* wanted. He seemed to believe there might be other Opens.

Either way, it was a sharp reminder that despite the best efforts of the television coverage, winning was not the only thing that mattered. It also suggested that the modern preoccupation with focus might be misplaced: it seemed productive to have something else to think about.

Of course, even Fisher wanted the best of both worlds. 'I've got through three days, she's got through three days. Let's just hope that we can both hold on.'

Some of the spectators had already taken up this theme and were out there right now, sporting caps saying, 'Hang on Mrs Fisher'. When he missed a tricky putt on the 18th (for the outright lead), some wag in the stands shouted: 'Ross! Rossy! There's a phone call for you!'

There were a couple of late casualties. The nightly half gallon of St Mungo's failed to carry Calcavecchia through another day; he stumbled round in 77. And Steve Marino fell away too. Perhaps

Graeme Storm had a point about that 15th pin placement, because Marino went for it and landed on the bank to the right. He found the ball, but it was buried deep.

'My only options were to take an unplayable or go back to the tee.'

He dropped it back on the neighbouring fairway, chipped to the far edge of green, and took a six – no way to claw a path to the top of an Open.

It was a bitter lesson. 'I was going along well, and suddenly it was like bam. It was a combination of the good, the bad and the ugly, I guess.'

He was quick to pay tribute to his playing partner, however. During his travails at the 15th, Watson had prowled the green patiently, even holding the flag high so that Marino could see the line in.

'There's a reason why he's won five Claret Jugs,' said Marino. 'It was just super special for me to watch him do his thing at this golf course.'

Watson could afford to be generous, because he was performing wonders again. And although he kept talking about how calm he felt out there, this was no magical walking-on-water kind of performance. It was all skill and tenacity. He had clung on in the early part of the round, slipped a couple of times, but kept fighting back. He too had had trouble at the 15th, finding the bunker at the back and failing to hole out for par, but he still came to the 16th on two under par, one behind the leaders, and two crisp strikes put him on the middle of the green. The silence that fell over the crowd was heavy. Surely he couldn't do it again.

He could. The ball filtered down and darted into the centre of the cup. He was back at the head of things, with two holes to play.

No one expected him to miss out on a birdie at the 17th, and he didn't. His drive slanted right, though, and he was fortunate to find an aggressive bounce that turned it back towards the fairway.

The golfing gods truly did seem to be smiling on him. He came to the 18th on minus-four, one ahead of Goggin and two clear of Fisher and Westwood. Par at the last was hardly a problem for a man of his ability. Here came the tournament leader.

This was no joke. History might be at hand.

Once again, he suggested that he was in the grip of a strange external force. 'For some reason today I just didn't feel real nervous out there. I was just – I guess "serene" again is the right word for it. Even though I messed up a couple of times, I didn't let that bother me.'

His approach to the last green mimicked Cink's: it landed just short and leaped on, leaving him a straightforward two-putt for par. He marched into the giant acclaim, and on television he might have looked as if he were unaccompanied. In fact he was following a cameraman on an upright two-wheeler reversing a few yards ahead of him. Golfers must in part also be actors: Watson gave every appearance of not noticing.

Ten minutes later he was up before the media again.

'You guys must be sick of me,' he smiled, knowing it wasn't true.

He was happy to condense his feelings into a concise, tabloid version of the week so far. 'The first day here, yeah, let the old geezer have his day in the sun, you know, 65. The second day you said, well, that's OK, that's OK. And then today you kind of perk up your ears and say, this old geezer might have a chance to win the tournament.'

While happy to deprecate himself, however, he was not about to permit anyone else to cast aspersions. One reporter thought it 'ironic' that Watson should be riding the very instrument – his putter – that had given him so many problems over the years, and Watson was terse.

'It's not ironic. Every now and then it works, you know.'

This divided tone was becoming characteristic. On the one hand he was happy to play the sentimental old fool. 'It is kind of emotional out there,' he agreed. Coming up the 18th, he said, he mentioned his late friend and long-time caddie Bruce Edwards (who had died six years earlier) and said to his new bagman: 'Bruce is with us today.' And of course he was happy to invoke the distant, mighty spirit of Jack Nicklaus himself ('I know my friend is watching').

But Watson was also, when pressed, as tough-minded as any cattle trader.

'I do know one thing,' he said, cutting short a line of inquiry about how improbable this adventure was becoming. 'I feel good about what I did today. I feel good about my game plan. And who knows, it might happen. It would be something special if I did what I intend to do tomorrow.'

Intend? It sounded almost as if he were playing well on purpose.

Matthew Goggin would be paired with him the following day, and at least knew what to expect; they had been paired at Royal St George's in 2003 (the year Watson won the Senior Open here at Turnberry).

Goggin recalled it well. 'It was shocking just how good he was. I mean, it was ridiculous. I was thinking, He's getting on in years and not playing so much, but he was just smashing it round.'

All in all, it was another victory for the golf course. Only five players managed to get round under par, and when South Africa's Thomas Aiken joined Molder, Fisher, Jaidee and Goggin in that magic circle, he made it a clean sweep for inexperience. Matteo Manassero had also steered his ball through the wind with enviable brio, and was still in touch.

The initials 'TW' were still leading, however (as predicted), and there was magic in the air. One of Watson's achievements was already evident. Win or lose, he was banishing the cynical expertise that assumed he would falter; he was turning jaded golf watchers into bright-eyed innocents.

Perhaps the best compliment to his terrific play was that the Ailsa was still claiming scalps. The best form of defence, in these conditions, was . . . defence, but Sergio Garcia tripped every wire in a seven-bogey 76.

'I'm not surprised we didn't see a charge,' he said, swallowing his dejection. 'It's tough even hitting fairways with a four- or five-iron.'

Once again, debate focused on what Watson's performance said about golf. In the most obvious sense, it confirmed the fact that it was, for the most part, a game for older people – despite the protestations it was, more often than not, taken up by men and women no longer fit enough to play runaround games. Jack Nicklaus came to the rescue by declining to insist that things were better in his day. 'I think there are more good players now than there were when I was playing,' he said. 'But because there were fewer back then, they had more exposure to winning.'

This was a neat explanation, but it fell to Justin Rose to put his finger on the prevailing mood.

'If I don't win,' he said. 'I'll certainly be rooting for Tom Watson.'

Letting slip something that had not been widely mentioned, he added: 'He said to me earlier this week, and I'm sure he's said it publicly too, that he wants to win this Championship so he can keep playing it.'

This touching news added a fresh dimension to Watson's valiant challenge: the man was striving not just to be the greatest Open winner of all time, but to extend his own golfing life by a few more years.

It was another sign that golf was part of life, not the other way round.

'The greatest links player of all time,' added Rose, 'deserves to play the Open Championship as long as he wants, in my opinion.'

Hear, went the world, hear.

CHAPTER THIRTEEN

Day Four

The final day of the Open is not like other days. Overnight, the myriad possibilities distil into a single urgent question: who will win? So if the qualifying process often resembles a marathon, this last dawn is the moment when the leading group bursts into the stadium for the final lap.

It was a grey, pale morning. The cold sea slopped on the rocks and the beach. But brightness over the hills suggested a fine day.

There was only one thing to be resolved. Could Watson do it? As the hours passed, a second question pressed to the fore. Why not?

Daniel Gaunt might have been the best player in the world on Friday, but his form had dipped the next morning, so he was the first man on the tee for the finale, the first to explore the new wind direction (helping and off the left on the first hole) and the first to experience the slightly belittling sense that the crowd is no longer much interested in your efforts – it is merely claiming good viewing spots to watch the later challengers.

Unlike Edfors, he invited Turnberry's director of golf along as a marker and companion. Things didn't go too well for either of them. The marker, faced with a task that called for tact as well as skill, found the bunker four times in the first three holes, while Gaunt himself missed the green on the 1st, chipped on and then missed the par putt too. On the 2nd, his ball came to rest on a cigarette end beside the edge of the path behind the green, and as the rules official stooped to inspect the lie, a roar of applause erupted from the 1st tee, where Darren Clarke was being introduced. Gaunt made a brave up-and-down, and snapped up a birdie at the 3rd, but then dropped two more at the beastly 5th to lose ground on the players ahead of him. He had some other good moments, but Turnberry gave him a stinging parting slap at the 16th, when his wedge spun into the burn (again) and handed him a quadruple bogey to think about on the way home. His 4th shot, from the top of the green, pretty much summed up his week. It looked like a beauty; it checked when it pitched and slowed up at the pin. The crowd began to clap. But then the ball crept on, gathered pace, and dived back into the watery gully below the hole. He had shot 67 on a tough day two, but too many seemingly good shots had wound up like this one.

This hole in particular had been his nemesis, costing him seven shots in the last two rounds alone. 'As we walked to my ball, I said to my caddie, "I wonder what it'll hit us with now." I struggled with it all week.' It all meant that he would come last of those who had made the cut. But he knew that he had come 73rd out of several thousand competitors, and the experience as a whole had been a thrilling high point in his golfing career. 'I don't think it will ever go from my mind what I achieved, and the experience of playing in the Open will definitely make me feel different. I've always believed I could do it. Now I know I can. And I'll work even harder now.'

He had won £9300 – a sum worth celebrating. From somewhere he scared up a bright yellow 2009 Open flag from the 18th green, signed it as a gift for his parents, and headed back to his life.

*

Behind Gaunt, the rest of the field flowed out on to the course and saw their scores, and their hopes, rise and fall like the tide. Up in the hotel, Tom Watson watched the television to see how the course was playing, and found a message from Greg Norman on his phone: 'Remember your comment on Monday night.'

It was during dinner. Watson had been talking, hypothetically, about how much an Open win would mean to him, and this was sufficient to indicate to Norman that he was at any rate thinking of it. 'It was in his mind,' he said. 'He believed he could do it.'

They both knew how hard it was to take the lead into day four of a major championship. It was a built-in golfing fact. It would be crazy to do what Norman himself had done more than once – to go for flags and lose shots on the breeze like torn betting slips. But conservative play was perilous too: at least one of the expert golfers queuing up behind was bound to have a good day.

The best approach was to go out fast, grab a lead, force others to press, and watch them fall away. That, in recent times, had been the Woods way; but though fine in theory, it was no easy task.

For a while it looked as though Ross Fisher would be destiny's child. He seemed not to have read Dan Jenkins's disparaging remark on Twitter – 'Ross Fisher says he'll do the Phil Mickelson thing and leave the Open if his wife goes into labour. OK by me.' When he rolled in a birdie putt at the 1st, and then chipped in at the 2nd, he found himself sitting on five under par, two shots in the lead, with the round barely begun.

But on the 4th he carved his tee shot on to the right-hand slope, hacked it out and dropped a shot. And at the 5th . . . disaster. He took an iron from the tee (playing safe; always risky), but it sheared away on the wind and fell right into thick grass. His caddie asked the crowd to step back.

'This could go anywhere,' he said – not the most encouraging line.

Fisher's first attempt – down the grip, with a quick stabbing swing – to move the ball succeeded only in lumbering it a foot or so forward; his second sent it slashing across the fairway into an equally impossible lie on the other side. This time he was forced to take a penalty drop (if only he had done this in the first place) so after four shots (par) he was still in the rough, and nowhere near the green. He almost holed a putt for a brave seven, but had to settle for what the pros sometimes called a 'double par'. In the space of ten ugly minutes, his run at the title had faltered. He was one over par, and as good as out of it. The golf-dad story was over. His wife, if she were watching his torments on television, was probably having kittens instead.

Watson took care to do nothing boastful on the practice ground; he just drilled shot after shot low into the wind and smiled his grim, clenched half-smile, disguising his fierce will under a bemused expression. In 1951 a would-be winner, Max Faulkner, was asked for an autograph on the way to the 1st tee and impishly wrote 'Open Champion' beside his name. He did have a six-shot lead, but this was still tempting fate, and Watson showed no such gall. When he climbed into the buggy to be driven to the course, only to be stopped by a gaggle of period-dressed reps from a local gin distillery and ceremoniously presented with a rose, he forced himself to smile without unfixing his mind from the task ahead.

'Thank you,' he said, as if he had been presented with the trophy itself.

Out on the course, things were bunching up. Paul Lawrie birdied the 3rd, and saw his four-iron second shot roll improbably into the cup at the 7th for an albatross, only the eighth in Open history. But he was too far behind to repeat the feat of Carnoustie, where he came from ten shots back to dash the jug from Jean Van de Velde's lips.

Westwood was looking unflappable; Els, Kaymer and Leonard were within a fluke or two of contention; and some unfancied players – Aiken, Hansen, Johnson – were enjoying the day. So was Matthew Goggin, whose horse-loving Tasmanian family was pricking up its ears as he entered the straight.

At first, Goggin had accepted the role assigned to him and begun to fall away. So, for a while, had Watson himself. Bogey at the 1st was inevitable; at the 3rd it was forgivable. But he was still up there on the leaderboards; he pushed his head into the wind and made it to the lighthouse in good shape. As did Goggin, who rallied to birdie the 7th and the 10th to go to three-under and right up there. An exhilarating two at the short 11th from Watson put him back on top with the Tasmanian. It looked as though both of them were going to ride this thing to the end.

For a moment or two it was possible that the Open could be won by either its oldest or its youngest player. When Matteo Manassero trickled in a birdie at the 15th, he had no way of knowing that Ross Fisher was floundering in the dunes, and that one more birdie would move him to within a shot of the lead. His father, however, could hardly contain himself. The Manassero family was not troubling to hide its boisterous amazement at the derring-do of their son, who was grinning and waving and making putts like a young Seve, the silver medal already in the bag. His father strode in circles, hitting himself over the head with his umbrella. Could he breathe? There was a rapid translation. '*Si*,' he said. 'Of course.'

Maybe Manassero, like Watson, was bringing all his experience to bear. He never could have played like this when he was fourteen.

The globalisation of golf was proceeding apace. It was still possible that a Colombian might win; one of the referees was Russian; someone said that Vietnam had approved the construction of 60 courses. But history was pressing on the day as well. Before setting out, Watson had glanced at his phone and found another text, this time from Jack Nicklaus. 'You know how to win,' he wrote – knowing from personal experience how true this was.

Lee Westwood had eagled the 7th to take the lead, but

bogeyed the 10th to rejoin the chasing pack. Chris Wood, meanwhile, his hairstyle still modelled on the Turnberry rough, was picking his way home as well as anyone. In the radio and television booths the opinion-formers kept saying that he was sliding 'under the radar' – a clever-sounding phrase for players they themselves had chosen to overlook.

Stewart Cink was coasting along unremarked as well. He did nothing special early on, but didn't slide back either. He bogeyed the 5th and the 10th but pulled these back with birdies at 7 and 11. A long birdie putt on the 13th took him to minus-two, and suddenly he was in the thick of it. He dropped a shot at 14, regained it at 15, and even the TV cameras began to swing his way.

An hour earlier, Thomas Levet, one of the last men to be summoned to this event, had aced this 206-yard hole with one clean five-iron. There was room, even at this moment of extreme competition, with the Open in the balance, for a subsidiary celebration. Asked what he thought of as the hardest shot in golf, Groucho Marx once said, 'The hardest shot in golf I find to be the hole-in-one.' It is one of golf's magical possibilities, and this hole had a famous history of such deeds. In August 1963, a woman called Margaret Gordon played from the ladies' tee and achieved a 137-yard ace. Her husband George smiled, took a breath, played a nine-iron from eight yards further back, and middled it straight into the same cup.

Levet was not in the running, but championships can turn on such events. An hour later, Westwood hit an equally lovely tee shot, which threatened to go in too; but it missed the flag by inches and rolled on into the nearby back bunker. He flopped out and missed the putt. A luckier bounce and he would have been the clear leader. Now, after so much sure play, he was slipping back.

Up ahead, out of sight, Luke Donald was picking up shots. He had been a good player for a long time now, but was no longer young enough to get away with being 'promising'. He too was coming back after a wrist injury which had not inspired quite the same degree of public interest as Woods's knee. Indeed he had been attracting some bad press for picking up cheques without showing the 'drive' to be a major-winner.

This is what they used to say about Harrington. Or Cink.

It was true, however, that it was easier for any player to shoot low in the last round, like a fast-finishing horse that has left its run too late. And this couldn't help reminding one again of Harrington's pet observation that only a select few 'knew how to win'.

Was it true, perhaps, that the pressure at the top was so severe (in golf's intense, playful way) that only a few could plough down the last few holes with their game intact? If so, could anyone match Watson?

Even the weakest golfer presides over an inner quarrel between the adventurous thrill seeker who wants to smash towering drives over distant lakes, swing from the topmost rigging with gold doubloons gushing from his pockets, and the fearful realist who does not want to top it into brambles out of sheer deluded vanity, and have to endure the insincere, bad-luck-never-mind sympathy of his colleagues and rivals.

Perhaps it is this that lies at the heart of that other great golf cliché. As has been seen, it is often said – of players such as Sergio Garcia – that if they once 'broke through', they could go on and win repeatedly. Perhaps this was science. So far this year, however, it had not turned out like that. The Masters had been won by Angel Cabrera, and the US Open by Lucas Glover – good players having a superb day at the right time. In all the excited pre-Open talk about what sort of 'year' this would turn out to be, no one thought that it might be the Year of the Very Good Player We Have Forgotten About. On today's form, Donald, Westwood, Goosen and Cink were all pressing. It wouldn't be a shock if any of them broke through.

Ernie Els had an eagle chance on the 17th to catapult himself into the reckoning, but missed, and celebrated by bogeying the last. Donald's 67 took him to level par (280) and joint fifth for the Championship.

The galleries were large, but corporate hospitality was still lifeless. Martin Kaymer (285) and Ross Fisher (282) marched past without inspiring a flicker of interest.

The final tally was falling into place. Chris Wood missed out on the 18th – his adrenalin-powered nine-iron approach having flown the back of the green – but posted the Championship score to beat: 279, one under par. Goosen eagled the 17th for the second round in a row, but he needed a birdie three on the 18th to lift him alongside the Englishman. His four gave him level par for the Championship.

Wood remained in front until Cink holed his birdie putt on 18 for a clubhouse lead (278, two under par) that looked only half-relevant. Watson and Westwood were still out there. So was Goggin, although three straight bogeys, on 14, 15 and 16, looked like the end for him. Cink headed into the clubhouse, ignoring the souvenir Turnberry passport holder in the pro shop (£45) and even the grand collection of old clubs in their frames (the elliptical plain-faced jigger, the hand-forged cleek with dot-punched face, the wry-necked putter by Gourlay of Carnoustie), and watched the television, breath held, as Tom Watson played the closing holes.

He saw Westwood narrowly miss an eagle putt at the 17th ('Oh, it's all tingly tingly tingly,' whispered Peter Alliss) and then three-putt the last, after one of the Open's all-time great bunker shots. He saw Watson birdie the 17th to go to three-under and the outright lead, a single shot ahead of him, with that famous final hole to play.

Par at the last.

The crowd held its breath.

I was standing a few yards from Watson when he speared that eight-iron on to the 18th green and over the back. I then raced to the viewing area behind the green, where reporters were allowed to sneak in and watch. The stands, of course, were crammed full – and so, it turned out, was the standing-room-only zone. So I did not see the denouement. Along with a sizeable knot of other luckless spectators, I could only listen. I was behind the 18th, on the path by the recorder's cabin, the interview area and the practice green. I could see the stands, the flags, the sky, the faces of the spectators, but could only imagine the golfers striding into the swelling noise, and the Royal Navy personnel – as per tradition – linking arms on the fairway to hold back the crowd.

I could have run to the media tent, where televisions were broadcasting the now-classic footage. But it seemed silly to retreat from so decisive a moment. Anyway, you can hear a lot at a golf tournament. Even at the highest level, different levels of applause indicate varied outcomes: the polite, formal shuffle when a player is announced on the tee – plain punctuation. The ripple of firm appreciation for a birdie, the that'll-do-fine support for a tap-in par, or the notional, damning-with-faint-praise murmur that attends a bogey. The rapturous roar that greets a chip-in, and the sigh-groan, like air coming out of a balloon, that follows a missed putt.

The extreme silence now told us that Watson was settling over his ball off the back of the green. We had a vacant moment in which to remember that, for all the talk about his experience and the 'spirituality' he felt here at Turnberry, the reason he was lead-ing this Open was that half a dozen missable putts had rolled in. And of all the sources of golf's relationship with the uncanny, this was close to the heart. Golfers dedicate their lives to precision, but work within a margin of error compounded of physical motions, mental strains, invisible geological nuances and mere happenstance: a spike mark, an echo of a caddie's heel, a blade of scuffed grass. The best players negotiate these things with amaz-ing skill, but still, some putts go in and others don't. One of the most common mantras in the post-round interview is that putts 'just wouldn't fall', and this is usually true. 'I'm not being funny,' said Ross Fisher when he nearly won the US Open, 'but if I'd made a few more putts I honestly believe I could have won.'

This was both a statement of the obvious and a clear-headed insight. Similarly, there was much to be said (and was said) about Watson's amazing effort, but in the end he was in this situation simply because the putts *did* fall. Had they crept past, as usual, he would have been three or four over par, and everyone would have marvelled that he was still so competitive at his grand age – but it would not have been Watson's Open.

Here came the noise. A rumble turned into a roar, studded by a few sharp yells ('Get in the hole!') and then descended into a long, keening titter. Even without the benefit of a view, we knew exactly what had happened: the ball had missed and rolled past. There was more to do. And suddenly it seemed impossible that he could hole it – however long or short it was. The sheer weight of the crowd's anxiety would surely throw it off. If Watson had driven into trouble, hacked out and nailed a wedge to eight feet, or ten feet, you would have put your house on his holing it. But this was the last thing he wanted or planned to face.

No one was crossing their fingers more fervently than the hotel staff. The general manager, Stewart Selbie, admitted that a Watson win would have been . . . helpful. 'It would have been historic,' he said. 'It would have been absolute history.' He had been troubled by the sneers, in the press previews, especially the American press, that Turnberry was an easy 'resort' course that would be no match for top stars. 'The winners beat the golf course by two shots,' he smiled. 'What's wrong with that?'

We know what happened next.

The Open was over, almost – but the four holes ahead (the 5th, 6th, 17th and 18th) were an entirely new game. The play-off. Sunlight gushed across the green links, making it impossible to refer to this as the 'Duel in the Shade'. As the photographer

Dave Cannon later observed: 'The amazing thing about the whole week is that I had not pointed my camera at Stewart Cink until the play-off.'

He was not the only one.

CHAPTER FOURTEEN

The Play-Off

The first port of call for one large segment of the crowd was the gents behind the grandstand. The design and administration of these facilities – the one-way system in and out of the main stand – means that it is dangerous to give up a seat without careful thought, because at the end of a dramatic Open there is always a queue of people waiting to seize a vacated place. Now, released and bursting, they clattered down the scaffold stairs and hurried to the Portakabin, shaking their heads and grinning at the turn of events.

It wasn't the most beguiling venue for a conversation, but golf fans are good at making the best of things, and had a strong urge to put what they had just seen into words. So they formed an orderly queue where they could swap confident remarks about how they *knew* Watson was going to miss that putt, how they sensed Cink might be the man, and above all, how absolutely bloody rotten Lee Westwood must feel.

'Must be kicking himself,' said one man over his shoulder.

'Yeah. Went for birdie, didn't he?'

'Had to, I suppose.'

This was not true. It was an understandable error, but

Westwood was wrong (demonstrably, if only with hindsight) to think that he needed that birdie. A routine two-putt par would have put him in the finale. He did not know this at the time, but there was no hiding the fact that he had guessed wrong. Par would have sufficed. Many Opens have been lost by men who pressed for a score they did not need, including one on this very course. In 1994 Jesper Parnevik needed par at the 18th, but rashly believed (he had an eccentric rule against consulting scoreboards) that he needed more. In striving for birdie he dropped a shot, surrendering the title to Zimbabwe's Nick Price. This was not a rare event, and Matthew Goggin, in the interview tent, was even now expanding on the idea.

'It's the best I've played in a major,' he was saying, 'but at the end of the day they're probably, because so many guys get pepped up and fired up about them, the easiest tournaments to win. Of course they are the most difficult, but also the easiest, just because guys are freaking out.'

This seemed spot-on. A glance at the leaderboard indicated how many fancied stars had leaked shots in this tense final round. Watson, Goggin, Westwood, Fisher, Goosen, Furyk . . . of the six golfers in the last three groups, not one broke par. Victories in majors do have a lot to do with keeping things together under what sportswriters like to call 'the cosh' – the nerve-rattling drama of playing for high stakes. Lee Westwood was only the latest in a long, impressive line.

The other popular theory in the gents was that it 'must have been' the adrenalin surge that led Watson to pound his ball over the back of that final green. It was even possible to hear this corny theory being tossed around in the media tent, where people might have known better. It was possible that the man himself, a multiple major-winner with a superlative golf career behind him, might know more about the effects of adrenalin than the blokes in the gents, or even (heaven forbid) the journalists, but it is one of the happy delusions of sports-watching that we know more than the players. In some respects it is true – fans enjoy a superior view of the course (the way putts break, the way the ball rolls on certain holes) and can compare approach shots better than the golfers themselves. But it is safe to say that arm-chair fans know less about the difficulties of putting with sweaty palms or major-jangled nerve-endings than the players.

Still, it's a game of opinions, they say, and it was natural that everyone should want to interpret what they had just seen. There wasn't much time to reflect, though, because the play-off was due to begin in five minutes, and the only opinion that mattered now was where to go and watch it.

The crowd was split. Some – most – stayed in their seats, gambling that the drama would come down to the last roll of the last ball in this great amphitheatre; but thousands of others headed across to the high mounds above the burger concession that had been spewing out fatty smoke all week by the 17th green. This was one of the high points of the course: it gave commanding views of the 5th green, the 6th tee and 17th fairway, and also offered glorious glimpses out to sea, where the Ailsa Craig rose out of the water behind a cloud of indifferent gulls.

Only a handful of people, it turned out, went to the first play-off tee (the 5th hole), tramping over the abandoned 1st and 3rd fairways. I was one of them. We took our places around the ropes and waited for the players to arrive.

It took longer than the promised five minutes, so we had time to exchange muttered thoughts about the way these play-offs were organised. Everyone accepts that they are necessary – if you accept the convention that there can be only one winner – and they can often be thrilling; but they take different forms. Mostly they are staged on a single hole (usually the 18th, where the crowd is) and continue until someone loses. The US Open stages a full 18-hole play-off the following day, while Britain's Open (we are urged never to call it 'the British') opts for a compromise: a four-hole contest which goes to sudden-death if the scores remain level.

This solution is usually presented as ideal, especially by the journalists, since it does not require them to rearrange their lives and travel plans. The American route is commonly presented as dull and cumbersome. But while it might be irritating for those present at the event, who itch to see things resolved, for the television audience it has much to commend it – it presents an additional match between expert players on a course that armchair viewers now know. Better still, viewers get to see not just every shot but the unobtrusive action between shots – the caddies pacing out yardages, the moments of indecision and consultation, the blades of grass thrown into the air, the club selected and then rejected. We can examine every lie and each angle of attack, without cutting away to watch some other player holing out on the 11th or chipping close at the 14th. We can study every divot, in super-slow-motion.

The British way, while beguiling and immediate, can itself seem unbalanced. In particular, it has an alarming tendency to favour the player who has finished earlier, the one who by definition has shot a lower score (in order to draw level with the later starting times) and who has thus both more momentum and more time to regroup and compose himself.

The early finisher aspires to the play-off – it is the best he can hope for: one last crack. It is harder for those who have slid backwards into it, and are still berating themselves. In the 1999 Open at Carnoustie Jean Van de Velde tossed away his three-shot advantage with erratic decision-making at the last, but somehow salvaged his place in the play-off, only to lose to Paul Lawrie, who had been sipping coffee with his feet up for hours. In 2007 Padraig Harrington suffered a similar fate on that 18th hole, dumped it in the burn twice, and made double bogey only by dint of a tenacious chip and putt. Half an hour later Sergio Garcia, having led the Open throughout, missed the par he needed after his eight-footer kissed the hole and wandered on by.

Like Van de Velde, he was too unsettled to perform in the

play-off. Harrington, on the other hand, dandled his small son, let his heart rate return to normal and kept his swing warm on the practice green. When the time came, he grabbed a two-shot advantage on the very first hole.

Everyone knows that golf is game of fine lines, but it is worth recalling that if Garcia had holed that final putt in regulation play at Carnoustie, Harrington would have gone down as a man who had flung away the great prize through an abject failure of nerve. As it was, he was justly celebrated as a charming, industrious and deserving winner. It was Garcia who had to live with the self-lacerating feeling that he had failed to rise to the occasion.

The photographs of Garcia slumped over his wayward putter captured the soul-haunting moment to perfection, and now we had a fresh version of the same image: Watson walking after his own weak jab with a testy shake of the head. It was hard to think of him as a choker: he had won this event five times and had this week hung on to his lead, against all the odds, with superb tenacity. But it was equally difficult to imagine that he was relishing the hour to come. He had taken on the world's best, and none had beaten him. But could he possibly summon the energy and dexterity required to defy his advancing years one more time?

Something else had changed. For four days Watson had played his own sweet or 'serene' game. He had been favoured by fortune more than once, and had been able to smile a good deal as he defied the usual laws. Now, however, he had an opponent to contend with: a man. Golf is unusual among sports in that, as a rule, the actions of an opponent exert only an indirect impact on one's own game. Watson had not had to return a powerful serve, or keep pace with a Jamaican sprinter, or shake off a blow to the head. A major part of golfing psychology concerns itself with screening out the antics of your playing partners (just as a good part of golf gamesmanship concerns itself with getting through their defences). But a play-off resembles matchplay: you can play well and still lose, or poorly and win. It invites a markedly different cast of mind.

Not many competitors stayed to watch this final act, but Justin Leonard was spotted in the jostle; Tom Lehman tramped the dunes with his 18-year-old son, and here came someone who had not even been playing for the past two days. Jeremy Kavanagh, one of the first men to earn his place in Turnberry's starting line-up back in February, was one of the last to leave. He had enjoyed the wonderful practice round with Watson, and wanted to cheer him on. He wasn't alone. Thousands of spectators had invested part of themselves – their hopes, their own idealised dreams – in the prospect of a Watson victory. Defeat would be personal and painful. Fans always believe that the outcome of the game depends to some tangible extent on their own will power and faith, and this strange but deep illusion gripped hard now. It felt necessary, given the evidence of frailty we had just witnessed, that we believe. A sceptical voice would have seemed petty and affected, with no purpose other than to spoil sport.

Cink had a clear psychological edge, however. He had hunted his way into contention with an inspiring late lunge, since when he had been keeping himself warm in the clubhouse, praying that the play-off would come to pass. Watson, however, was still semi-stunned by his stumble on the 18th. There are entire books devoted to those who have laid one hand on the Claret Jug only to see it end up in someone else's arms. On this, the most recent page in Open history, Tom Watson hadn't just touched it – he had raised it to his lips, cradled its curves in the crook of his elbow, and sensed the engraver's tool cutting the letters of his name. Even now, there was only one man standing between himself and the grand prize . . .

It also seemed that the holes selected for the play-off favoured the younger man. They were a neat, coherent loop ending in a grandstand finish, and they were varied – two par-fours, one par-three and one par-five. But the first two – the 5th and 6th – were beastly, giving an edge to the longer hitter, and as for the 17th and 18th, well, Cink owed this career-changing new lease of life to his lacerating birdies on these two holes.

Finally, and worst of all, Watson had to wait. He stepped out of a golf cart and stood patiently at the back of the fifth tee as the crowd swelled around him, staring down the daunting hole that lay ahead. His memories of the view were happy enough. There was a high sand ridge up on the immediate left, which sheltered players from the sea breeze, and at the beginning of this long afternoon he had swept a four-iron to the centre of the green and two-putted for par – a score he would gladly settle for now. But there were ghosts and gravestones here too. This was where Ross Fisher, the early leader on this final day, had sunk his ball into the impenetrable long grass and suffered a ruinous four-over-par eight.

No sense thinking about that. But Watson had to hang about, letting the chill into his bones, for what seemed an age before Cink came marching back down the fairway – plenty of time to regret or at least brood on his miss at the 18th – a hole he would soon have to play again. Was it possible that a crack opened in his sangfroid? He had just foozled the best chance he would ever have to win this thing again. It was hard to say, but he certainly wasn't smiling.

It was a spellbinding evening. All week the weather had been kind – there had been no sustained rain, only the odd squally shower – and now, as if inspired by the occasion, sunshine poured out of the western sky and lit up the coast. It gilded the Ailsa Craig, which rose out of the Irish Sea like the crown of a giant's skull. One of the reasons the Open is so at home in Scotland is that the long northern day allows play to run from early in the morning till late at night (indeed it may be that the endless twilight is one of the reasons why golf took such a hold in Scotland in the days before television filled people's evenings). Tonight the sun was no longer warm, and cold air was settling on the links. But there were crisp shadows in the dips, and a quiet sea glittered across to those islands humped like colossal whales above the icy depths. It was not warm enough to be the 'Duel in the Sun Part II', and Cink (we have to be honest) was no Jack Nicklaus. But if Watson won this, it was only a question of time before it became the 'Duel in the Sunset'.

Ivor Robson appeared from somewhere, smart as always in a pressed green blazer, and with no frills in his matter-of-fact voice announced the players as if it were a beginning, not an ending.

'On the tee, from USA . . . Tom Watson.'

The gallery was small, partly because of the loftier vantage points on the grass turrets behind the green, and partly because the drop off the back of the teeing area was sheer and slippery. But there was a deep, low growl of encouragement as Watson swished his club in preparation.

As always, he wasted little time before swinging his driver with that familiar loop and snap of the hands, and cuffing the ball arrow-straight up the centre of the fairway. It was like looking at a Swiss watch. After all these god-knows-how-many years, there was still something rock-steady and perfectly tooled at the centre of his swing.

Cink, as if to emphasise his power advantage, took a two-iron. It is nice to think that had he known he was going to be in this position, he might have chosen different clothes. He was dressed in head-to-toe Nike – black and white with a livid green trim – which made him look like a poisonous beetle, or perhaps some lethal frog. He seemed too big for this game – he had to scrunch his frame to address the ball – but when he drew the club back he became tall, compact and elegant; he raised the blade high, brought it down fiercely, and battered the ball up the right-hand side.

The difference in flight was marked. Cink, a well-seasoned American pro, had the high, soft-landing trajectory ideal for inland courses with receptive greens. Watson, the links player par excellence, propelled the ball on a low and decisive path, making up for his lack of aerial carry with roll and forward thrust. And he may have taken more club, but he had outdriven his power-packed opponent. It would be Cink to play first.

Commentators love this. They call it 'getting your blow in first', and of course there is an edge to be gained if you can fire yourself close to the pin. But there is an equivalent advantage in being free to inspect the shape and outcome of the other man's shot, and the effect of the wind – stronger above the line of dunes than it seemed down here – and there is also the natural swagger inspired by distance off the tee.

Honours even, in other words. When Watson wandered off, hands in pockets like a man walking his dog, he looked relaxed. Perhaps, the crowd wished itself into thinking, he was not finished after all.

Jeremy Kavanagh certainly hoped so. 'He's definitely going to do it,' he said. 'Cink can't win . . . he can't . . . it's not his time. This is all about Watson. The world needs him to do it.' In most circumstances this would have seemed a wild overstatement, but as we strode along the ridge it seemed a rational and acute observation, as well as a calm expression of the prevailing mood. I felt the same. For Watson to let this slip now would feel like an outrage, a violation, a cold and surly slap in the face.

'Honestly,' added Kavanagh. 'I've had a feeling since the day I played with him. I'm telling you. I had a feeling.'

He wasn't the only one with his fingers crossed. Dan Jenkins had been putting his wit online this week, and reached for his laptop. 'If he wins the play-off,' he twittered, 'Stewart Cink has a chance to become the most hated man in the world.'

Professionals see the game quicker than fans. When Cink's four-iron tore off the clubface it looked perfect to me, but it was only yards above our heads when Kavanagh said, 'Bunker!' Sure enough, the ball fell with a silent splash into the sand some 220 yards up on the right. The noise from the crowd up there was, in its own special way, hideous: a huge, audibly insincere sigh shot through with a shiver of barely restrained glee.

Here came the decisive blow. This, right now, was Watson's opportunity to regain the initiative. It was obvious what would happen. He would take out that four-iron and, like a reluctant assassin, lace the ball to the centre of the green. The crowd – and there were thousands up there now, waiting with hands poised to celebrate – would erupt like Texan thunder, and Watson would surf to glory on a fresh wave of high emotion.

But for some reason Watson did not take the four-iron; he went for the five-iron. Maybe he was mindful of the doomed eight he had just pushed over the back of the 18th green. Perhaps he felt (rightly) that it was less windy now. Who knows? He had been making decisions like this all week, and most of them had been correct. All he had to do was fly the bunkers at the front. Cink was in the big one on the right, and Watson was damned if he was going there. But the other two were right in the way: they were small, deep and close-set, like a pair of goggles. They stared back down the fairway with eyes like dead sockets.

Watson's swing looked as it always did: neat, dapper and well-grooved. And as the ball rose up into the evening sky the crowd's murmur grew. It was like an approaching train. In a few seconds' time it would hit the turf with a thud and ignite a roar the like of which had not been heard on a golf course for years. People cleared their lungs and prepared to bellow.

But then, at the very top of its flight, the ball tottered as if punched. The breeze was strong up there, and the contact had not been quite so pure as usual (Watson called it 'chubby') and the temperature had dropped . . . whatever the reason, the ball ran out of zip, stalled, and fell into the sand.

Connoisseurs of the Scottish game, aggravated by the American name for bunkers, insist that 'traps' are for mice; but Watson was trapped all right. His ball lay jammed below the tall front lip; the pin was some twenty yards up the hill, far above his head.

'He can get it out,' said Kavanagh, pressing forward. 'He's on the upslope. But I don't know how far he can carry it up the green.'

Watson arrived, calm-faced, and took out his wedge.

Then a polite American voice carried from the other side.

'I think it's me, Tom.'

Cink was sizing up his own shot. His bunker was also deep, and his stance was troubling – the ball sat on sand that sloped away from him. Unlike Watson, he had plenty of green to work with, but it was a strange green: it leaned away to a low point, then rose again to the flag. A long-remembered tip from some golfing magazine flashed into his mind. Land your ball at the lowest spot. The downslope would throw it forward; the upslope would kill it dead. Cink pulled out his 60-degree wedge (the front lip was waist high) and followed his usual bunker method, picking a spot a few inches behind the ball, focusing on it, and not looking at his ball any more ('I didn't want to thin it into the lip'). His final thought was easy enough to say, but hard to do: Be aggressive. 'I wanted to make sure to give it enough to reach the hole.' His swing was shallow and unhurried; you could hear the soft, musical thump as the wedge bounced and splashed. Here came the ball, floating through a swirled mist of sand and running out towards the flag. It pulled up seven feet short: a fine recovery but not a certain par. The terms changed: perhaps Watson didn't need to get it close; so long as he got it out, he might have two putts for a half.

This was what he did, but it was all he did. The ball popped up and came to rest only a yard or so on to the green. And it was all very well talking about two putts as if they were inevitable, but all of a sudden this looked like three-putt country. An awful thought dawned. If Watson did take three, and Cink drained his, this could be as good as over right here.

Once again, as always, there was room for chagrin. If only Watson had taken the four-iron, as per the script, then Cink might not have felt so calm over his own bunker shot, might not

have been able to get it so close. It was no consolation that both
players had made the same error; Watson had enjoyed the luxury
of seeing his rival's fate, but had only repeated the mistake. In the
blink of an eye, Cink had seized the driver's seat, and the pas-
senger seat, and now he was sprawling all over the back seat as
well. He was a big fellow, in fine form; he would not be easy to
knock over.

It was still Watson to play. He took two quick practice strokes,
then rolled an absolute beauty just inches from the cup. It was a
tap-in, and now it was up to Cink to make his advantage count.

I found myself hoping that he could not feel the intensity with
which the crowd wanted him to miss (in the kindest and most
polite way: it is one of golf's embedded virtues that the gallery
resists vulgar partisanship). Alas, it did feel that everyone not actually related to Cink was urging his ball to stay out of that cup.
Watson may have erred, we told ourselves, but surely his grand
effort merited a reprieve. Some pretended that, like Wimbledon
crowds eager for a fifth-set decider, they wanted no more than a
close match, but this was a fig leaf. The truth is that few would
have minded if Cink had four-putted. It could not be mentioned,
but if he had yanked a hamstring and been forced to quit, it
would have struck most onlookers as only fair. The mood was
unanimous: the crowd craved a Watson win.

Some of the reasons were obvious. There was a generous-
hearted desire to see a seemingly decent man get what he
wanted. But a Watson win would also affirm a slew of worthwhile verities: that class is permanent, that advancing years can be
contested, that dreams do come true, that phoenixes can rise
from the flames, that the world really could offer a chap one last
turn in the limelight, and that there might be life in all the other
old dogs who slashed away at golf balls at weekends. It would
represent the triumph of skill over strength; hell, it would be
history.

There was another force at play – perhaps the most telling of all. Golf is delighted when unknowns steal into the early lead, but it does request that they not outstay their welcome. Like the pacemakers or 'rabbits' in 1500-metre record attempts, they are supposed to run one quick lap and bow out. It is a game, in the end, for überdogs.

It goes without saying that the winner-takes-all commercial culture of golf, boosted by the celebrity-fixated support of the media, helps to focus our allegiance on those few prominent names – Tiger Woods being the most obvious example. But it is also inscribed in the rubric of the Open that it identify the best, the 'champion' golfer of the year. Michael Bonallack, one-time chairman of the Royal and Ancient, used to wave aside complaints that the Open was too tough with the lofty phrase: 'This is an honours degree, not a common entrance exam.' And it was a source of pride at Turnberry, often cited as proof of the venue's calibre, that it had been able, in the form of previous winners Watson, Norman and Price, to locate and reward the world's 'best player at that time'.

This argument felt like a syllogism – those players surely seemed like the best golfers of their day in part because they won the Open: the Open was a cause of their greatness, not a mere symptom of it – but it did confirm golf's faith in the hierarchy of talent and its desire to anoint those we already believe to be the best. Topsy-turvy outcomes sit awkwardly with this ideology, so there was a sense that the results in the year's two earlier majors – Cabrera's Masters and Glover's US Open – were in some way 'bad for golf'. Some sports would have loved the idea of a free and fluid meritocracy, open to new winners – even football likes it when some team of part-time cloggers takes the super-rich glamour boys down a peg. But golf feels that its senior figures deserve to be recognised as such. While it makes much of the role of fortune, it does not want the outcome to be decided by sheer dumb luck. It wants greatness to prevail.

Tom Watson's magical performance at Turnberry thus represented a unique merger between two conflicting ideas. On one hand he engaged all the classic human-interest reflexes inspired by being a no-hoper; he was a perfectly bred underdog. But he was an underdog of whom we had heard, one who suited our equal desire that the laurels go to a proven winner. He was Rocky Balboa with a groaning trophy cabinet. No one else could combine these qualities with such grace. A comeback by Nick Faldo would call forth some of the same feelings, but Faldo was a driven monomaniac who suffered the handicap, up here in Scotland, of being English. He could never have been so popular a candidate as Watson.

There was, in other words, a powerful collection of forces trying to blow life into Watson's hopes. The crowd, as crowds do, was swaying as one. No one wanted to see evidence of other, bleaker truths – that you win some, you lose some – or see signs that sport is not moral, and does not award victory on the basis of justice or deserts. Deep down, we know that golf is blind, and that the Claret Jug goes to the man who plays the fewest strokes, so perhaps there was a faint rebel streak in the feeling running for Watson, a revolt against the callous tyranny of numbers. We wanted George to slay the dragon; we wanted good to prevail; we wanted virtue to be rewarded. We wanted the whole damned fairy tale, and we had paid good money to see it happen. So this wasn't only about Watson, in the end; we deserved a happy outcome too.

As I say, I stood there half-hoping that Cink was unaware of the depth of these feelings; it could not have made the putt any easier. Top golfers speak a lot about 'focus', about the need to achieve tranquillity over the ball: they spend much time and gold on narrowing their minds. In Cink's case it seemed to have been money well spent, because he did manage to ignore the larger drama in which he was involved, fold his long, sturdy frame over the ball, and with a sure touch roll it right in.

The applause was generous, though tinged with bitterness. After just one hole Cink was a stroke to the good, and Watson looked tired as he clambered up the path that led through the churning crowd to the 6th tee.

A couple of policemen were groaning at the size of the throng.

'They shouldn't be coming through here,' said one.

'Want to try stopping them?' said his colleague, swept uphill like everyone else.

The thin blue rope that functions as crowd control at the Open is not designed to channel a gallery of this size. Sensibly surmising that no one pressing after the players harboured the smallest criminal intention, the policemen shrugged and decided to watch the golf instead.

Could anyone recover from such an early setback? It had taken Watson four days to be two shots better than par; could he overcome a one-shot deficit in just three holes? It did not look hopeful, because Cink had the wind in his sails: in the last two holes he had overhauled Watson by three clear shots. And the next play-off hole was another monster, a 231-yard par-three across a valley to a raised green, with a bustling breeze off the sea to the left. It would take an expert tee shot to find the putting surface.

It was Cink's honour. Once again he reached for his favourite weapon: the two-iron. He looks tall and clumsy over the ball, but he swings with surprising delicacy and an emphatic downward thump, squeezing the ball up and away at impossible velocity, like a child firing cherry pips. Or, as he put it himself, 'I'm not real long, but I'm up there.' It seemed to be sailing right, and the crowd rustled with false concern, but when it landed it inched back down to the putting surface. It wasn't close, but it was safe.

The truth was that no matter how well Watson played, he now needed his opponent to foul up somewhere, and Cink had avoided the grave trouble surrounding this shot – the cavernous bunkers at the front and to the left, the sheer drop down to the right. It was a fine, strong shot which deserved a bit more than the polite, cool applause it received.

It does not take long for hopes to revive. Watson pulled out his hybrid, the old man's biffer that had been a trusty companion these past few days, and suddenly it seemed possible that he might blaze the ball to the side of the hole and twist the tables back in his favour. But the serenity had leaked out of his swing, and he made a hasty pass at the ball, tossing it firmly to the right. It toppled into the crowd on the side of the steep bank and lurched down to the bottom of the hill. 'I got stuck,' he said.

Cink didn't have to imagine that the crowd was against him any more: there were shrill voices ringing across the hollow when the players dipped off the tee after their balls. Some had a plaintive tone. 'Goo Tom! . . . You can do it, Tom! . . . Garn Tommy! . . . Go get 'im, Tom! . . . You're still my hero, Tom! . . . We love you, Tom!' It cannot have been easy for either man to listen to these panic-stricken cries, but Cink looked calm and unhurried. He had booked his seat on the putting surface, and knew that it would take a while for the gallery to arrange itself around Watson's ball: an untidy loop was already forming around it, pushing in close.

Watson walked up and down the slope, measuring the carry and sizing up a safe place to land. Marshals were spreading their arms and urging people to back away, to give the man room.

'It's OK,' said Watson, his voice unruffled. 'Just stay still. I'm going to come right over you guys.'

He swished his club, feeling the resistance in the grass. The hillside had been trampled by spectators, so the ball was perched on a raised nest of dry straw and air. It didn't need gouging out; if anything, the risk was that the club might slide under the ball and flop it forward only a foot or two.

He was aiming up through a narrow chute of bodies, with pale faces turned to watch. But he didn't seem fazed. He once wrote that he was fortunate to discover, early in his career, that he did possess something of the showman in his temperament, and this served him well now, because this was like playing a shot on a crowded railway platform. He did not fret or cower. A quiet turn, a firm move down, and up the ball floated, clean over the heads of the people on the crest, straight at the setting sun. It melted in the glare, so we could not see it finish, but it was evident from the shout of joy up there that Watson had pulled off a fine recovery. This wasn't over. If he could hole out, and if Cink happened to three-putt . . . these were big ifs, but what else was there to cling to?

Watson and his caddie did not have a smooth time forcing a path through the crowd and on to the green, and when they finally made it, Cink spoiled their mood by curling his putt downhill to the hole. For a moment it looked as though it might scurry past, and Cink had to raise his voice.

'Sit!' he called. 'Sit!'

The ball obeyed. It was not a gimme, but it looked an odds-on three.

Silence fell as Watson inspected his line. The putt was make-able, but it was stretching credulity to believe he could hole another one. The electric crackle was dissolving in the melancholy dusk, because this wasn't one you could see him holing, not after everything that had happened in the last half-hour. The truth − a sad one, but we had to face it − was that this was no longer a contest; these were the last rites. Watson was going through the usual ritual of bearing down, naturally, but once this missed, it might be best if the pair of them shook hands and called it a day. No one wanted to watch a beaten Watson plod the last two holes.

There are moments in action films when the hero falls into the fast-flowing waters beneath a bridge or a cliff, or over the edge of a yacht, and the villains zing bullets into the ripples and prowl around to make sure that they have finished him off. After a while they exchange glances, grimly agree that there is no way a man could survive a fall like that, and head back to the warmth to tell dirty jokes. And at that exact moment − hurrah! − up bobs the hero, alive and barely even kicking.

Something of this emotion is what inflamed the crowd when Watson holed his par putt. It wouldn't be true to say that the dunes shook, but the stunned roar did have a clubbing, percussive effect. It was equal parts glee, hope and shock; it may have been the loudest gasp in history.

By his own high standards Watson had played two holes poorly, and wasn't moving well, but he was still on his feet. And Cink's par putt suddenly looked teasing. To those who hate it, golf seems achingly slow, but here we could see how fast things change. Should Cink miss, the scores would be level and the momentum would be Watson's; he would again be favourite in a play-off that only seconds earlier seemed quite lost.

Cink didn't miss. He hadn't missed anything for a while now, and though it was hard to wish him well, exactly, we had to hand it to the guy: he was timing the ball sweetly and holing out in trying circumstances and with lukewarm support. In its own sad and unpopular way, it was impressive.

A platoon of red-jacketed marshals fanned out on the 17th fairway to act as ball-spotters. The hole runs parallel and in the opposite direction to the 16th; it dips into a deep valley before rising to a green 559 yards away – easily reachable in two, and a clear eagle or birdie opportunity for players as good as this. Both had picked up a shot here in regulation play.

The crowd around the 6th skidded to the bottom of the hill, past where Watson's ball had been, to the expected landing area. Cink took a three-wood and cracked the ball up the far side, where it sauntered into the fringe of the fairway some 300 yards from where he stood. Mouths tightened in grudging approval: another fine shot, damn his eyes.

From the bottom of this chute it is not possible to see players on the tee; they are back over a high mound. But there was the titanium crack of a driver – Watson's ball was on its way. We looked – the smartest place, usually – to the middle of the fairway, but the ball never arrived.

'Anyone see it?'

'Must have pulled it.'

Some of the spectators were listening to headsets tuned to Radio Open Golf, the dedicated station providing dawn-to-dusk commentary. According to the presenter Robert Lee, Watson's ball had dived into the left-hand rough – what he liked to call the 'cabbage'. His co-commentators shared his anguish. The airwaves filled with the sound of gnashing teeth and wringing hands.

Even the marshals didn't seem to know where the ball was. A few of them began to climb the hill short and left, in very thick grass. It was an awful spot to end up in – Watson would not be hitting this green in two.

Once again the script seemed to have been lost. 'My legs didn't work,' said Watson. His hands flipped ahead of his turn, and the ball dived into this long grass where hares trembled amid nesting skylarks (or so it was said: they were rarely glimpsed) as if determined to disappear for ever.

It was all too easy to lose balls here. Turnberry had been closed for the whole winter in preparation for this event, and when it reopened, only a week or so before the Open, the members came out for a welcome-back day and lost several hundred balls in these fiendish seaside grasses.

Not this one, please.

There didn't seem to be any sign of it. Watson arrived and strode into the waist-high fluff, but he hadn't seen the ball land, and had no idea if he was looking in the right place. By now there were dozens of people tramping the slope, poking and peering. Here came someone who seemed to know: he was pointing higher up the hill with a confident air. A camera crew trotted across, hungry for a sadistic close-up.

Then an arm went up, and a cry broke the air, and there it was, twenty or thirty yards short of where the main group was looking. Watson stooped down, identified the ball as his own, and straightened. He should have been relieved, but there was a sad note in his body language: he looked impatient, as if he couldn't wait to get this blasted thing done with.

'I don't know if I can get it out, Ox,' he told his caddie. 'But I'll try.'

The camera crew was still wandering in the fairway, but he took a thrash anyway. And perhaps here, at last, he had found a place where younger muscles were needed. The ball hopped up like a winged bird and died back into the same rough only a few yards ahead. This was a wreck.

He had a better lie this time and was able to slash it on to the fairway, but there was no point constructing fanciful models of what could – might – happen, because Cink was already knocking the ball up to the green, and the Open was falling into his hands. Two putts would increase his lead.

Who said play-offs were exciting? This was agonising: a sad implosion performed in hideous slow-motion. Cink made a clean two-putt birdie; Watson staggered on and missed for double bogey. 'The lead is four entering the final hole,' twittered Dan Jenkins to those of Watson's fans who were not watching television. 'I've been to funerals that were more uplifting.'

So Cink stood on the 18th tee with a four-stroke lead. Even if he turned round and whacked his ball into the sea he could still win, and he did not look willing to do anything so eccentric or rash. He scorched his two-iron into a perfect area beyond the safe landing zone, leaving himself with only a pitching wedge to the green. Just like his play-off partner all those years ago (32, if anyone needed reminding), he took dead aim and dropped the ball by the flag for a scintillating (so far as he was concerned) finishing birdie.

As for Watson, well, if it was Young Tom who had given a masterclass in links golf for four days, it was Old Tom who now had to hobble home like a wounded veteran. His tee shot at the last toppled into the crowd and had to be dropped back over the railings. 'I apologise,' he said, and it was if he were saying sorry not for wounding a spectator but for losing. It seemed appropriate: he had promised a historic finale, and failed to write the ending. Those watching felt sympathy but also loss. Watson had tried valiantly, so we did not blame him in the least – but we too felt sick.

Expressionless, he gave the ball a sod-it shove forwards, just missing the green. His chip was no better than routine, and the putt that followed . . . but there is no point reliving those last horrible shots. For all the chance he had of winning Watson might as well have been kicking it up the fairway. The applause was rapturous, grateful and sustained – even Cink joined in, sportingly clapping-in his beaten opponent – and Watson doffed his cap with a courtesy accumulated over many years. But there was no hiding the dejection on his embattled features. His blue eyes were watery, and that windswept half-smile trembled on the brink of a sob.

That was it. Watson had missed out. And as the crowd filed in silence over the temporary bridge to the car parks, whipped and hurting, the Open revealed its final irony. All these slumped, dumbstruck spectators, along with the multitudes glued to it at home (the Open was watched in 600 million households, according to Royal and Ancient estimates), were dazed with sorrow on behalf of a man who had just won £450,000.

By most standards that is a decent return on one week's stick-and-ball fun at a luxury resort. It would cost a tourist around several thousand pounds to enjoy such luck. Yet here we were, awash with sympathy for the guy.

I suppose we could, if we wanted to be vulgar, have noticed that he had also just lost £300,000 – the baffling difference between first and second place. And while it didn't seem cultured to be dwelling on financial matters at a time like this – everyone knew that the money meant nothing beside the grief of falling short – it was an arresting fact that Watson had, in coming second, won more treasure than in all his previous 31 Opens put together. At Carnoustie in 1975 he earned £7500; the 1977 Duel in the Sun netted him just £10,000. There could hardly have been a more telling sign of the riches that had fallen on golf in recent decades.

Now, for the first time in years, it was all under threat. The recession was putting cold claws around both the elite tour and the public game. Events were struggling for sponsors; clubs were struggling for members. Golf had not been a poor man's sport since its earliest days, when industrial-age artisans eked out a living by mastering the mashie shot and forging clubs for aristo-cratic no-hopers; but in recent years it had become a byword for fat-cat prosperity. The squillion-dollar pro tour, a plush fantasia of golden endorsements, ravishing cars, five-star luxury and bling watches, was the showy public face of a sport more tightly woven into the commercial mesh of finance and elite villa development than any other. And now, in 2009 (at last, some said), it was hit-ting a reef.

Perhaps this, finally, was why everyone had been so eager for Watson to prevail. He reminded us of a simpler time, a time when golf was a game rather than a multi-billion-dollar industry. He himself had been quick to remind the media how greatly things had changed. 'Isn't it amazing?' he said in a post-round conference. 'In 1975 there were about 15 press people after I won in the play-off. And then here we are . . .' He looked across a temporary hall containing at least 30 times that number. 'And you know, it was raining and wet and all this and all that. And now here we are in 2009, talking about text messages. Who would have thunk it?'

Watson's tumultuous performance stopped the clock. By find-ing victory in defeat, his brave effort had a redemptive quality, as if there might be fixed points in our spinning world. And by encouraging us to dwell on the past, he exposed the game's ancient and precious roots in this harsh and daunting Scottish wilderness. Watson's wintry smile and clever play offered us reminders of a different world. His own stirring past – the prospect of a historic sixth win – invited us to dwell not just on the resonant names from bygone times (Willie Park, Old and Young Tom Morris, Harry Vardon and Jack Nicklaus), but also on this unique links landscape, the unearthly weave of salt, sand and heather to which the Open was eternally devoted. Watson glorified the event by illuminating its most cherished traditions. As it entered its 150th year – that first Open, in 1860, at Prestwick, was only a few miles up this rocky shore – he had walked, waved and putted down these green alleys like the ghost or spirit of Opens past.

'I tell you what,' Robert Lee was saying to his radio listeners as the gleaming silver jug was handed to Stewart Cink on the sun-polished 18th green. 'This will still be remembered as Watson's Open.'

He was right. And it may well have been an unlucky bounce for Cink, because this was the high point of his career, perhaps even his life – but for a few bright days in July, Watson demonstrated for all the world to see that winning was not, in fact, everything. Golfers like to assert, as fuel for their single-minded drive for glory, that second place is worthless, that nobody remembers guys who come up short – as if there is something feeble and lily-livered about beating all of your opponents bar one. Watson took this unpleasant cliché and tore it to ribbons. In the months to come, golf fans would shake their heads at the memory of Watson's sterling effort and struggle to recall who it was – hang on, it'll come to me in a minute – the name of that tall fellow who actually won in the end.

CHAPTER FIFTEEN

The End (Again)

The Open was not quite over. There was time for some light but intent booing (not screened, for some reason) when the crowd was told that there would now be a pause while the players gave TV interviews. The rancorous response was understandable. Spectators who have spent £55 and a good deal of sweat chasing the game do not like being pushed aside by the very cameras that have been such an intrusive presence all day; they resent the brute reminder that they are mere scenery.

Everyone knew that the age when golf (like all sports) invited fans to marvel at excellence up close was passing. In the brave new digital-marketing complex we had invited into our homes, we would be seduced into watching golf only on screens, inhaling the advertising that kept the show on the road. And the players (even Woods) would be offered as exemplars of the qualities corporate sponsors most wanted to emphasise: steadfastness, reliability, trustworthiness, goal-getting.

The end of the Open is a historic ritual sanctified by a renowned lineage of poignant deeds. To have this compromised in favour of a few instant – and instantly forgotten – televised platitudes felt as hollow as a missed putt.

'It's fair comment,' said David Hill. 'But the big world of television is where the money is paid, and they do like that quick interview at the end. We have looked at doing it on the 18th green [the Wimbledon approach], but you get a large gaggle of people coming forward, so it's not done in an orderly manner, and doesn't work well. So we take the players off the green into the recorder's area. Each TV company gets its one-minute spot. The fact is, like it or not, Americans in particular don't always stay for the presentation. Ratings plummet. We try to be fair to everyone . . .'

The pause was especially costly because it let the emotional pressure of the moment leak into the chilly air. By the time the presentation party walked on to the square of green grass where the last rites had taken place, the atmosphere had lost its edge; it had become merely polite. The presentation party blinked in the sunlight, like a cabaret firing-squad.

The winner of the silver medal (for the leading amateur) was announced, and Matteo Manassero beamed in the sunshine. Over the first two days his fortunes had been so closely entwined with Watson's that it felt fitting that he should now be part of the pre-liminaries in the older man's coronation, so it came as a shock, even now, when Stewart Cink was declared the winner. His speech – a routine statement of gratitude and pride with an uncomfortable (to most British ears) expression of his recently rekindled faith, would have been fine in most circumstances, but at this hour, in this place, it felt leaden. The occasion called for something much more self-effacing, stirring and in keeping with the valiant, knightly nature of Watson's fall . . . like this:

Thank you. I know what you're thinking. It is obvious to all of us that this has been Watson's Open. Tom was writing a new chapter here, and if I'd been out here watching, I would have been rooting for him too. But I wasn't watching; I was competing. And as a competitor I can only say that victory is sweet precisely because of the calibre of the man I beat.

Tom has five of these, so knows how it feels. To stand here on this

green, on this course, in this Championship, in this place, in this sun-
shine – as someone once said: this is what it's all about, isn't it? I've been
dreaming of this since I was the height of the rough out there. I wish we
could share this jug, but sport is hard sometimes. I'm sorry.

I'd like to thank the Royal and Ancient, the greenkeeping staff, every-
one involved in this great tournament – even the media – [laughter] and
especially all of you, the fans, for your great courtesy – even now, when
I know you are sad. I hope that when the dust settles you won't regret
having me as your champion too much. For my part I will cherish this
famous title with enormous pride. Thank you all.

It is wildly unfair, of course, to expect too much of such
speeches. It is hard enough to win the Open, and we certainly
can't expect champions to turn into Abraham Lincoln in the time
it takes to sign a sponsored hat. But Cink was presented with a
unique opportunity to put himself into golf history by saying
something resonant or at least generous, and, misled by the idea
that winning was enough, he muffed it.

As the green cleared, and the crowd thudded down the metal
stairwells one last time, Tom Watson was driven to the media
tent, where he installed himself on the raised stage and waited as
the world's press, few of whom were as wirily fit as he was, scurried in and found seats.

The marquee filled with a heavy silence, tinged with sadness.

'This ain't a funeral, you know,' said Watson, self-deprecating
to the last.

It was not quite original. Boris Becker said the same thing
('Nobody died') to the mourners present when he lost his
Wimbledon title – it was an exemplary way for a sportsman to
demonstrate that he, at least, was rising above the disappointment.
But in one sense it was not true. This *was* a funeral: a dream, a
wish, a hope had died out there; and there was little useful to say
about it. Watson spoke easily and at length about his day, as if it
had been just another round of golf ('I kept the ball in play off the
tee, which is critical here'), but kept getting dragged back to the

emotional wave he had set in motion, and then ridden, and then fallen off.

'It was fun,' he said, invited to summarise the experience. 'It was just like my son said. "Have fun, Dad." It was fun to be in the mix again. There was something out there. I still believe that. It helped me along. It's Turnberry. Great memories here. This would have been a great memory. Unfortunately it didn't happen.'

Now that was more like it. And it wasn't that these were per-ceptive insights in themselves; it was enough that they trembled with the drama of what we had just seen unfold.

Cink, alas, was too happy to be swayed by such considerations. With the Claret Jug in front of him, eyes bright with pleasure, he could not bring himself to see Watson's heroics as anything other than an obstacle he had successfully overcome. In paying lip serv-ice to Watson's achievement ('It's mixed feelings because I've watched him with such admiration all week'), he committed an alarming faux pas by referring to his opponent as 'the same Tom Watson that won this tournament in, what was it, '72?'

The collective gasp made the room judder. Cink might have been the only person within two-iron distance who did not have 1977 seared into his golfing memory as the year of the Duel in the Sun. Even given the excitement of the moment, it was a bleak lapse (generously amended by the official transcript). It seemed that he had not yet registered the dizzy sentiments that had been raised by Watson's effort.

One Scottish reporter tried to impress on him the way the world was likely to see his victory. 'You've effectively put a red pen through one of the greatest stories in golfing history. Can you fathom that?'

Cink could not. 'In the end, you know, it's a tournament to see who lasts the longest. It's a survival test out there . . .'

It was sad. The truth was that he had no need to apologise; no one really begrudged him the prize he had landed. But he was certainly missing the chance to write himself into the annals of sportsmanship. The most charming thing he said was that he had played a lot with Tiger Woods over the years, so was well used to people rooting for the other guy.

It was true. He was an experienced party-pooper. Back in March, when Woods made his comeback at the Accenture Match Play in Arizona, after eight months of waiting, he actually delayed the entrance of the maestro. Golf's treasurers were hugging themselves: on the day it was announced that Tiger would play, an additional 41,000 tickets were sold. The media geared up; indeed, on the first practice day the cameras were so preoccupied with the return of He-Who-Must-Be-Named that they sent a unit out to follow his caddie Steve Williams as he walked the course, squinting into the sun and measuring yardages.

When the time came, Woods was due on the tee at 12.05 p.m., just two minutes after the TV coverage began (what a coincidence). But Cink had already commandeered the 1st tee for his play-off against Richard Sterne. 'He's waited eight months,' said Cink. 'He can wait two more minutes.'

Now as the Open champion, he was able to smile at his own lack of renown. 'I never really heard my name tossed in there with the group of best ones not to have won,' he said. 'So maybe I was starting to believe that, that I wasn't one of the best.'

That was more like it. Modesty. Humility. Who could possibly object? A worthy winner.

The day after the Open resembles every other drained aftermath in the sporting world. 'I always think this is the worst day of the year,' said Peter Dawson, and it was easy to see what he meant. The marquees lay deserted, with flapping panels of canvas lifting on the wind. There were cracked, empty plastic beer cups strewn on the worn-out grass, along with drinks cans, crisp packets, half-chewed sandwiches, useless ticket stubs and torn sweet wrappers. The bunker beside the practice green had new furniture – a

cigarette packet, a takeaway coffee canister, a ripped-up programme, even an inside-out umbrella – and had not been raked:
there were drifts of breeze-blown grass, stray weeds and muddy
footprints.

This time the feeling was worse than usual. People formed
small knots and confided that yes, they felt sick, hollow . . . just
plain damned awful. No one was acting: the common sense was
of a monstrous collective hangover. People felt personally
deprived, if only because they had so wanted to be able to boast,
when this amazing story happened in front of their eyes, that they
were there. They were implicated. For one long, perfect weekend
they had been willing Watson to victory, and they had failed. It
was a severe blow, and as a result the most popular analyses echoed
Watson's own remark: 'It would've been one hell of a story.'

This was the view in most of the newspapers. 'Fairytale Not
To Be' said the *Scotsman*. 'Dream Almost Came True' sighed
USA Today. *The Times* said it was 'six inches from being the
greatest sports story ever told', and the *Telegraph* agreed: 'Cink
Ends Watson Fairytale'.

So far as I was concerned it still was one hell of a story; it was
just a slightly different story from the one we thought we were
being told. It had a twist in the tail, that's all. You could even argue
that this made it even better; not happier, of course, but richer.
Watson had corralled the spirits of the game's original storytellers,
Old Tom and Young Tom; he had carried them on his shoulders,
his steel-blue eyes clear and cloudless, and then delivered the most
unexpected ending of all: defeat. Perhaps we have all developed
an immunity, fuelled by the narrative absolutes of Hollywood-age
television, to the idea of a sad ending: we just don't get it. Instead
we interpret a sad tale as a happy one that 'almost' happened.

Workmen and technicians were nosing down empty walkways,
pulling high-performance cable out of the gorse bushes and
rolling it into hoops, while trucks reversed across the abandoned
acres, collecting railings and piling up refuse sacks. Young men

and women sat on the damp hessian floor of the merchandising tent, folding up unsold sweaters, waterproof jackets, hats, shirts, brand-name umbrellas and souvenir tee pegs. Rhod McEwan's books were flying off the shelves – into packing cases.

Flaps hung low over the once-welcoming entrances to the Open Arms. Pot plants were loaded on to racks and wheeled up ramps into the dark interiors of the lorries and vans that growled in the broken 'village'. Squads of Biffa kids speared litter into their groaning sacks.

The set was being struck, but the golf course belonged to the R&A for one more day (as a prudent measure against postponement or delay, it does not return the course to the resort until the Tuesday). Lucky invitees headed out to see how their games fared against the Championship set-up, on the ground where yesterday's heroes came and went. (How many sports permit fans to compare notes with the stars in this direct way? A football supporter will never know what it is to play a Rooney, a Messi, a Drogba.) There were no marshals or ball-spotters to speed them on their way, but the fairways were still lined with crowd-control ropes – the thin blue twine – and (deserted) grandstands still towered over the greens.

It was a bright morning, and the wind was ripping at the roofs of the marquees. Where Garcia and company were hitting mid-irons down to the bunkers on the right, today's players were flaring drivers left and right into the billowing gale. Real life came back to Turnberry with a crunch.

The starter stepped out of his trim hut, handed out scorecards and greeted the intruders as if they were international stars, tactfully hiding his disquiet at the diminished level of ball-striking.

I broke with etiquette by mentioning it. 'Looks like there may be a slight decline,' I murmured, 'in the standard of play.'

'I'll not argue,' he said, keeping his voice low. 'Though you'll have to forgive me for objecting to your use of the word "slight".'

Actually, some of the players leaning into the wind were pretty good. The hotel's top brass (Stewart Selbie and his marketing

Open Secrets

manager, David Walker) treated themselves to a pat on the back
by grabbing their clubs and hurrying down the hill. 'When we
got to the 18th we all dropped balls where Watson had been, to
see what we could do,' said Selbie. 'I think every group did the
same.' The outcome was brutal: three out of the four players in
Selbie's group managed to get up and down in two. The sad fact
was that any single-figure golfer worth the salt in his porridge
would curse if he failed to make par from there. 'It's not a difficult shot,' said Selbie. 'Though it's fair to say that we didn't have
the huge crowds and the whole situation to contend with. That
might have made a difference.'

He wasn't joking. It sure might.

Over at the media tent, the R&A top brass strolled through the
morning, no longer in jackets and ties, to give their final press
conference.

One of the chief lines of enquiry concerned the number of
spectators. Journalists fastened on to this as if seeking a stick with
which to beat the administrative body, but it seemed an odd
question: surely everyone knew that gate receipts counted for
almost nothing in the context of the immense fees raked in from
TV contracts. The Open, Peter Dawson pointed out with a smile,
was watched by some 600 million households around the world.
A small fluctuation in the number of paying spectators in Scotland
was – no offence – neither here nor there. It was something to be
grateful for, surely, that the R&A was not required to show year-
on-year growth to shareholders, and that, as David Hill kept
repeating, this whole subject of Open venues was treated on a
long-term basis, as a ten-year cycle, not as a series of one-offs.
Turnberry hadn't been auditioning; it had been hosting, and it
could hardly have gone better. These links seemed to produce
exhilarating Opens, and that was enough to secure its place on the
Championship list. It was worth losing a few spectators for the
burst of prestige generated by a gripping on-course climax.

'It's a funny one,' said Hill. 'The fact is, the media would slaughter us if we said we were taking Turnberry off the list, but that's the way of it sometimes. You can't win.'

The other issue concerned Tom Watson's age. The Open at St Andrews in 2010 would, unless he won it, be his last: former winners were welcome until they were 60, but after that they had to qualify like anyone else. Watson had proved this week that he was still a competitive force, but there seemed no sign that the rules would be relaxed. Twice, Watson had urged this very room to take it up with Peter Dawson, and since he was now sitting here in person (this is what is meant when people talk disparagingly about those who communicate 'through the media'), that is what the room did. Dawson was tactful, and said that of course it was something they would 'keep looking at', but when he met Watson himself, on the eve of that final round, he was more direct. 'Tom,' he said. 'You could make this whole thing moot by winning tomorrow.'

Watson had nodded. Having toyed with the media all week, urging them to tackle Dawson on this subject, he now revealed that he did not want the older generation to be overindulged. 'I agree with what they do. The age limit is correct,' he had said. 'They have to make room for younger players.'

Maybe there was a simple motive at work here: dejection. Sports journalists pose as impartial witnesses, but they are also fans, and have the same bitter response to defeat as any other diehard. It isn't the done thing to be mean about the winner, so the media bent over backwards to compliment Cink, through gritted teeth. Quite a few forced themselves, with grim fair-mindedness, to sympathise with him for winning the Open in such circumstances. The Claret Jug was depicted as a poisoned chalice.

It was odd to be invited to pity a man who had just been granted his life's most fervent wish. But such is golf.

Only a handful of journalists stayed for these last rites. Most had turned for home, or the next tournament, the evening before.

Some were standing in line at Prestwick or Glasgow Airport, waiting to board flights to Tokyo, Madrid, New York or Miami. Others were driving home. A few headed south to Sunningdale, to watch Tom Watson all over again, in the Senior Open – in three days' time. A heretical thought dawned: was it possible that this whole Turnberry-magic thing was a front, and that Watson was simply warming up for the greater challenges down south?

Lee Westwood went to Harrogate to deliver a masterclass to junior golfers, hiding his disappointment from the seven-year-olds he was there to encourage. It hurt, but he did not need to feel too dreadful. He had not, in the cold light of day, been foolish to believe he needed birdie at the last – there was no reason at that moment to think that Watson would bogey it. Things had simply not fallen his way. But he had played superbly and banked a quarter of a million pounds. Worse things happened at sea.

Retief Goosen crossed the Atlantic, played the Canadian Open in a downpour and lost the play-off. Marc Cayeux and Graeme Storm headed east to the Czech Republic, where they came joint fourth in the Moravia Silesia Open and wondered how come they hadn't played like this in Scotland. Golf wasn't stopping just because the Open had finished.

Ross Fisher went back to Surrey to hold his wife's hand and await what the *Sutton Guardian* called 'the putter of tiny feet'. A week later (some ten days after the deadline), she gave birth to a daughter. There had been much debate, among people who had never met either of the happy couple, concerning the name. At Turnberry it was widely felt it had to be Craig, if a boy, or Ailsa, if a girl. In fact she was called Eve. Fisher didn't celebrate for long. He was soon on a transatlantic flight for the PGA.

Padraig Harrington and Rory McIlroy went to lend their glamour to the launch of a spanking new golf resort in Fermanagh, Northern Ireland. Daniel Gaunt, Jeremy Kavanagh and the Saltman brothers shook their heads, tried to resume their normal lives, and found themselves playing together in a pro-am at Burhill, near Weybridge. Rhys Davies and Steve Surry were in Wales fighting the rain at the Swalec Wales Challenge (they had to sweep puddles off the green for Davies's winning putt).

Stewart Cink, meanwhile, flew home to Atlanta and took a big gang of family and friends to a local restaurant, where he celebrated in style, with Guinness in the Claret Jug and plenty of happy laughter ('Had a good ole time for a few hours'). He was feeling generous, and why not? He even offered to buy dinner for anyone close by who felt that he was noisy or disruptive. Who could begrudge him a bit of fun? It wasn't his fault that everyone wanted his opponent to win. Indeed, the sweetest thing about his victory was the stature of the men he outlasted. The world was still wondering how Watson lost, but Cink could distinctly remember making three birdies in the last four holes. That took some doing, and he knew it.

As for Tom Watson, well, what is a man to do who has just let go of the great prize? He went to a 'family-run' seafood restaurant at Maidens (only a few blows with his two-hybrid from the hotel) called Wildings, to eat tiger prawns, sea bass and that great Kansas delicacy: sticky toffee pudding. It was comfort food: he had eaten here five times this week, once with Greg and Chrissie. This time, when he walked in, the whole room stood and clapped. He ended up signing trinkets and posing for photos; he even went out back to thank the boys and girls in the kitchen.

He didn't sleep too well in the short Scottish night – 'It was dark when I went to sleep, and dark when I woke up.' The next morning he went to the airport. When he walked on the plane, there was another ovation.

It was a strange feeling. Defeat hurt ('It tears at your gut, as it always tears at your gut'), yet he felt like the most popular man on the planet. Messages were flying in from all over, some from people he could barely remember: 'How so many people got my email address, I don't know.'

It was said, when he passed through security at the airport the next morning, that his hip triggered a security alarm. This was fanciful: if new joints tripped the system, airport terminals would sound like amusement arcades. It must have been his steely resolve that beeped the bell.

Sunningdale was where some players' Open had begun. It was only six weeks since International Qualifying, but it seemed an unfeasibly long time ago. A lot of golf balls had gone into the water under the bridge since then. Still, there were lessons to be teased from the memories. Branden Grace had played well here, and managed to take his fine play north. But Graeme Storm had been unable to reproduce his Berkshire ball-striking in Scotland. Here he had beaten the hapless Johan Edfors by a dozen shots; at Turnberry, they were tied in 52nd place. Some of the other qualifiers – Rafa Echenique, Raphaël Jacquelin – made no impression at all. After his last-minute heroics to come through the play-off, Scotland's Richie Ramsay sank to a drab 77 on the Ailsa links, and faded from sight. Oliver Fisher fared even worse. The smart young Englishman followed a chaotic 79 with a grim 78. In all, only four of Sunningdale's qualifiers made the cut, but there was no shame feeling the halfway sword at an Open, not when you consider the calibre of the others (Montgomerie, Woods, Scott, Duval, Glover, Faldo, Ogilvy, Poulter) who also fell by the wayside.

For one player Sunningdale came as a relief. The defending Senior Open champion, Bruce Vaughan, had qualified for Turnberry, but had endured a wretched few days of uphill golf. 'Probably the lowest point of my career,' he said. 'I hit it so bad. I mean, I had no clue where it was going.' As a Kansas man, he was eager to lavish praise on Watson. 'I tell you, I played with him this year at Newport Beach, and I started off birdie, par, birdie, birdie, and on the fifth tee I'm still hitting last. The guy is great.'

When Watson reached Berkshire he allowed himself a pang of self-pity, but only a brief one. Then he told himself not to 'wuss out', unpacked his clubs and headed out for a practice round: 'Played a nice round with Bob Gilder, who took ten pounds off me on the back nine. Didn't like that.'

Next day he played in a pro-am, and over evening drinks smiled his usual gracious smile and said he was optimistic about his chances because he had – on the quiet – been putting in some high-quality practice up in Scotland. Naturally, he was happy to submit to further questioning from the media. 'There's still quite a vacuum in the stomach,' he said. 'I'm not crying, but I've been affected by it. But this too shall pass.' Asked to sum up how things stood, he said simply, 'It's been a great go. It's been a great go for me.'

He harboured no ill feelings towards Stewart Cink. How could he, when he himself had played the Cink role, right there at Turnberry, when he won the Senior Open in 2003. A luckless Carl Mason double-bogeyed the last and ended up losing to Watson in a play-off. 'I said to Jack Nicklaus right after that, that evening, I said, "I was really lucky." And he said, "No. You've got to play 72 holes. You've got to do it."'

The next morning it was competition time again. Watson stood on the range (the converted 18th hole of Sunningdale's New Course) and, wearing the same light-blue sweater he had in Scotland, loosened up that famous snappy swing. On the putting green he ran into his playing partner, Greg Norman. 'See you have the same guy caddying for you,' he said, smiling at Norman's son. Norman shook his hand and congratulated him on his work at Turnberry. 'Well, you know what it's like,' said Watson.

And off they went together, like knights of old.

On the first tee, under full midsummer foliage, Ivor Robson was waiting in his R&A green jacket.

'On the tee from USA,' he said, time folding in on itself, 'Tom Watson!'

It was a soft, warm day in the Surrey woods. Norman blazed

it right; Watson drilled it up the middle, found the green, and lag-putted to the hole for an easy tap-in birdie. Who said golf was difficult?

Greg Norman, not a man to be upstaged, trickled in three birdies on the first four holes, but Watson wasn't fazed, and picked up three of his own. It looked as though his touch on the greens at Turnberry was no fluke. He shot 67 ('I made some early putts I probably shouldn't have made') and rode high for four days without quite finding a winning surge. In the end he came eighth – a fine showing – behind Loren Roberts, who rolled in a ten-footer to step past Mark McNulty in a play-off. Roberts couldn't stop smiling. It was his first look at Sunningdale, and he pronounced himself smitten.

There was one more thing. He had just qualified for next year's Open.

The debate about Watson's age continued to grip the world's 19th holes. He was clearly an unusual case, but then, so was Norman the year before. For two years in a row a senior golfer had contended . . . was this a coincidence? It was clear that thanks to modern medicine, people stayed young for longer these days; Watson himself had (perhaps literally) the hips of a mere stripling. The growth of the Seniors Tour too seemed to be making a difference. Great players now had the means to keep their games sharper than used to be possible.

Some were still comically anxious to argue that Watson's excellent effort put golf in a poor light – an amusing and affected response to such a rare event. There are plenty of reasons to dislike golf – its addictive triviality, its giddy dress sense, its self-satisfactions, its sanctimonious platitudes – but none of these prevent it from being a sport. One might (to repeat) as well argue that football and rugby are not sports, since they require such babyish pitches (a golf course could hold half a dozen and still have room for a squash complex). Why should muscle or willpower be regarded as superior to the blend of balance and timing required to fly a golf ball 300 yards. Golf is a unique game with a rare history, requiring physical and mental composure. Anyone who has tried it knows it to be difficult and nuanced. Its fans are evangelists, which is off-putting, and it has a strict code of conduct, which invites would-be Bohemians to reject it with a sneer. In all of these ways, golf sports with its own opponents. It enrages them, mocks them and leaves them empty-handed in one haughty breath.

The sad truth, however, was that had Watson won (however brilliant the 'story'), it would have led golf's younger stars to be pilloried, and would have loudly undermined golf's claim to be a stern athletic discipline.

All of this was trumped in the end by the simple fact that Watson did not win. The debate could rage as long as it liked, but his performance proved nothing. By coming close he hinted that older guys could win; but he also proved that they couldn't – that they would falter at the last. People could say whatever they liked; both sides were right.

Watson himself – surprise, surprise – wasn't buying the idea that his grand effort was 'bad for golf'. 'I don't agree that a 59-year-old almost winning reflects badly on the younger generation,' he said. 'The notion that they can't finish; well, Stewart Cink finished. He drilled me in the play-off. And I feel bad he didn't receive the adulation he deserved.'

We can say what we like, but when the world thinks back to the 2009 Open it might remember just one bounce of just one ball. When Cink hit his final iron to the 72nd green, he caught it a trifle heavy; it pitched short, lurched and curled its way towards its target, and left him a testing 15-footer which (brilliantly) he holed. Watson's final iron, on the other hand, seemed perfect. In mid-air, a record-equalling sixth Open was as good as in the bag. But here came that ping-pong ricochet on the wind-dried turf, and there went his hapless ball, trickling on and on over the back edge.

Watch it again. The ball pitches a yard on to the front: it could hardly have been more finely judged.

'You'd think I could stop it,' said Watson. 'But that crest was probably the driest part of the green.'

How can such things be explained? Are golf's grand outcomes decided, in the end, by nothing more profound than mere dumb luck?

Golf – especially links golf – is famously that game of fine lines: players are invited to take the rough with the smooth, to smile at misfortune and press on into the wind. There is no doubt that Scotland's variable weather does give luck a major role. Early starters can get calm sunshine while late starters find themselves in sideways rain (or vice versa). Fortune also lies in the stray rebounds from trees, fences, galleries and grandstands. Everyone remembers Jean Van de Velde's stupidity on the 18th hole at Carnoustie, but his second shot hit the corner of a grandstand and could easily have bounced into a playable lie. It is not luck that sends a ball clattering into the trees, but it is luck that decides whether it is lost or found. Some balls get mud on them; others don't. Van de Velde was foolish, but also unfortunate.

Coping with random blows is an everyday part of the game, but some near-misses are so decisive that it is easier to see them as agitations of fate or providence. The fact is that golfers have to live with a margin of error and a range of influences that lies beyond human control. They can practise as much as they like, all day and all night if they want to, but they can only compress the margin for error, not eradicate it entirely. A fly might land on the ball. It is not, as the saying (and the book) goes, a game of perfect, and one of the challenges it imposes on its adherents is that they must cope with its (and their own) imperfections.

A lot of what we take to be luck is just part of the architecture of the game. Those fairway bunkers, that stream, that steep incline behind the green . . . these are not divine thunderbolts, sent to try us: they have been placed deliberately, to punish errors that may be either physical (a thinned wedge, a fat pitch) or mental (too greedy, too impatient, too unrealistic). Horrid breaks – the ball that caroms off the trees into the base of the wall, the bunker blast that plugs in the lip – these are difficulties intrinsic to the game. Without them, golf would be snakes and ladders without the snakes, and those fine, sunlit days would lose their sheen. A cricketer can be given out lbw first ball when he has hit it; he can be caught off a fielder's boot, or blamelessly run out. Such extreme mishaps happen in golf too, but the routine disasters cannot be put down to ill luck. People who hit it straight rarely lose their ball.

Here is the paradox. A well-struck putt can miss; a mishit putt can fall. As Bobby Jones said, 'You get bad breaks from good shots, and good breaks from bad shots.' This is hard to swallow, so we tend to describe the whole arena of close shaves as a matter of sheer crazy luck. But a ball that trickles into a lake is not unlucky (there was no need to be anywhere near it); a bad lie in the rough is not unlucky (it is what the rough is for); and a ball that lips out is not unlucky: it was a whisker off-line, or a fraction too firm. If putts that miss are unlucky, then putts that fall must also be flukes, and few golfers want to admit that.

Speaking of putting . . . while it is true that a missed putt is by definition a weak putt, the margin for error here is demonstrably small. A putt is a difficult stroke. On television it looks as though the top professionals roll them in for fun, so it comes as a surprise to learn that, on average, even the world's best players regard six-foot putts as a 50–50 game: they hole them only half the time. Television misleads us by showing more hits than misses: it follows the tournament leaders, who by definition are the ones holing putts that day. Nor can one blame the producers: an endless pageant of missed six-footers would hardly make gripping viewing.

The reason why so many putts are missed is that the hole is tiny relative to the distances involved. A four-inch target from six feet leaves scant room for manoeuvre. Multiplied out, it means that in the case of a 100-yard approach, the target (the green) would be no more than 18 feet wide – a daunting landing area. Add to this the inscrutable scoring madness by which a one-inch putt carries the same weight as a 300-yard drive, and you have a recipe for some very scrambled brains. No wonder we prefer to attribute close shaves to Lady Luck. Just as the ancient Greeks personified the indecipherable workings of fortune into the whims of capricious gods and goddesses, so modern sportsmen enlist luck (the 'lap of the gods') as an emblem of the incalculable precision required.

This is why luck is invoked more often when it comes to putting than with driving. Hardly anyone curses the golfing gods when they zing a drive into the trees on the left or the water on the right – though the margin of the error may be no greater than the shaking hands that push putts at the edge rather than the centre of the cup. The harrowing irony is that if the hole were bigger there would be more bad luck, not less: the edge would be larger, and an even greater number of putts would flirt with it. The role of 'luck' would expand.

It is true that invoking luck can be a way of ducking responsibility (witness the so-called 'lottery' that is football's penalty shoot-out), but in this context, 'luck' is no less than a point of view, a way of seeing. An ageing Seve Ballesteros, his powers dwindling, once said, 'When I was young, no matter where I hit the ball, I always had a shot to the green. Now when I go off-line, I am always dead.' He was right. 'Luck' was another word for his own decline, and it was big of him to admit it.

Someone once calculated that in a normal round of golf ill fortune outranks good by about five to one – but this seems typical, if anything, of our natural tendency to attribute good luck to our own hard-won skill. Gary Player is often held to have written the chapter-and-verse on this subject when he agreed (after a fortuitous chip-in) that he had been lucky, but added: 'And the harder I practise, the luckier I get.'

This immediately became the anthem of the self-help gurus. If luck were merely a by-product of hard work, why, we could all be lucky. It seemed a neat and useful billboard slogan for the protestant work ethic. As it happens, it was not quite original. Thomas Jefferson appears in books of quotations saying exactly the same thing ('I am a great believer in luck, and I find the harder I work, the more I have of it') a couple of centuries before Player. And Ralph Waldo Emerson was also keen to insist that the whims of fate were no match for can-do American willpower: 'Shallow men believe in luck. Strong men believe in cause and effect.'

Many excellent golfers echo this determined maxim. 'There is no such thing as bad luck,' said Greg Norman – surprisingly, since he was the victim of a good deal of it himself over the years. 'Fate has nothing to do with success or failure . . . I'll have nothing to do with it.' As a result, when he lost (some say blew) the Masters in 1996, he wasn't looking for excuses. 'I screwed up,' he said. 'It's all on me. I know that.'

This is brave talk. But the trouble with the self-reliant creed is its blatant conceit: luck, it asserts, can be earned, even deserved. This is quite a serious form of egotism, and it shares something with the common (and equally unsettling) tendency of some golfers to attribute their success to divine grace. John Updike once smiled at it by lampooning the 'personable blond pro' who pops up on television to say, 'I just come to do my best each week, and I leave the rest of it up to the Lord.'

This in part explains that shimmer of unease that ran through the crowd when Stewart Cink (like Zach Johnson after winning the Masters in 2007) made this connection in his victory speech, thanking his wife for helping him unlock the power of prayer. Modern Britain is secular (unlike America) and this strikes most people as an awesome conceit. If the Lord wanted Cink to win, then we have to believe that the Lord wanted Watson to lose. Surely not!

Of course, Cink was attributing his calmness under pressure to his faith, not to actual divine intervention. But evangelical players, and there are plenty pacing the fairways ('I try to work with God as a partner' – Gary Player) seem happier to attribute good fortune to God's mysterious ways than they are to mention the wicked moments – the putt that fails to drop, the drive that finds the trees – for which the Lord must also be thanked.

There may well be some logic to imagining golf as a spiritual progress, a Bunyanesque ramble through sloughs of despond and vales of tears (not for nothing is the sharp swale below the 18th at St Andrews named 'the Valley of Sin'). It certainly invites (not always with success) the pursuit of self-knowledge. 'In no other walk of life,' wrote P. G. Wodehouse, 'does the cloven hoof so quickly display itself.' The tributes to golf's infuriating nature are legion. 'No matter how badly you play,' goes the saying, 'it is always possible to get worse.' Ray Floyd once remarked, 'They call it golf because all the other four-letter words were taken.' And Updike put his finger on the game's willingness to shine a torch on our defects. 'A putt that rims the hole is definitely not in,' he wrote, 'no matter what you write on your scorecard. The game and your swing provide a barrage of criticism that there is no evading. What other four hours' activity can chasten a magnate with so rich a variety of disappointments?'

It seems greedy, in this light, to make the ebb and flow of fortune junior to one's own resolve. So it is preferable, and humbler, to think of luck as neutral. Jack Nicklaus once called golf 80 per cent mental, 10 per cent ability and 10 per cent luck, and, while as clumsy as all generalisations (see the famous quip that 90 per cent of golf is half mental), this at least recognises that luck is indifferent, neither benign nor hostile.

Tiger Woods, as hard-headed a golfer as ever lost a ball, moved this thought forward when he stated, years ago, that he chose to see himself as a lucky player. Of course there were sound empirical grounds for this: his was a wildly successful life, and there was

little sense frowning (except when he flared a drive). The pragmatic point remained: if on-course luck evened out, it was better
for one's mental equilibrium to think oneself blessed rather than
tormented. Woods was often to be heard, after his tournament
triumphs, saying that he had a good break here or a lucky bounce
there, and he had even thanked his stars for the agonising knee
that kept him out of the game for so long. It was, he said, 'a blessing in disguise' that he was getting to spend the time at home
with his wife and their two infant children. 'I was very lucky
there.'

Later events would reveal this to be even harder-headed than
it seemed at the time, since it was not necessarily sincere.

It may not be a coincidence that Tom Watson shares Woods's
view, considering himself a lucky player. 'You tend to look at fail-
ures instead of good bounces,' he says. 'The eight-footer you miss
instead of the 60-footers you make.' In his last press call he was
prodded to bemoan his luck (the media often try to tickle players into self-pity; it is the next best thing to having them lambast
someone), but Watson wouldn't have it. Instead, he dwelt on
some earlier flukes. 'On 12,' he said, 'I caught a break when the
ball hit a spectator and dropped into a perfect lie. And on 13 on
Friday I hit a hybrid off the tee and I pushed it, and good thing
I did push it, because if it had gone where I aimed it, it would
have been in one of those pot bunkers.' This sort of candour
didn't make such a good 'story'; it meant that he couldn't be
depicted as crushed or agonised. But it was the simple truth.

There is a humility in acknowledging luck, a concession that
there may not be such a thing as a winning 'mentality' (from
which enormous sums can be extracted, of course); at any rate
it is not so self-aggrandising as the conviction that success is merited, or some kind of divine thumbs-up. And it requires players
to admit that bad breaks are often just weak play. Half-full players do not shirk responsibility for blunders; they take the blame,
live with it, leave a tip for their mind coach, and move on.

In this light, 'luck' emerges as a mode of interpretation, a retrospective analysis. Some players are disposed to imagine themselves lucky; others scowl at their constant ill fortune. Some see the glass half full; others see it half empty, if not drained to the dregs. Some players are quick to curse the bad breaks that come their way, while barely remembering to thank the outrageous favouring wind that occasionally lends them a hand.

It has been apparent for years that Colin Montgomerie, for instance, is a half-empty man, tut-tutting at the golfing gods or at far-off cameras – what Wodehouse would call 'the uproar of the butterflies in the adjoining meadows'. Off the course Monty could be breezy and self-mocking. At one Open media conference, asked if he was glad that mobile phones had been banned, he grinned and said, 'Actually, they don't bother me too much.' But on the course he could be prickly, easily stung, and prone to moaning that people should have more respect for his 'office'. This was an unwise metaphor, because a golf course isn't an office – it is a stage; the players are paid (very nicely) as performers, not executives, with an audience (or two audiences: one present, and the larger one reached by those noisy cameras). As it happens, few offices are as silent as a golf course where a player is about to hit the ball. The hush is sudden and tense, and it is immediately clear that a Montgomerie-style unease makes it worse. Nothing is louder than a thousand people trying not to make a sound.

A final thought on luck as a way of interpreting events. On the 18th at Carnoustie, back in 2007, when Padraig Harrington stood on the tee with a two-stroke lead, he smeared his drive right. This we know; we know too that the ball tried to scramble across a bridge, but it clipped the wall and fell into the burn. At the time it was an awful moment, but with the benefit of hindsight Harrington was glad it happened that way. 'People say to me, "Well, your tee shot on 18 was really unlucky that it didn't cross the bridge." But if it had, and I hit it up around the green and made five and won, people would have said it was lucky. I would have been the "Bounce Across the Bridge Champion" or something.' As it was, victory was put down to his skill and industry.

Even so, if Garcia had holed his own putt at the last, Harrington would not have been hailed as hard-working, likeable, or even unlucky; he would have been jeered at as a weakling. This is how golf analysis, under time pressure, works: solid character traits are reverse-inferred from stray outcomes. No one was grittier, if we were honest, than Stewart Cink: he carried on striving to the last, even though victory never seemed likely or even possible. There may have been advantages in being 'under the radar', but by any standards his was a determined and resolute effort. Yet it would always seem a lucky win, since if Watson and Westwood had not faltered, his resolute effort would have been for nothing.

Nothing? What are we saying? Coming second is not nothing. Nor is coming third. Nor is coming 73rd. Daniel Gaunt would never forget the Friday of Open week, the day he was the best player in the world. Nor would Watson, and the thousands of fans who saw him come so painfully, achingly close. It is the one-dimensional idea (sponsored by players themselves) that everyone who doesn't win is a loser that makes second place seem like 'nothing'. No one who was there will ever think it so.

It was neither desirable nor possible to present Watson as a weak-spined choker. A man who has won eight majors cannot be described as an edgy finisher. The fact remained: we could fetishise and reward sporting skill as much as we liked, but asking someone to hit so small a target – a sweet wrapper! – from 190 yards was too much. So as the caravan melted away from Scotland, golf couldn't help feeling queasy. Watson, Westwood, Wood – all of them had three-putted the last. Quite what this place had against people whose name began with a 'W', we could not say. (Tiger Woods hadn't fared well either.) But we knew, since this turf had been so very kind to Watson in the past, that (like form) it was not permanent.

There is never a shortage of dotty explanations for the way things turn out. The central appeal of sport is that it is unscripted drama, so nothing is written – things really could go either way. But sport fans are weak – they demand reasons – and it was hard to accept the idea that the Open turned on pure chance, an idle trick of fate. We felt cheated. If Watson's ball had flown a foot further it might even have found a soft bounce and pulled up, leaving him an easy two-putt. It might also have been that if Cink had messed up his putt on the second play-off hole, Watson would have found a fresh wave of optimism to escort him to victory. It wasn't a case, as one newspaper put it, of coulda woulda shoulda; it was mighta mighta mighta. Nothing was destined; nothing was preordained. That was why people pulled off highways in America to find a bar with a TV. That was why the audience at Lord's swivelled away from the Test match to watch the finale in Scotland. Until the very last shot the Open was . . . open. And that, if you want to talk about fate, is how it was meant to be.

Either way, it was over. It had been absorbing fun, and some of it would glow in the memory for years. When Watson left Sunningdale, however, he was feeling vexed. In the endless contest that is high-level golf, he was going straight from England to the US Senior Open at Crooked Stick in Indiana, but he was fretting about his 'lack of preparation'.

It seemed incredible. He had played world-beating golf for two straight weeks. What on earth could he need to work on?

'I'm just going to try to weaken my grip a little bit,' he said, 'so I can feel both hands together a bit more, make myself release it. You know, we've always got to try something.'

Golf is incessant, and there is no such thing as steady-state: the game is a continuous process of adjustment and flux. Just ask Harrington.

Or maybe Bruce Vaughan put his finger on it when he mocked his own constant tinkering. 'It's the same old stuff,' he said, his warm Kansas accent echoing across the Bagshot sands. 'A guy wins a big tournament, and then makes some changes in his swing.' He paused for a brief laugh. 'Nobody ever accused golfers of being smart.'

CHAPTER SIXTEEN

Aftermath: A New Beginning

The day after the Open I went to the place where it all began, a century and a half ago: Prestwick. It was a dull day; clouds hung over the airport to the east, and drizzle blurred the lines between land and sea, dune and sky, past and present.

A narrow approach road dips below the railway line that has flanked the course since its earliest days; the grey sea lies ahead, with guest houses on the left, and there, behind a low stone wall on the right, is the famous course itself, a rough, bumpy expanse of 150-year-old turf running north towards Troon. It is hard to make out a single fairway in that bewildering wilderness of grass and sand. For once the links really do feel 'out there'.

I watched a group of elderly Japanese chipping it away from the first tee, half-wondering if they would ever be seen again. The holes had old-fashioned, storybook names: 'The Alps' (the hillocks by the 17th green), the 'Cardinal's Knob' (the 3rd), the treacherous 'Himalayas' by the 5th, and the daunting 'Sahara', where a million dreams have turned to dust.

The warm, airy clubhouse is full of heirlooms. Some form an active part of today's club: the formal dining room is like a Victorian officer's mess, and members lunch beneath portraits of their predecessors (the Earl of Eglinton stares hungrily down at the weekly roast). Some are vestigial: the velvet-coated brass scale for weighing local grandees is not much in demand these days. The walls of the club room, meanwhile, are studded with classic memories. Here hang proud images of the founders, Old Tom Morris and Young Tom Morris, with scorecards to prove the wonders they performed in this place. Over there is Willie Park, and the Morocco-leather belt that used to be the champion's prize; there is the 'Great Triumvirate' (Vardon, Braid and Taylor) captured in watercolour with Ted Ray and Arnaud Massy above the heroic caption, 'Paladins of the Golf Course'. Here is a ball used by Braid 101 years ago, alongside photographs signed by Open winners: Sandy Lyle, Payne Stewart, Paul Lawrie. In pride of place hangs an irreplaceable antique plan of St Andrews signed by all the Open winners: a terrific living record of golfing triumph and disaster.

In case anyone thought the previous day a dream, there was, up there already in a tight, black scrawl, the signature of 2009's champion. I am ashamed to say I could not help wincing when, groping in thickets of golfing greatness, I found Cink's name sandwiched between two colossi, Ben Hogan and Seve Ballesteros.

I can only apologise. It just didn't feel right. I mean, once we dropped the pantomime bluster, Cink deserved to win as much as anyone else. He was a fine player with a strong swing and now, it seemed, a calm temper. Good for him. It was a golf tournament, not a popularity contest. The Open did not eject players for failing to top some nationwide phone vote. He had won the Claret Jug fair and square, and that was that.

It was just that he seemed to belong to modern rather than ancient times, to the world of the Fedex Cup and the Race to Dubai rather than to this bleak, dog-eared nest of time-honoured golf. In Tom Watson, the modern game had unearthed that link to its own past, and it was nice, while it lasted.

When I walked outside the rain had stopped, and there were

blue breaks in the sky. A rusty train clanked along the raised
embankment. It was not hard to imagine the gaggle of sturdy
linksmen, dressed as gentlemen mountaineers, heading into this
dappled burial ground to test themselves against the land, the elements and one another. It wasn't hard to see them lifting dented
hip-flasks and hunching coats up to keep out the cold. It was
harder to fathom what they would make of today's scene: the aircraft roaring over the sheds to our right, the gleaming German
saloons, the phone lines where the birds stood in rows, the aeri-
als that jabbed at the sky, the electric lights that blazed across the
gloomy afternoon.

I climbed into the car and headed to an exhibition of golf history in a country park outside Ayr. Here were more memories:
the scorecards for the Duel in the Sun, showing Watson's closing
65 in 1977's final round (if only). Here was a 'Far and Sure' guide
to the golf links published by the Glasgow and South Western
Railway Company; here were some of those angry letters protest-
ing against the introduction of Sunday golf at Turnberry ('There
are still a few men in Scotland who are not altogether carried away
by the golf craze'); here wreckage from wartime plane crashes; and
more of those magnificent old golf implements, resonant with the
craftsmanship of golf's workaday past. Look at this: a 'water-iron'
with holes in the blade for scooping the ball from puddles. What
was this? A baffing spoon by Tom Morris (not at all unlike the
hybrid used 25 times by Tom Watson in the last few days). And
there, in the glass cabinet next to the Claret Jug itself (or one of
them), a beech-headed driver made by Willie Dunn Sr. If only, I
thought, today's players made their own clubs. What we wouldn't
give for a 'Downball!' driver carved by Tiger Woods himself, or
a 'Staytrue' putter forged by Sergio Garcia.

I went home after that, and the Open began to fade in the
memory, forced out by new feats. In Akron, Ohio, golf got the
story it wanted when Tiger Woods and Padraig Harrington tussled

for the Bridgestone Invitational. The latter looked a certain winner until, after a warning for slow play, he made a few rash swings on the 16th and let Woods snatch the trophy.

The following Thursday, at the PGA, the fourth and most junior major, the pair put on a similar show. This time Harrington blew up a few holes earlier, but Woods was beaten by some silky putting from the Korean Y. E. Yang. Here was another of the year's juicy stories coming true. As the newspapers were quick to declare, Asia had a major-winner, the first of many. None (that I could see) ran the obvious pun: 'My Brilliant Korea'.

A few weeks after that, American golf reached its climax at the Tour Championship, the big-money equivalent of Europe's Race to Dubai. It was held in Atlanta at East Lake, home of Bobby Jones, keeper of the flame for golf's amateur heroes. And it was close, but no surprise, when Woods hit the $10-million jackpot. Those who had spotted flaws in his swing at Turnberry had to eat their words. The man seemed over his 'setback'. Victory, it was said, eased him to that billion-dollar-mark in total earnings.

There was time for one last Open jaunt. Since this was Stewart Cink's home club (he was a member), he brought along the Claret Jug, packed in its distinctive suitcase. But when he set it down in the locker room, Harrington recognised it as his missing ladybird vase, hid it in his own locker and went off to the putting green. The attendant did not make Cink suffer long, and soon put him out of his misery. Badly jolted, he went out and lit up the front nine with four birdies. Since the Open he had struggled to break 70, but he too was beginning to get over it.

It was time to pore over the final statistics; perhaps numbers, shaved of emotion, would tell the true story. They didn't. Stewart Cink was 30th for driving distance (averaging 292 yards), 33rd for fairways hit (Watson was 4th), 23rd for greens-in-regulation and 9th in putting. Were these figures enough for a winning performance? A clue lay in the fact that Cink was 103rd in the list of double bogeys or worse: only once, at the par-three 4th on day two, had he dropped two shots. In an Open where lost strokes were hard to regain, this was decisive. But Watson had not carded a single double bogey. The tall Australian Michael Wright had seven such slip-ups, which was why he was tied in 144th place.

Some of the numbers were easy to interpret. Paul Casey was the fifth-longest driver (301 yards) and equal-first in greens-in-regulation, hitting 53 out of 72 putting surfaces. But he hit 132 putts, 15 more than Cink. Better form on the greens would have put him right in at the death.

At the death . . . an odd expression. Golf has a marked enthusiasm for allusions to mortality, and often deploys them in the service of longed-for outcomes. A wedge close to the hole is said to be 'stiff'. He's knocked that one dead, murmur the commentators, or 'that one's stone dead'. Big drives draw the same gruesome praise. He's 'crushed' or 'killed' it, they say, as Garcia (the tournament's longest driver, with an average of 311 yards) 'slaughters' another one. 'Nailed it,' we say modestly, when a five-iron flies sweetly. Very well, says Mr Determined, I'm going to 'bury' this one. Weak putts 'die' left or right, just as wedges 'die' on the breeze. St Andrews has a set of fairway bunkers known as the 'coffins'.

No one has to be a psychoanalyst to detect the stirrings of desire and fear trembling here. If we factor in the extent to which 'getting the ball in the hole' has inspired locker-room banter down the years, well . . . let's just say that Freud could have made a mint as a mind-coach out on tour.

Actually there was some chewy food for thought in the driving distance chart. Only one of the top-ten long drivers (Henrik Stenson) finished in the top 20 – one in the eye for those who felt that distance from the tee counted for too much these days. Daniel Gaunt could reflect that being the sixth longest driver (301 yards) was not enough to prevent him coming 22 strokes behind Cink and Watson. Direction beat length, every time.

If Paul Casey were looking for someone to dine with, he could have done worse than have fish and chips with Thongchai Jaidee. Thailand's best player had come top of both fairways-hit (42 out of a possible 56, two better than Luke Donald) and (along with Casey) greens-in-regulation. He was the best player tee-to-green, so why didn't he win? Could it have been that 128 blows with the putter (11 more than Cink) was too many?

One of the common criticisms of big-money golf is that it is, effectively, a putting contest. Putting, it is said, is where the players collect their dough. They are all excellent, so trophies merely fall to the one who happens to hole a few putts in any given week. There is some truth in this. Watson played wonderfully, but the reason he was in contention for four days was because he holed that slew of putts ('no-brainers', he called them) from improbable distances (he could have been half a dozen shots back – and we still would have had to hand it to him). But this is not straightforward, because Cink (on 117 putts – impressive, given that you are allowed 144) was by no means the stoniest holer-out at Turnberry. David Howell needed only 112, and it got him no further than a tie for 52nd; Fredrik Jacobson took two fewer putts than Cink, but ended up 17 shots behind. The week's low scorer with the putter was Søren Kjeldsen. He took only 110 shots, seven fewer than Cink, and he came joint 27th.

Of course we no longer expect statistics to tell the truth, and in this case they hide the extent to which some players miss greens, chip close, and take fewer putts than those who hit greens from further away. But no amount of hand-waving can obscure this simple fact. Lee Westwood drove the ball a yard further than Cink; he hit five more fairways and four more greens-in-regulation. For four days, in other words, he outplayed his American nemesis. But he took three more putts than Cink; Watson (despite all those long bombs) took four.

In all, seven of the 25 international qualifiers made the cut (four from America, three from Europe, and none from Africa, Asia or Australia). Two of the nine final qualifiers survived. This doesn't prove much. Some who failed in the qualifying events – Nick Dougherty and Johan Edfors – sneaked in through tour rankings and played well. Matthew Goggin didn't qualify, and was invited only when Trevor Immelman withdrew, and he came fourth.

As for the idea, touted by some newspapers, that English players had once more failed to perform, well, England was the top-performing nation by far, with three in the top five and six in the top 25, ahead of America (five), South Africa (three), and Sweden (two). In all, 12 Englishmen made the cut, so if you include three Northern Irishmen and two Scots, that made 17 British players in the final stages of the Open. This didn't seem a bad effort to me (there were 18 Americans, two of them in the play-off).

Something else about all these numbers: they didn't sweat. They didn't have wind watering their eyes, adrenalin flooding the valves of their heart, or stress (This for the Open!) tightening the synapses in their brains. The Championship was measured in statistics, but they obscured to the extent that every one of those thousands of shots mattered like hell to the player who stood over it. Each of them could have gone wrong. Each brought into play years (not many, in the case of Manassero) of skill, practice, thought, resolve and – yes – luck. And it was framed by 149 years of dim echoes, which hung above the gorse like gulls buffeted by a gale – pale, still and staring at the familiar scene with incurious eyes.

It would be nice to say that the sun never sets on the British Open, but of course it isn't the British, it is only the Open. And as the autumn shadows began to lengthen, and the European season slid towards its lucrative climax beside the Arabian Sea, David Hill settled back into his office at St Andrews. There were television contracts to negotiate, jubilee events to plan, and a rather special birthday to look forward to.

There was good news from Lausanne. Golf would indeed be included in the 2016 Olympiad, which would be held, it had just been decided, in Rio de Janeiro. Padraig Harrington, Matteo Manassero and Michelle Wie supported the bid, and won the day. It was, said Tiger Woods, 'great . . . a perfect fit'.

In Brazil, in the summer, they would not need hand-warmers.

The news from Dubai was more ominous: after grim-faced negotiations with the European Tour, the prize fund for both the Dubai 'World Championship' – the end-of-season mega-tournament – and the Race to Dubai was being reduced ('slashed', as the papers put it) by 25 per cent. This was not the end of the world: none of the contenders were going to starve because they were reduced to competing for $7.5 million instead of the pledged $10 million. But it was a sign that the foundations of the gold-plated desert swing were built (not only literally) on sand. Much worse news was to come at the end of the year: days after Lee Westwood scooped the gulf bullion by winning the Race to Dubai, the state-backed Dubai World, owner of Nakheel, Leisurecorp (and Turnberry), declared itself unable to honour its debts. When word emerged that its oil-rich neighbour, Abu Dhabi, was unwilling to stand behind Dubai, the entire property bubble looked like a mirage. In the same week Tiger Woods drove his car into the fire hydrant outside his Florida home (driving into the water, as they said), it seemed as though a certain exceptionally lavish golfing era might be over.

David Hill could not afford to frown over such tidings for long. The Open was too old to be bruised by trifles, but there was a lot to do: sites to inspect, people to hire, ticket prices to announce, sponsors to woo and on-course modifications to complete (a delicate matter, at St Andrews).

It helped that when he looked out of his office window he could see next year's venue. The Old Course at St Andrews is a special place, and this would be its 28th Open, making it by far the most popular venue. It is a place of pilgrimage for all the world's golfers, however unskilled, and remains – incredibly, in this commercial day and age – in public ownership.

In 1552 permission was granted for a rabbit warren on the land, which enshrined the right to play golf while permitting the acres to be trimmed and reshaped by decades of nibbling and scraping. Until the 18th century there were 12 holes, ten of which were played twice – once on the way 'out' and once on the way 'back' – using huge shared greens. It is not a coincidence that these terms are an embedded part of golf's lingua franca; they echo the unique St Andrews design, which really does send golfers on an outward run before asking them to 'turn' for home.

In 1764, while James Watt was fiddling with steam engines at Glasgow University, four of the short holes were condensed into two, producing a narrow circuit of ten (eight of which were now played twice). This is how golf arrived at the 18-hole structure that seems so natural and permanent.

In 1797, citing 'temporary impecuniosity', the links were sold as an out-and-out rabbit farm, but in 1805, the year of the Battle of Trafalgar, the tide turned and golfers were granted the right to kill the rabbits. There followed an almost 20-year squabble, a 'rabbit war' (modern geographers would call it a 'land-use con- flict'), that ended only when a merchant called James Cheape bought the links outright, making them safe for sticks and balls.

The layout has never truly been imitated, and in some ways is not ideal. The first nine holes run north (more or less: there is a hook at the far end) and the back nine comes south to the town. Half the course plays with one direction of wind; the other runs the opposite way. Originally it was played clockwise: players went out inland and came home with the sea to their left. Now it is played anti-clockwise. In theory (and sometimes in practice) it can be played either way. Some of the bunkers still look as though they belong to the right-handed original circuit.

In 1893 Cheape sold the links for £5000 to the Royal and Ancient Club, which outbid the town by £500. The council petitioned the government and secured the guarantee of common ownership that survives to this day. The Links Act guaranteed public access, and when the old town council was legislated out of existence in 1974, Parliament established a new body – the Links Trust – to run the golf courses on the public's behalf.

It is the home of golf, but also the biggest golf playground (with seven courses) in Europe. Half the tee-times are pre-sold to the town's hotels, or reserved for VIPs and corporate 'guests', but anyone can enter the daily ballot. Cards must be handed in by 2 p.m. the day before the game. There is a draw, and then tee-times are posted. There is no play on Sunday.

In Allan Robertson St Andrews boasted the world's first out-and-out golf professional, and in Old Tom Morris it found its eternal father figure. If he seems to the outside world a Victorian patriarch as distant as Darwin or Carlyle, in Scotland he is an agile presence: a folk hero. One of his less-known achievements is that he gave the Old Course its title: it wasn't until his 'New' course appeared in 1895 that the original needed a name of its own: for 150 years it had been the only course in town.

It is golf's greatest cathedral, and the famously harsh weather only adds to its stubborn appeal. It would be the best place in the world, the saying goes, if it weren't for the fact it is so horribly damp, grey and cold – and then of course you've got the winter.

Almost every leading player has had something to say about it. Arnold Palmer, who reinvigorated the Open almost single-handedly with his charging enthusiasm in the 1960s, said: 'This is the origin of the game, golf in its purest form, and it's still played on a course that seems untouched by time.' As it happens, far from feeling untouched, St Andrews feels utterly and entirely saturated in time, as distilled by the years as a local malt whisky. But we know what Palmer means. By some improbable miracle (and thanks to the efforts of committeemen who must have seemed pedantic bores), it has barely changed. Not everyone's memories are warm. This is where Doug Sanders missed a tiddler to let Jack Nicklaus win an emotional victory. 'It doesn't hurt much any more,' he said years later. 'These days I can go a full five minutes without thinking about it.' But the connection to the past is intact. 'If a golfer is going to be remembered,' said Nicklaus, 'he must win the title at St Andrews.'

The most brilliant leading-light of golf's reputation for sportsmanship is Bobby Jones. He was such a beacon of 24-carat courtesy that he appears in Stephen Potter's lovable guide to gamesmanship as a byword for the golfing conscience ('Heads are shaken when his name comes up').

He was not always thus. In 1921 he came to St Andrews for the Open and hated it. He liked the town well enough, but the flat, featureless course, all blind shots and hidden bunkers, made his golfing instincts shrink. He did not complain, but in the third round topped his first drive, foozled irons, took 46 strokes to reach the famous 'turn', stumbled to a double-bogey six on the 10th, and took four shots in the notorious Hill Bunker on 11. Red-faced with fury, he picked up his ball and quit. Some say he tore up his scorecard in disgust. Bernard Darwin, in *The Times*, stated that Jones actually teed up a ball and smacked it into the water, but he was not on hand at the time, so this may be fanciful. Either way it was a gaffe, and Jones was disqualified. He never forgot the remorse – it was, he said, his 'principal regret'. That afternoon he went back out for his final round, though he was no longer in the contest. He shot a meaningless but face-saving 72, and never looked back. 'I've often wished I could offer a general apology for picking up my ball,' he said. 'It means nothing to the world of golf. But it means something to me.'

He returned to St Andrews in 1930 with a changed attitude, and won the Amateur Championship, the first leg of the so-called 'Impregnable Quadrilateral (the four-majors-in-a-year clean sweep known these days as the Grand Slam). In 1958 he was named a 'Freeman of the Burgh', an honour he was delighted to accept, since by now he was a warm disciple. 'I could take out of my life everything except my experiences at St Andrews,' he said, 'and I'd still have a rich, full life. The more I studied the Old Course the more I loved it, and the more I loved it the more I studied it.' After his death in 1971, the R&A held a memorial service and even named a hole (the 10th) after him. Only one other player has ever enjoyed such an honour: the 18th is called – what else? – 'Tom Morris'.

Later golfers have queued up to accept Jones's notion that links golf is a game that does not flaunt its virtues or yield its pleasures lightly. In 1946 Sam Snead reportedly took one look at St Andrews, took it to be disused ('It looks like an old abandoned kinda place'), and asked where the golf course was. Pete Dye, the celebrated American golf architect, played one round here in the 1963 Amateur Championship and called it a 'goat ranch'. Tom Kite once said of the 17th, the famous 'Road Hole' (where Tom Watson once drove himself, almost literally, up the wall), 'It's a great golf hole. It gives you a million options, none of them worth a damn.' This is a fair working definition of the ancient game.

Hardly anyone would compare Bobby Jones with John Daly. The one was the epitome of the gifted amateur, the other is a drug-haunted, bloated wreck, forever picking up his ball, walking off in disgust, spending nights in custody and trying the patience of golf's ruling authorities. At Turnberry he was virtually in rehab, hauling those 'fun' trousers around the links in an attempt to scrabble together his £10,000-a-month alimony bill. Go down to the range and you could watch Woods, Singh and a hundred others work through their bags in sober routines that took them from club to club in a well-rehearsed drill. Daly was different. He'd whale a ball over a distant fence, spark up a cigarette, chat to a pal, lean on someone's brolly, grab a mouthful of bacon roll, let fly again, drain a can of fizz and amble off like a hungry bear in search of fresh dustbins.

He had been suspended from the US Tour for being arrested outside a branch of Hooter's ('intoxicated and unco-operative') and spending a night in a cell. He had starred in a topless golf film clip on YouTube (not the prettiest sight). When he went to Australia he said that he had enjoyed his last visit there, forgetting the time he shot 78 and threw his putter into a lake. Stewart Appleby spoke for quite a few when he remarked, 'I don't think John's here because of his world ranking.'

It was true. He was the world number 603, and his richest commodity was his bad-boy notoriety. He was not an obvious poster-boy for golf's cherished traditions; indeed he was the last golfer anyone would expect to be moved by the game's ancient folklore. Yet in 1995 even he was lifted by the aura of St Andrews. In his (ghosted) autobiography, *My Life In and Out of the Rough*, he recalled how he came to Scotland in thorough disarray ('I was a train wreck'), and how the Old Course sneaked past his defences.

On the evening before the tournament (he wrote), he walked on to his balcony and let his big American gaze drift on the fabled links. It had been a blustery day, but now the sky over the 'auld grey toon' was washed clean; it was a pure, crystal northern dusk. 'The wind died down some, and it was cooling off fast.' Daly shivered, but those golf-haunted, rabbit-nibbled swales were a balm to his fidgety soul. He turned to his agent, and bared his beleaguered heart. 'I love it,' he said. 'I've never felt more comfortable on a golf course in my life. This is my home.'

The field was full of shades, and the glimmering coast was possessed (as always) by unquiet echoes. Those green alleys bore the footprints of Old Tom Morris and his heartbreaking son, along with those of Vardon and Braid, Nicklaus and Watson, Ballesteros and Woods; somewhere out there slept the spirit of Jones himself. In the face of such a history, Daly grew quiet. 'I'm not big on golf traditions,' he wrote. 'I don't get weepy because Bobby Jones made a birdie here or Walter Hagen used to drink there.' He was stirred. 'This is where the game began, in a damned sheep pasture next to a beach in a cold, rainy, windy corner of Scotland. Golf clubs? Take a look at a shepherd's stick, and think two-iron.'

He may not have known it, but if he had stopped by Rhod McEwan's bookstore he would have discovered that he was quoting from *The Art of Golf* (1887) by Sir Walter Simpson, the original author of this delightful whimsy ('A shepherd tending his sheep would often chance upon a stray pebble, and having his crook in his hand, he would strike it away.')

It was no surprise that a conservative traditionalist like Tom Watson should find 'serenity' in this landscape, but in 1995 Daly – with his yo-yo diet, tantrums, trailer-park idioms and multiple addictions – seemed the last man likely to fall under its sepia-tinged spell. He was captivated, however. 'I felt so good about being there that I played two practice rounds. Hell, I never play two practice rounds. A lot of times I don't even play one.'

For the next four days he kept his eye on the ball, loved the wind, didn't party, gulped down the same room-service menu every night (spaghetti with meatballs, Diet Coke and chocolate ice cream) and hit the sack at 9.30 p.m. He had a tense moment on Sunday afternoon, when Constantino Rocca holed a monster putt from off the 18th green ('A 75-foot putt to send us into a play-off? You've got to be fucking kidding me!'), but for the most part he played in the approved one-shot-at-a-time manner. He wasn't a big fan of positive-thinking guides, so when he found himself in the play-off he had to devise his own demotic slogan – 'Go out and bring that sonofabitch home!' When it was over he put ice cream and chocolate sauce in the Claret Jug and pronounced it 'the best food I have ever eaten'. He had won more than a golf match. 'The happiest four days of my life in golf,' he wrote, 'were the four days of the 1995 British Open.'

If the officers of the R&A had heard him refer to it as the 'British', they might have torn the Claret Jug from his grasp, chocolate sauce and all. But what could they do: the next Open was already under way. Tiger Woods, to universal astonishment, was about to hit the fire hydrant and fall from grace like Icarus. And at the end of August 2009 a long-haired French teenager, Victor Dubuisson, qualified for St Andrews 2010 by winning the European Amateur at Chantilly, north of Paris. His five-under-par final-round 66 was enough to push the Italian wonder-*ragazzo* and silver medallist Matteo Manassero into seventh place. Dubuisson was thinking about turning professional, but victory made him delay: he could not bear to relinquish the place he had won as an amateur. 'I came here with a great motivation,' he said. 'A win to play the Open!' On the 71st hole it looked as if he might fall short, but he snaked in a 40-foot putt that left him needing par at the last. Par at the last! Dubuisson knew, after Turnberry, that this was no easy task, but somehow he managed to stop his hands shaking, and made it.

When Dubuisson's putt rolled in, Scotland's Ross Kellet went pale. He had led the tournament since round two, but now his own six-footer for par looked prickly. He missed, dropped back to second place, and his Open dream was shredded. He hit the last in regulation, and for several splits of a second his long (50-foot) putt looked like it might – wonder of wonders – fall. But it glanced at the hole, wobbled, caught the edge and passed on.

Kellet ended up one shot short of making it to the Open.

It was tough, but nothing new. Golf had seen this sort of thing a thousand times. You win some, you lose some. Try again tomorrow.

It was all starting again.

Acknowledgements

A book such as this cannot be written without the assistance and camaraderie of a host of helpful people, but let's break with convention and not name them all here. Especially fervent thanks, however, are due to Richard Beswick and Iain Hunt at Little, Brown for their patient stewardship of the work-in-progress, even when it stalled. Thanks to Malcolm Booth and his team at the R&A for assembling such an extraordinarily media-friendly resource: the golf-writer's day may be long, but the information flow is rich and sustained – sport's equivalent of a chocolate fountain. Thanks to the players who – not always for contractual reasons – spoke so freely to gaggles of unknown reporters (including me, lurking at the back) about their day, their form and their prospects. Thanks to Ian Smith and Julian Winder for road-testing my thoughts without laughing too openly. Thanks to 'the man upstairs', as golfers like to call him, for supplying fine weather (rain is not kind to notebooks). And thanks to the man who has saved my own clumsy swing, Mr Neil Kitchen.

I must also salute the wealth of the online resources available these days. This may have been the first Open in which the champion (Stewart Cink) actually tweeted from the locker room, sharing with his fans a snap of the clubhouse vending machine (complete with its supply of condoms). Reports, interviews and photographs from across the golfing world are now only a few keystrokes away. If this book shows any signs of having trotted the golfing globe, it is, alas, purely a coincidence.